A Text Book of

FORMAL LANGUAGE AND AUTOMATA THEORY

(THEORY OF COMPUTATION)

Sem – V

THIRD YEAR DEGREE COURSE IN COMPUTER ENGINEERING

As Per New Revised Syllabus of
North Maharastra University of Jalgaon.

(Effective from June 2014)

Vinod S. Wadne
M. Tech (Computer Sci. & Engg.)
Assistant Professor
Computer Engineering Dept.
JSPM's Imperial College of
Engineering & Research
Wagholi, Pune.

Sarika S. Jadhav
M.E. (Computer Engg.)
Assistant Professor
Computer Engineering Dept.
JSPM's Imperial College of
Engineering & Research
Wagholi, Pune.

N 2292

FORMAL LANGUAGE & AUTOMATA THEORY (TE Comp. Sem – V, NMU) ISBN 978-93-5164-202-2

Second Edition : July 2015
© : Authors

The text of this publication, or any part thereof, should not be reproduced or transmitted in any form or stored in any computer storage system or device for distribution including photocopy, recording, taping or information retrieval system or reproduced on any disc, tape, perforated media or other information storage device etc., without the written permission of Authors with whom the rights are reserved. Breach of this condition is liable for legal action.

Every effort has been made to avoid errors or omissions in this publication. In spite of this, errors may have crept in. Any mistake, error or discrepancy so noted and shall be brought to our notice shall be taken care of in the next edition. It is notified that neither the publisher nor the authors or seller shall be responsible for any damage or loss of action to any one, of any kind, in any manner, therefrom.

Published By :
NIRALI PRAKASHAN
Abhyudaya Pragati, 1312, Shivaji Nagar,
Off J.M. Road, Pune – 411005
Tel - (020) 25512336/37/39, Fax - (020) 25511379
Email : niralipune@pragationline.com

Printed By :
REPRO INDIA LTD,
Mumbai.

☞ **DISTRIBUTION CENTRES**

PUNE
Nirali Prakashan : 119, Budhwar Peth, Jogeshwari Mandir Lane, Pune 411002, Maharashtra
Tel : (020) 2445 2044, 66022708, Fax : (020) 2445 1538
Email : bookorder@pragationline.com, niralilocal@pragationline.com

Nirali Prakashan : S. No. 28/27, Dhyari, Near Pari Company, Pune 411041
Tel : (020) 24690204 Fax : (020) 24690316
Email : dhyari@pragationline.com, bookorder@pragationline.com

MUMBAI
Nirali Prakashan : 385, S.V.P. Road, Rasdhara Co-op. Hsg. Society Ltd.,
Girgaum, Mumbai 400004, Maharashtra
Tel : (022) 2385 6339 / 2386 9976, Fax : (022) 2386 9976
Email : niralimumbai@pragationline.com

☞ **DISTRIBUTION BRANCHES**

JALGAON
Nirali Prakashan : 34, V. V. Golani Market, Navi Peth, Jalgaon 425001,
Maharashtra, Tel : (0257) 222 0395, Mob : 94234 91860

KOLHAPUR
Nirali Prakashan : New Mahadvar Road, Kedar Plaza, 1st Floor Opp. IDBI Bank
Kolhapur 416 012, Maharashtra. Mob : 9850046155

NAGPUR
Pratibha Book Distributors : Above Maratha Mandir, Shop No. 3, First Floor,
Rani Jhanshi Square, Sitabuldi, Nagpur 440012, Maharashtra
Tel : (0712) 254 7129

DELHI
Nirali Prakashan : 4593/21, Basement, Aggarwal Lane 15, Ansari Road, Daryaganj
Near Times of India Building, New Delhi 110002
Mob : 08505972553

BENGALURU
Pragati Book House : House No. 1, Sanjeevappa Lane, Avenue Road Cross,
Opp. Rice Church, Bengaluru – 560002.
Tel : (080) 64513344, 64513355,Mob : 9880582331, 9845021552
Email:bharatsavla@yahoo.com

CHENNAI
Pragati Books : 9/1, Montieth Road, Behind Taas Mahal, Egmore,
Chennai 600008 Tamil Nadu, Tel : (044) 6518 3535,
Mob : 94440 01782 / 98450 21552 / 98805 82331,
Email : bharatsavla@yahoo.com

niralipune@pragationline.com | www.pragationline.com

Also find us on   www.facebook.com/niralibooks

Dedicated to ...

Our Beloved Mother

Late Smt. Kamal S. Wadne

& Father

Shri. Subhash Wadne

...Vinod

Dedicated to ...

Our Beloved Mother

Mrs. Anita S. Jadhav

& Father

Shri. Subhash Jadhav

...Sarika

PREFACE TO THE SECOND EDITION

We are glad and excited to announce that the First Edition of this book received an overwhelming response from the engineering student community, compelling us to release its Second Edition within a very short period of time.

This thoroughly revised Second Edition has been updated with additional matter, many solved papers, including university examination problems and numerous exercises for practice.

Special care has been taken to maintain high degree of accuracy in the theory and numericals throughout the book.

We take this opportunity to express our sincere thanks to Dineshbhai Furia of Nirali Prakashan, a reputed pioneer in the publication field. Our special thanks to Jignesh Furia for their effective cooperation and great care in bringing out this revised edition. We also appreciate the efforts of M. P. Munde and the entire staff of Engineering Books Deptt. of Nirali Prakashan for bringing this book to the students in a timely manner.

We sincerely hope that this "Second Edition" will also be warmly received by all concerned as in the past.

Valuable suggestions from our esteemed readers to improve the book are most welcome and highly appreciated.

Pune   –Authors

PREFACE TO THE FIRST EDITION

It gives us immense pleasure to present this book **'Formal Language & Automata Theory'** to the students of Third Year Degree Course in **Computer Engineering** of the North Maharashtra University, Jalgaon (2014).

Authors has tried to introduce the subject to the average students. The subject matter has been developed in a logical and coherent manner with neat illustrations along with a fairly large number of Solved Problems of Finite Automata and Regular Grammer.

The Objective of this text are :

Unit I Covers : Introduction to Basic Concepts of Finite State Machines.

Unit II Covers : Regular Expressions and Finite Automata.

Unit III Covers : Context free Grammar and Normal forms for context free grammars.

Unit IV Covers : Concept of Pushdown Stack Memory Machines and Production Systems.

Unit V Covers : Construction of Turing Machines.

We take this opportunity to express our thanks to **Shri. Dineshbahi Furia**, **Shri. Jignesh Furia** and **Shri. M. P. Munde** and team of Nirali Prakashan namely, Mrs. Deepali Lachake, Mrs. Shilpa Kale and Miss. Mandakini Jadhavar.

We are also thankful to **Mr. P. M. More**, Branch Manager, Jalgaon Office for his valuable help and efforts for promotion of our book.

Our special thanks to our family members, students, and all those who directly or indirectly supported us in this project.

Any suggestions and feedback shall be appreciated and acknowledged.

September 2014

Pune   **Authors**

SYLLABUS

Unit I : Finite State Machines   **(08 Hrs)**

Mathematical Preliminaries:

(a) Sets, Relations and Functions
(b) Alphabets, Words / Strings, their Properties and operations
(c) Graphs and trees
(d) Basic machine

Finite State Machines:

(e) State tables, Transition graph
(f) Adjacency matrix
(g) Description of a Finite automaton
(h) Transition Systems
(i) Properties of Transition functions
(j) Acceptability of a string by a FA
(k) Deterministic and Non-deterministic FSM's
(l) Equivalence of DFA and NFA
(m) Moore and Mealy Models
(n) Minimization of Finite Automata
(o) FSM with Epsilon moves

Unit II : Regular Expressions   **(08 Hrs)**

(a) Definition, Identities for Regular Expressions
(b) Finite Automata and Regular Expressions
Transition System Containing ^-moves, NDFAs with ^-moves and Regular
Expressions, Conversion of Nondeterministic Systems to Deterministic Systems
(c) Building RE
(d) Construction of Finite Automata Equivalent to a Regular Expression
(e) Conversion of RE to FA
(f) Converting FA to RE
(g) Equivalence of two FA
(h) Pumping lemma for regular sets
(i) Applications of Pumping lemma
(j) Closure properties of Regular sets

Unit III : Grammars   **(08 Hrs)**

(a) Definition
(b) Derivation trees
(c) Leftmost and Rightmost Derivations
(d) Ambiguous grammar

(e) Removal of ambiguity
(f) Chomsky hierarchy
(g) Construction of Reduced Grammar
(h) Eliminating Useless symbols
(i) Eliminating Epsilon productions
(j) Eliminating Unit productions

Normal Forms for Context – free Grammars
(k) Chomsky Normal Form
(l) Greibach Normal Form
(m) Reduced Forms – CNF and GNF
(n) Reduction to CNF and GNF
(o) Pumping Lemma for Context – free Languages
(p) Decision Algorithms for Context- free Languages

Unit IV : Pushdown Stack Memory Machines & Production Systems (08 Hrs)

Pushdown Stack Memory Machines
(a) Definition, PDM examples
(b) Acceptance by PDA
(c) Power of PDM
(d) Deterministic and Non-deterministic PDM
(e) Construction of PDA from CFG
(f) Construction of CFG from PDA

Production Systems
(a) Definition, Post canonical system
(b) PMT systems
(c) Markov algorithm

Unit V : Turing Machine (08 Hrs)

(a) Turing Machine Model
(b) Representation of Turing Machines
(c) Language Acceptability By Turing Machines
(d) Design of Turing Machines
(e) Techniques for TM Construction
(f) Variants of Turing Machines
(g) Composite and Iterated TM
(h) Universal TM
(i) TM limitations
(j) The Halting problem

CONTENTS

Unit I : Finite State Machines	1.1-1.70
Unit II : Regular Expressions	2.1-2.44
Unit III : Grammars	3.1-3.50
Unit IV : Push Down Stack Memory Machines & Production Systems	4.1-4.38
Unit V : Turing Machine	5.1-5.32
University Question Papers (May 2015)	P.1-P.2

◈ ◈ ◈

Unit - I

FINITE STATE MACHINES

1.1 INTRODUCTION

A formal language is an abstraction of the general characteristics of a language. A formal language consists of a set of symbols and some rules of formation by which these symbols can be combined into entities called as strings or sentences. A formal language is the set of all strings permitted by the rules of formation.

1.1.1 Symbols/Alphabets

Alphabet is a finite, non-empty set of symbols.

For representing alphabet, we are using the Σ symbol.

Example 1.1 : $\Sigma = \{0, 1\}$ It is a set of binary alphabets
$\Sigma = \{A, B, C \ldots Z\}$ It is a set of capital letters
$\Sigma = \{a, b, c \ldots Z)$ It is a set of small case letters
$\Sigma = \{0, 1, 2 \ldots 9)$ It is set of decimal numbers
$\Sigma = \{0, 1, 2\}$ It is a set ternary alphabets

1.1.2 Strings

Finite sequence of symbols from alphabet is nothing but a string or word.

Example 1.2 :
1. 0110110 : It is a string of binary alphabet.
2. abc : It is a string of lower case letters.
3. ABCD : It is a string of upper case letters.
4. 5922 : It is a string of decimal alphabet.

"Hello" is one string, then the length of that string is $|Hello| = 5$.

Suppose w is a string, then we are using $|w|$ for calculating the length of that string.

1. w = Hello
   $|w| = 5$
2. w = Hi
   $|w| = 2$
3. Length of empty string is 0.
   $|\epsilon| = 0$

Reversal of String :
- In this, we are taking the reversal of a string.
- Suppose w is a string, w^R is the reverse of that string.
  Example :   w = Hellow
             w^R = olleH   ($\because$ Reversal of w)
- Exponential notations are used for representing the set of all strings of particular length.

$$\Sigma^K = \text{set of strings of length K}$$
$$\Sigma = \{a, b\}$$
$$\Sigma^1 = \{a, b\}$$
$$\Sigma^2 = \{ab, bb, aa, ba\}$$

In the above set, we are having those strings which are having length as 2 over an alphabets a, b

$$\Sigma^3 = \{abb, aaa, bbb, aba, bba\}$$

1.1.3 Language

- Set of strings is nothing but a language.

OR

Finite set of strings is nothing but a language.

OR

A language is a subset of strings over an alphabet Σ.
- Mathematical representation of language is

$$L \subseteq \Sigma^*$$

Meaning of the above expression is, L is a language and it is a subset of strings over an alphabet present in the set.

Examples 1.3 :
1. $\Sigma = \{0, 1\}^*$
   L = {0, 1, 01, 11, 00, 110, 0110 ... }
2. Set of all strings ending with 01
   L = {01, 001, 1101, 11001, ... }
3. Set of all strings starting with 11
   L = {11, 110, 1111, 110110, ... }
4. ϕ is the empty language.

1.1.4 Kleene Closure

Given an alphabet Σ. The Kleene closure of Σ is given by

$$\Sigma^* = \Sigma^0 + \Sigma^1 + \Sigma^2 + \Sigma^3 \ldots$$

$\quad\quad\quad\quad\quad\quad\downarrow\quad\quad\downarrow\quad\quad\quad\downarrow$

$\quad\quad\quad\quad\quad\epsilon$ string $\quad$ string of $\quad$ string of
$\quad\quad\quad\quad\quad\quad\quad\quad\quad$ length 1 $\quad$ length 2

If $\Sigma = \{x\}$
  $\Sigma^* = \{\epsilon, x, xx, xxx, xxxx \ldots\}$
If $\Sigma = \{a, b\}$
  $\Sigma^* = \{\epsilon, a, b, ab, ba, aa, aaab, baab\}$

1.1.5 Natural and Formal Language

Natural Language :
- Natural language is a piece of jargon to refer to languages like English, French, German etc.
- They are called natural because, we do not invent them; we naturally acquite them.
- A language is neither good nor bad considered in itself, for example, it is not designed or invented for a purpose.

Properties of Natural Language :
1. **Syntax :** It refers to the way in which words may be combined to form phrases and sentences.
2. **Semantics :** It is an exceptionally complex and confusing area. Just what is part of semantics as opposed to syntax is a question much disputed.
3. **Pragmatics :** It is used as a general term for referring to all kinds of effects on what we say - the thought we express.

Formal Language :
- A formal language is one we invent for some purpose or other.
- A programming language such as LISP, for instance is a formal language invented for the purpose of programming computers.
- A formal language consists of :
  An alphabet of symbols 'A' and
  Rules (syntax) for their combination.
- A formal language is based on rules which are explicitly stated :
  List of symbols is explicitly stated.
  Rules for forming a string (word) are explicitly stated.
  Rules for forming a sentence are explicitly stated.

1.1.6 Basic Machine

Definition :
A machine is defined as a system where energy, materials and information are transformed without direct intervention of human being.
In computer science, a machine used for transformation of information.

Characteristics of a Machine :

(1) Input, (2) Output, (3) States, (4) State relation, (5) Output relation.

- **(1) Input (I/p) :** This is a sequence of symbols from the set of alphabet that is applied to the machine.
- **(2) Output (O/p) :** It is a sequence of output symbols from the finite set of output symbols.
  This sequence is the output of the machine in response to any input.
- **(3) States :** Various states like q_0, q_1, q_2.
- **(4) State relation :** The next state of a machine depends on the present state and the next input.
- **(5) Output relation :** Output is related to either state only or to both input and the current state.

1.2 SOME MATHEMATICAL PRELIMINARIES

1.2.1 Sets

A set is determined by its elements. A set is a collection of elements without any structure other than membership

Some Important Points Regarding Sets

- A set is a Finite or Infinite.
  e.g. Finite: A = {11,12,21,22}   Infinite: A = {3,5,7,9,....}
- The order in which we write the elements in the set is irrelevant.
- A precise way of describing a set without listing the elements explicitly is to give a property that characterizes the elements.
  e.g. (a) B = {x | x is an odd integer greater than 1}
       (b) A = {x| x is a two digit integer, each of whose digit is 1 or 2}
- To say that x is an element of A, we write x ∈ A.
- For two sets A and B, we say that A is proper subset of B and written as A ⊆ B, if every element of A is an element of B.
- Two sets are equal, if they have exactly the same elements and this is the same saying that each is a subset of other.
  e.g. A = B says that A ⊆ B and B ⊆ A
- The complement of a set A is the set A' of everything that is not an element of A.
  e.g.   A' = { x ∈ U | x ∉ A }
  where U is Universal Set.

Operations on Set :

1. Union :

$$A \cup B = \{x \mid x \in A \text{ or } x \in B\}$$

e.g. $A = \{1, 2, 3, 4\}$ and $B = \{2, 4, 6, 8\}$

$A \cup B = \{1, 2, 3, 4, 6, 8\}$

Intersection :

$$A \cap B = \{x \mid x \in A \text{ and } x \in B\}$$

e.g. $A = \{1, 2, 3, 4\}$ and $B = \{2, 4, 6, 8\}$

$A \cap B = \{2, 4\}$

Set Difference :

$$A - B = \{x \mid x \in A \text{ and } x \notin B\}$$

The difference $A - B$ is the set of everything in A but not in B.

e.g. $A = \{1, 2, 3, 4\}$ and $B = \{2, 4, 6, 8\}$

$A - B = \{1, 3\}$

Properties of Set :

1. **The Commutative Laws :**

    $A \cup B = B \cup A$

    $B \cap A = A \cap B$

2. **The Associative Laws :**

    $A \cup (B \cup C) = (A \cup B) \cup C$

    $A \cap (B \cap C) = (A \cap B) \cap C$

3. **The Distributive Laws :**

    $A \cup (B \cap C) = (A \cup B) \cup C \, (A \cup C)$

    $A \, (B \, C) = (A \, B)(A \, C)$

4. **The Idempotent Laws :**

    $A \cup A = A$

    $A \cap A = A$

5. **The Absorptive Laws :**

    $A \cup (A \cap B) = A$

    $A \cap (A \cup B) = A$

6. **The De Morgan Laws :**

    $\overline{(A \cup B)} = \overline{A} \cap \overline{B}$

    $\overline{(A \cup B)} = \overline{A} \cap \overline{B}$

In order to visualize a set that is formed from primitive sets by using the set operations, it is often helpful to draw a Venn Diagram.

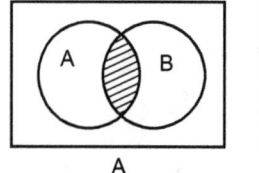
A

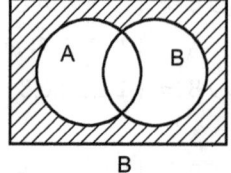
B

Fig. 1.1

Fig. 1.1 (A) represents set $A \cap B$. Fig. 1.1 (B) represents $(\overline{A} \cap \overline{B})'$.

1.2.2 Logic

Logic contains two things **Proposition** and **Logical Connectivity**.

Proposition :

It is a declarative statement that is sufficiently objective, meaningful and precise to have a truth value. (i.e. true or false)

e.g. (a) Fourteen is an even integer. – True
(b) 0=0 – True
(c) India is the largest country in the world. – False
(d) $x^2 < 4$ – It is not a proposition.

Logical Connectivity :

1. Conjunction : $p \wedge q$
2. Disjunction: $p \vee q$
3. Negation: $\sim p$

P	Q	p∧q	p∨q	~p
T	T	T	T	F
T	F	F	T	F
F	T	F	T	T
F	F	F	F	T

1.2.3 Functions

A function is a rule that assigns to elements of one set a unique element of another set. The first set is called as domain of function, second set is its range or codemain, and f is the function. We write

$$f : S_1 \rightarrow S_2$$

to indicate that the domain of S is a subset of S_1 and range of f is a subset of S_2. If the domain of S is all of S_1, we say that f is the total function on S_1, otherwise f is said to be a partial function.

1.2.4 Relations

Some Important Points :
- Relationship between objects.
- It is a set of ordered pairs.

  e.g. The first component of the pair is from the set called A and second component is from the set called B.
- In a relation, if A and B are the same set 'S', we say that relation is on S.
- If R is a relation and (a,b) is a pair in R, then we write relation as **aRb.**

Equivalence Relations :

If a relation R is Reflexive, Transitive and Symmetric, it is said to be Equivalence relations.

Properties of Equivalence Relations :

1. R is Reflexive if aRa for every a ∈ A.
2. R is Symmetric if for every a and b in A (a,b ∈ A), if aRb then bRa
3. R is Transitive if for every a,b and c in A (a,b,c ∈ A), if aRb and bRc then aRc.
4. R is an Equivalence relation on A if R is Reflexive, Transitive and Symmetric.
- The Relation which is Reflexive, Transitive but Anti-symmetric is called as *Partial Ordering Relation*.

Example 1.4 :

Find Transitive, Symmetric and Reflexive closure of the relation R = { (1,2), (2,3), (3,4), (5,4) }.

Solution :

1. **Transitive Closure**

$$R^+ = \{ (1,2), (2,3), (3,4), (5,4), (1,3), (2,4), (1,4) \}$$

Reasons : (1,2) and (2,3) Hence (1,3)

(2,3) and (3,4) Hence (2,4)

(1,3) and (3,4) Hence (1,4)

2. **Symmetric Closure**

$$R = \{ (1,2), (2,3), (3,4), (5,4), (2,1), (3,2), (4,3), (4,5) \}$$

Reasons : (1,2) hence (2,1) Similarly (3,2), (4,3), (4,5)

3. **Reflexive Closure**

$$R = \{ (1,2), (2,3), (3,4), (5,4), (1,1), (2,2), (3,3), (4,4), (5,5) \}$$

1.2.5 Trees

Definition of Tree

Tree is a finite set of nodes such that

- There is a specially designed node as a root node.
- The remaining nodes are partitioned into n ≥ 0 disjoint sets $T_1, T_2 \ldots T_n$, Where each of these sets is a tree. $T_1, T_2 \ldots T_n$ are the subtress of the root node.

Basic Concepts Related to Tree

- **Node :** Each element of tree is called as node
- **Edges :** The lines connecting the nodes are called edges or branches.
- **Root node :** Specially designated node and which does not have any parent.
- **Child node :** All the immediate successors of a node are its child nodes.

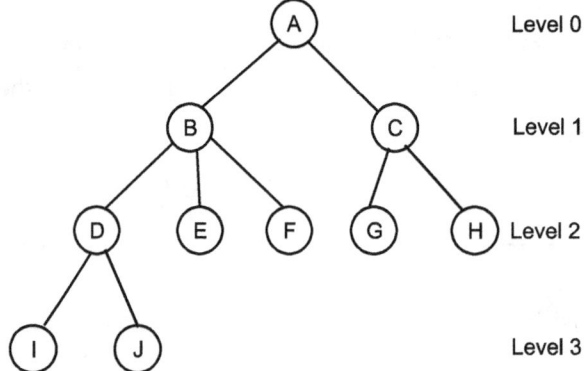

Fig. 1.2

See in Fig. B and C are the child of node A.

    D, E, F are the children of node B

- **Parent Node :** The immediate predecessor of a node is called parent node. e.g.
  - Immediate predecessor of D, E and F are node B then B is the parent node of D, E and F.
  - Immediate predecessor of G, H is node C then G is the parent node of G, H.
- **Leaf node / Terminal node :** A node that does not have any child is called leaf node or terminal node. e.g.

  Node J, J, E, F, G and H are the leaf node because they does not having any child node.

- **Level of Tree :** Level of any node is defined as the distance of that node from the root node. e.g.

  Level of root node A = 0

  Level of node B, C = 1

  Level of node D, E, F, G, H = 2

- **Height of Tree :** The total no. of levels in a tree is the height of that tree. e.g.

  Height of the above tree is 4.

- **Degree :** The no. of subtree or children of a node is called its degree. e.g.

  Degree of node A = 2

  Degree of node B = 3

- **Forest :** A forest is a set of n disjoint trees where n ≥ 0. If we removing root node from tree then we get forest consisting of its subtress.

- **Binary Tree :** In Binary tree no node can have more than two children i.e. node can have 0, 1 or 2 children. Each child is designated as either left child or right child.

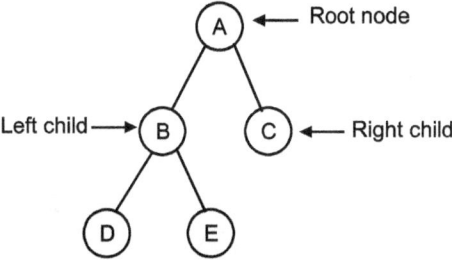

Fig. 1.3

- **Traversal of a Binary Tree :** Traversing a Binary tree means visiting each node in tree exactly only single time. Traversal of tree gives linear order of the nodes.

There are three main tasks for traversing

1. Visit root node
2. Visit left subtree
3. Visit right subtree

We traversing these task in different order. We are getting 3! = 6 ways for traversing the tree. But mainly we are using three ways for traversing the tree.

1. Preorder traversal
2. Inorder traversal
3. Postorder traversal

1. **Preorder Traversal :**
   - Visit root node (N)
   - Visit left subtree of root in preorder (L)
   - Visit right subtree of root in preorder (R)

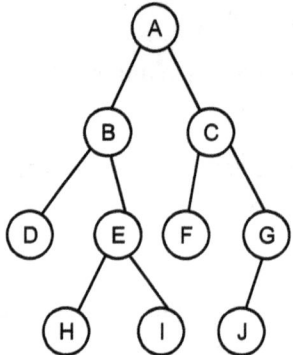

Fig. 1.4

Preorder traversal of above tree – AB DE HI CF GJ

2. **Inorder Traversal**
   - Visit left subtree of root in inorder (L)
   - Visit root (N)
   - Visit right subtree of root in inorder (R)

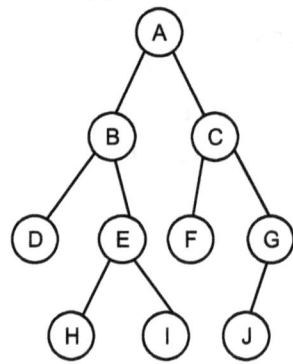

Fig. 1.5

In order traversal : OBHEJAFCJG.

3. **Postorder Traversal**
   - Visit the left subtree of root in postorder (L)
   - Visit right subtree of root in postorder (R)

- Visit root node (N)

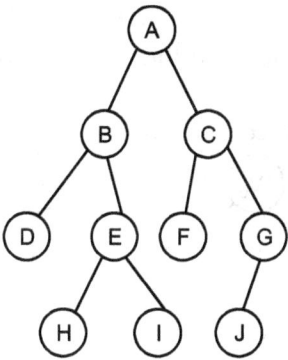

Fig. 1.6

Postorder traversal : DHJEBFJOCA

1.2.6 Graph

A graph is collection of vertices and edges. Graphs is represented as

$$G = \{V, E\}$$

where V = Set of vertices

E = Set of Edges present in the graph.

- Edge is line or arce which is used for connecting two vertices and it is denoted by pair (i-j) i, j ∈ v.

There are two types of graph.
1. Directed graph
2. Undirected graph.

1. Direct Graph : A directed graph is a graph which has ordered pair of vertices (u, v). u is the head and v is the tail of the edge.

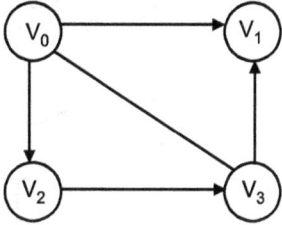

Fig. 1.7 : Directed Graph

$$V = \{V_0, V_1, V_2, V_3\}$$
$$E = \{(V_0, V_1), (V_0, V_2), (V_0, V_2), (V_0, V_3), (V_2, V_3), (V_3, V_1)\}$$

The above graph containing 5 edges which maintained in set of E.

2. Undirected Graph
- A graph, which has unordered pain of vertices is called undirected graph.
- If u and v containing the edge, then this edge can be represented by either (u, v) or (v, u),
- In this order of vertices are not considered.

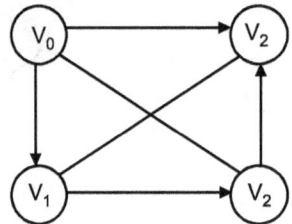

Fig. 1.8 : (a) Undirected graph

Representation Technique of Graph
- A graph containing mainly two parts
  1. Vertices
  2. Edges
- So we required data structure for storing the information regarding to each vertices and edges present in the graph.
- There are mainly two ways for representing the graph.
1. Adjacency matrix
2. Adjacency list

1. Adjacency Matrix
- For mainting the information regarding to adjacent vertices the adjacency matrix is used.
- From this matrix we are getting information reporting to adjacent vertices of a particular vertex.
- Example : Adjacency matrix for directed graph. Take one graph containing 4 vertices as V_0, V_1, V_2, V_3 and containing 8 edges as (V_0, V_1), (V_0, V_3), (V_1 V_3), (V_1, V_2) (V_1, V_0), (V_2, V_3), (V_3, V_2).

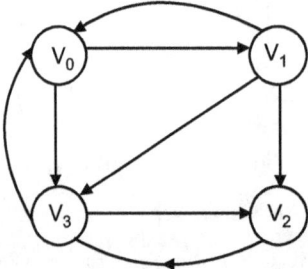

Fig. 1.8 : (b)

See how we are constructing the adjacency matrix for the above graph is as follows :

- The graph containing four vertices that why take the matrix order is 4×4

$$\begin{array}{c} \quad\quad V_0\ V_1\ V_2\ V_3 \\ \begin{array}{c} V_0 \\ V_1 \\ V_2 \\ V_3 \end{array} \left[\begin{array}{cccc} 0 & 0 & 0 & 0 \\ 0 & 0 & 0 & 0 \\ 0 & 0 & 0 & 0 \\ 0 & 0 & 0 & 0 \end{array} \right] \end{array}$$

- 1st row represents 1st vertex.

  2nd row represents 2nd vertex so on.

Similarly 1st column represents 1st vertex.

2nd column represents 2nd vertex and so on.

- The entries in the adjacency matrix are filled using this definition.

  $A(i, j) = 1$ if there is an edge from vertex i to j

  $A(i, j) = 0$ if there is an edge from vertex j to i

- Adjacency matrix for the above directed graph as follows

$$\begin{array}{c} \quad\quad V_0\ V_1\ V_2\ V_3 \\ \begin{array}{c} V_0 \\ V_1 \\ V_2 \\ V_3 \end{array} \left[\begin{array}{cccc} 0 & 1 & 0 & 1 \\ 1 & 0 & 1 & 1 \\ 0 & 0 & 0 & 1 \\ 1 & 0 & 1 & 0 \end{array} \right] \end{array}$$

In the graph V_0 to V_1 edge is present thats why matrix entry $A(0, 1) = 1$

edge from V_0 to V_3, so matrix entry $A(0, 3) = 1$

edge from V_1 to V_2, so matrix entry $A(1, 2) = 1$

edge from V_1 to V_3, so matrix entry $A(1, 3) = 1$

edge from V_2 to V_3, so matrix entry $A(2, 3) = 1$ and soon.

(i) Adjacency Matrix for Weighted Graph.

- If graph has some weights on its edge then the elements of adjacency matrix can be defined as

  $A(i, j)$ = Weight on edge   if there is an edge from vertex i to j

  $A(i, j) = 0$ otherwise

- Take one weighted graph containing 4 vertices and the graph is as follow

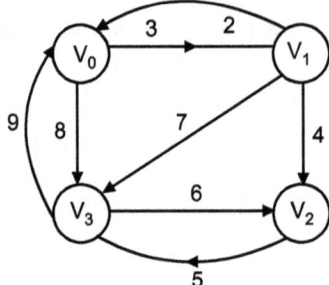

Fig. 1.8 (c)

Adjacency matrix for the above graph

$$\begin{array}{c} \\ V_0 \\ V_1 \\ V_2 \\ V_3 \end{array} \begin{bmatrix} V_0 & V_1 & V_2 & V_3 \\ 0 & 2 & 0 & 8 \\ 3 & 0 & 4 & 7 \\ 0 & 0 & 0 & 5 \\ 9 & 0 & 6 & 0 \end{bmatrix}$$

(ii) Adjacency Matrix for Undirected Graph

- If the graph is undirected graph then the elements of adjacency matrix can be defined as

$$\left. \begin{array}{l} A(i, j) = 1 \\ A(j, i) = 1 \end{array} \right\} \text{ if the edge is present in between vertex i and j}$$

Take one undirected graph and construct adjacency matrix for that graph.

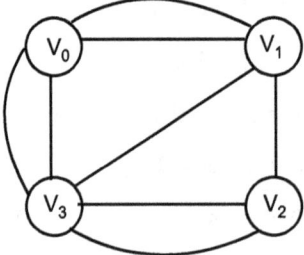

Fig. 1.8 (d)

Adjanency matrix for the above graph

$$\begin{array}{c} \\ V_0 \\ V_1 \\ V_2 \\ V_3 \end{array} \begin{bmatrix} V_0 & V_1 & V_2 & V_3 \\ 0 & 1 & 0 & 1 \\ 1 & 0 & 1 & 1 \\ 0 & 1 & 0 & 1 \\ 1 & 1 & 1 & 0 \end{bmatrix}$$

2. Adjancency List

- If the graph is not dence means if the graph containing less edges then we are using adjacency list for representing the graph.
- In this technique we are using two linked list one list for maintaing the every vertex present in the graph and second list for storing adjacent vertixes of each node we called that list as a edge list.
- Suppose graph containing n vertices then we create 1st list for n vertices and after that we are creating n list for storing the adjacent vertices of each vertex.

Example 1.4 (a):

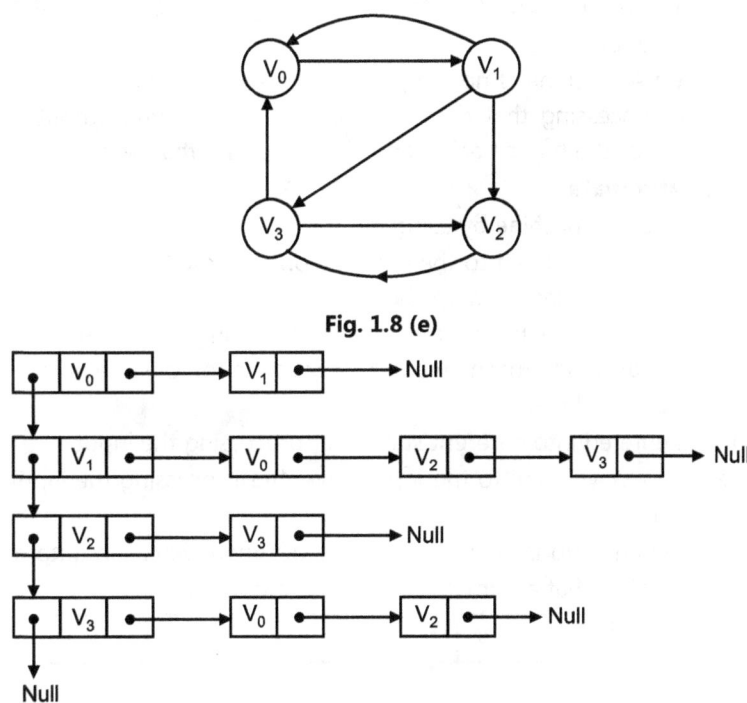

Fig. 1.8 (e)

Fig. 1.8 (f)

Edge list or adjacent vitices of vertex present in vertex list.

V_0, V_1, V_2, V_3 vertices are presenting in the graph.

We are adding the vertices in vertex list.

- Vertex V_0 having one adjacent node as V_1 so we are adding V_1 to adjacent list for vertex V_0.

- Vertex V_1 having three adjacent node as V_0, V_2 and V_3 so we are adding V_0, V_2, V_3 to the adjacent list of V_1.
- Vertex V_2 having one adjacent node as V_3. so add vertex V_3 to adjacent list of vertex V_2,
- Vertex V_3 having two adjacent node as V_0 and V_2 add V_0 and V_2 to adjacent list of vertex V_3,

1.3 FINITE AUTOMATA

- Finite automata is a severally restricted model of an actual computer.

OR

Finite automata is the study of abstract computing device or machines.

- Finite - limited / restricted

Automata Machine : A machine is nothing but one system in which we providing data to that system. System processing that data and come up with some output is nothing but machine. Machine reduce the human effort and time for doing that work.

Working of Finite Automata :
1. Input is provided to machine by using input tape.
2. Tape is used for giving input to the machine on tape multiple square boxes are there and each square contains input symbol.
3. The machine present in the box, machine containing the multiple states. q_0 state represent the start of the machine and * mark as the top of state name represents the final state of the machine.
4. Machine will entered into different state after processing the input.
5. Machine head always point to the input tape after processing the input head moved from left to right.
6. If the machine ends up in one of the final state then we called automata is correct, otherwise we called that automata as incorrect automata.

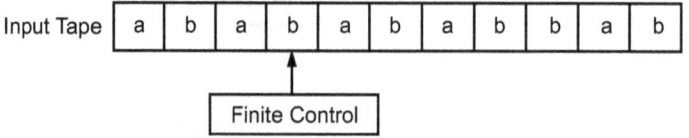

Fig. 1.9 : Finite state machine (FA)

Applications of Finite Automata :
- Designing and checking of digital circuits.
- String matching.
- Communication protocol for data exchange.
- Lexical analysis/analyzer in compilasation.

1.3.1 DFA : Deterministic Finite Automata

In deterministic finite automata, each transition is deterministic in nature. It means our machine can transist from current state to only one another state on each input symbol. Finite automata means in that finite number of states are present.

Definition of DFA :

Deterministic finite automata is a set of five tuple/quantiple.

$M = \{Q, \Sigma, \delta, q_0, F\}$

where,
- Q : finite set of states
- Σ : finite set of input symbols
- δ : this is a transition function
- $\delta : Q \times \Sigma \rightarrow Q$
- q_0 : q_0 is the start state of the machine, $q_1 \in Q$
- F : F is the final state of the machine and $F \subseteq Q$

Example :

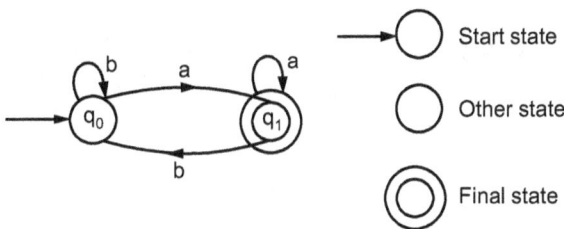

Fig. 1.10 : State transition diagram

In deterministic finite automata, states are represented by the circle. Start state is represented by an arrow. Final state is represented by a circle within circle. For representing the transition in between two states, we are using forwarded arrow from current state to next state and input symbols are mentioned it on the transition.

In Fig. 1.10, q_0 and q_1, there are two states present in automata.
- q_0 is start state.
- q_1 is a final state.
- input symbols are a, b.

From Fig. 1.10,

The definition of deterministic finite automata is

$M = \{Q, \Sigma, \delta, q_0, F\}$
$Q = \{q_0, q_1\}$
$\Sigma = \{a, b\}$
$\delta = \delta(q_0, a) \rightarrow q_1$
$\quad\quad \delta(q_0, b) \rightarrow q_0$
$\quad\quad \delta(q_1, a) \rightarrow q_1$
$\quad\quad \delta(q_1, b) \rightarrow q_0$

Transition in between two states is represented by state transition diagram.

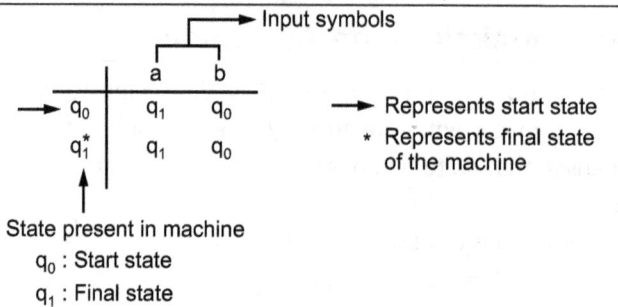

State present in machine
q_0 : Start state
q_1 : Final state

Fig. 1.11 : State transition table

Now we will check which type of language is accepted by the above machine.

Take one string as ababaa and check whether this string is accepted by the machine or rejected by the machine.

$\delta(q_0, ababaa) \rightarrow \delta(q_0, \underline{a}babaa)$

Start state   Input string

$\rightarrow \delta(q_1, \underline{b}abaa)$
$\rightarrow \delta(q_0, \underline{a}baa)$
$\rightarrow \delta(q_1, \underline{b}aa)$
$\rightarrow \delta(q_0, \underline{a}a)$
$\rightarrow \delta(q_1, \underline{a})$
$\rightarrow \delta(q_1, \epsilon)$

Final state   Empty string

At the last if we are getting final state and empty symbol then, we can say that the string is accepted by machine otherwise, rejected by the machine.

Properties of Transition Functions :

- Transition function gives the next state depending on the current state and current input.
- A transition function is problem specific and it depends on the problem.

e.g. give transition function for a "DFA to check whether a binary number has even number of 1's.

- Consider q_0 – indicates even number of 1's.

    q_1 – indicates odd number of 1's.

- As there is one more input symbol 0 which will not have no effect on number of 1's.

$\delta(q_0, 0) \Rightarrow q_0$

$\delta(q_0, 1) \Rightarrow q_1$
$\delta(q_1, 0) \Rightarrow q_1$
$\delta(q_1, 1) \Rightarrow q_0$

	0	1
→ q_0	q_0	q_1
q_1	q_1	q_0

(a) Transition table

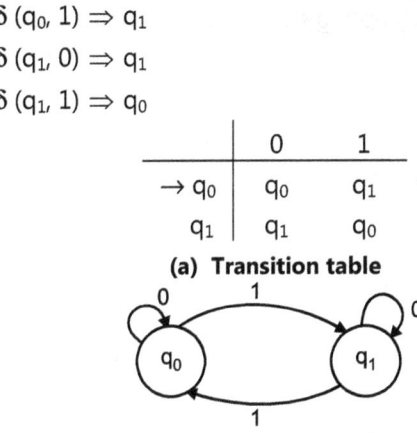

(b) Transition diagram

Fig. 1.12 : Transition table and transition diagram

Example 1.5 : Construct the transition table for the following :

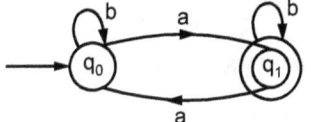

Fig. 1.13 : Transition diagram

Solution :

	a	b
→ q_0	q_1	q_0
* q_1	q_0	q_1

$\delta(q_0, a) \to q_1$
$\delta(q_0, b) \to q_0$
$\delta(q_1, a) \to q_0$
$\delta(q_1, b) \to q_1$

Definition of a DFA

$M = \{Q, \Sigma, \delta, q_0, F\}$

where,
$Q = \{q_0, q_1\}$
$\Sigma = \{a, b\}$
$q_0 = q_0$ start state
$q_1 = $ final state

Example 1.6 : Construct DFA for accepting the following language over an alphabet {0, 1}
   (a) Accept only 1 as a string.
   (b) Accept string as 01.
   (c) Number of 1's is even and number of 0's is even.
   (d) Number of 1's is odd and number of 0's is odd.

Solution : (a) Accept only 1 as a string

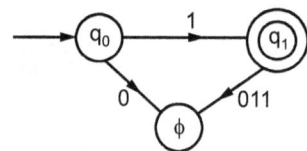

Fig. 1.14 : State transition diagram

Transition Table

	0	1
→ q_0	ϕ	q_1
* q_1	ϕ	ϕ

Definition : $M = \{Q, \Sigma, \delta, q_0, F\}$
where,
$Q = \{q_0, q_1\}$
$\Sigma = \{0, 1\}$
$q_0 = q_0$ start state
$F = q_1$

(b) Accept string as 01

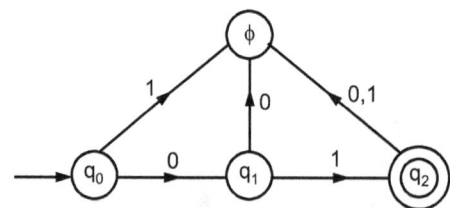

Fig. 1.15 : State transition diagram

Transition Table

	0	1
→ q_0	q_1	ϕ
q_1	ϕ	q_2
* q_2	ϕ	ϕ

(c) Number of 1's is even and number of 0's is even.

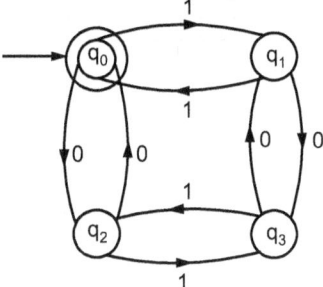

Fig. 1.16

Transition Table

	0	1
$\rightarrow q_0^*$	q_2	q_1
q_1	q_3	q_0
q_2	q_0	q_3
q_3	q_1	q_2

For example, take one string as 110011, and see this string is accepted or rejected by the above DFA.

$$\delta(q_0, \underline{1}10011) \rightarrow \delta(q_1, \underline{1}0011)$$
$$\rightarrow \delta(q_0, 0011)$$
$$\rightarrow \delta(q_2, 011)$$
$$\rightarrow \delta(q_0, 11)$$
$$\rightarrow \delta(q_1, 1)$$
$$\rightarrow \delta(q_0, \epsilon)$$

q_0 is final state and string is ϵ, means the above string is accepted by deterministic finite automata.

(d) Number of 1's is odd and number of 0's is odd.

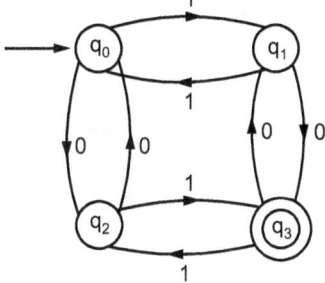

Fig. 1.17

Transition Table

	0	1
→ q_0	q_2	q_1
q_1	q_3	q_0
q_2	q_0	q_3
*q_3	q_1	q_2

Example 1.7 : Design a DFA which accepts the odd number of 1's and any number of 0's over an alphabet {0, 1}.

Solution :

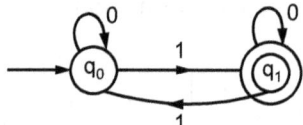

Fig. 1.18

From the given problem statement, the strings are accepted by our machine which are containing odd number of 1's and any number of 0's.

Transition Table

	0	1
→ q_0	q_0	q_1
*q_1	q_1	q_0

Example 1.8 : Draw DFA for the following language over {0, 1} :
1. All strings of length at most five.
2. All strings with exactly two 1's.
3. All strings containing at least two 0's.
4. All strings containing at most two 0's.
5. All strings starting with 1 and length of the string is divisible by 3.

Solution : (1) All strings of length at most five.
- Maximum length of string is five, so we require five + 1 states for forming the string.

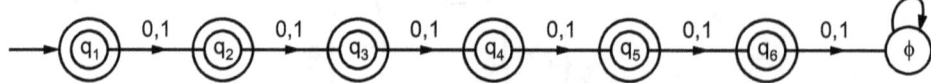

Fig. 1.10

- In above machine all strings should be accepted which are having length of strings equal to five or less than five.
- Those strings are rejected by machine which do not satisfy the condition.

	0	1
→ q_1 *	q_2	q_2
q_2 *	q_3	q_3
q_3 *	q_4	q_4
q_4 *	q_5	q_6
q_5 *	q_6	q_6

(2) All strings with exactly two one's.

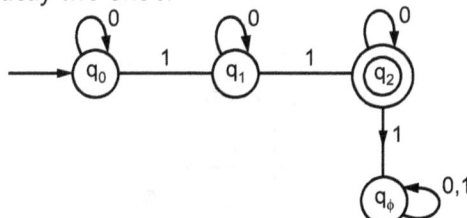

Fig. 1.20

(3) All strings containing at least two 0's.

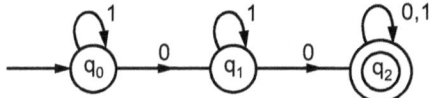

Fig. 1.21 : State transition diagram

(4) All strings containing at most two 0's.

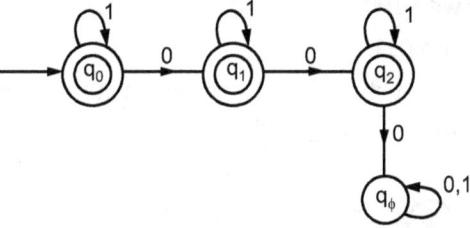

Fig. 1.22 : State transition diagram

Transition Table

	0	1
→ q_0 *	q_1	q_0
q_1 *	q_2	q_1
q_2 *	q_ϕ	q_2
q_ϕ	q_ϕ	q_ϕ

(5) All strings starting with 1 and length of the string is divisible by 3.

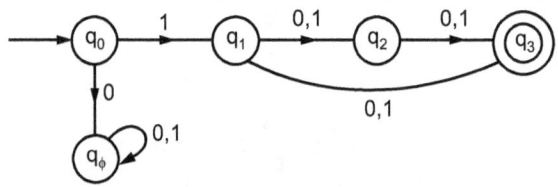

Fig. 1.23 : State transition diagram

- Each string start with 1 i.e. why we are taking the transition on 1, from q_0 to q_1 state.
- Second problem statement is that to accept those strings which are divisible by 3. For satisfying this condition, we are taking the strings in multiple of three.

State Transition Table

	0	1
$\to q_0$	q_ϕ	q_1
q_1	q_2	q_2
q_2	q_3	q_3
q_3^*	q_1	q_1
ϕ	q_ϕ	q_ϕ

Example 1.9 : Construct DFA for the following languages :
(a) All strings starting with 011.
(b) All strings starting with 100.
(c) All strings ending with 011.
(d) All strings with a as a substring i.e. 011 anywhere in the string.

Solution : (a) All strings starting with 011.

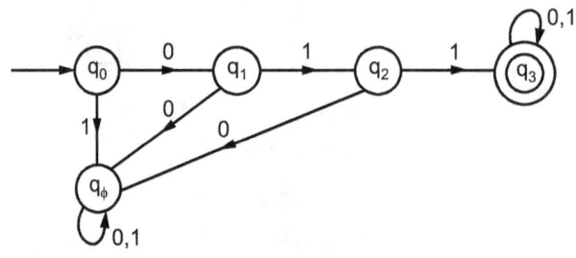

Fig. 1.24 : State transition diagram

- All strings start with <u>011</u> that is why first, we are taking 0 as the input followed by 11.
- If at the start, we are taking the input as 1 then machine goes into the dead state.

State Transition Table

	0	1
→ q_0	q_1	q_ϕ
q_1	q_ϕ	q_2
q_2	q_ϕ	q_3
*q_3	q_3	q_3
q_ϕ	q_ϕ	q_ϕ

(b) All strings starting with 100

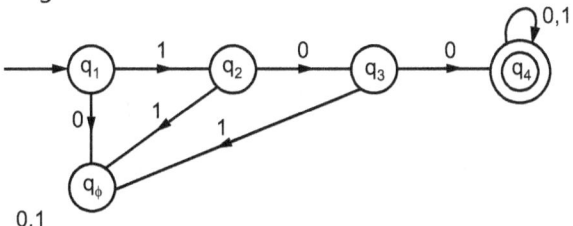

Fig. 1.25

State Transition Table

	0	1
→ q_1	q_ϕ	q_2
q_2	q_3	q_ϕ
q_3	q_4	q_ϕ
*q_4	q_4	q_4
q_ϕ	q_ϕ	q_ϕ

(c) All strings ending in 011.

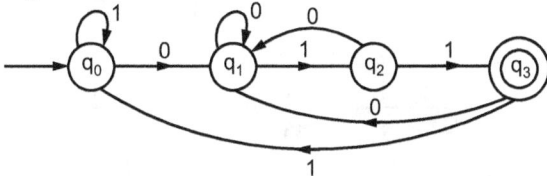

Fig. 1.26 : State transition diagram

State Transition Table

	0	1
→ q_0	q_1	q_0
q_1	q_1	q_2
q_2	q_1	q_3
*q_3	q_1	q_0

(d) All strings with 011 as substring

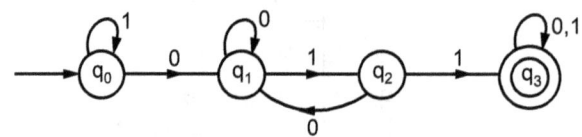

Fig. 1.27

Example 1.10 : Draw a FSM or DFA for the language L = {a, b, c} start with b and end with c.

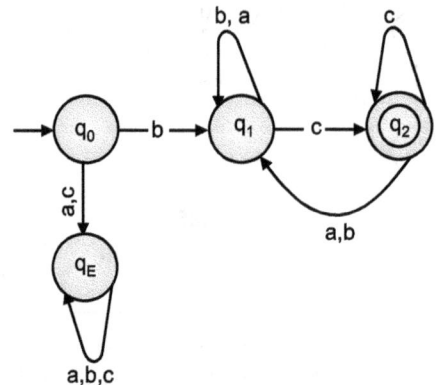

Fig. 1.28

Solution :

Input/State	a	b	c
q_0	q_E	q_1	q_E
q_1	q_1	q_1	q_2
q_2	q_1	q_1	q_2

Definition :   M = (Q, Σ, δ, q_0, F) where,
Q = { q_0, q_1, q_2}
Σ = { a, b, c}
δ = Transitions are given in state transition table.
q_0 = { q_0 }
F = { q_2 }

Simulation: (q_0, bacbc) -| (q_1, acbc) -| (q_1, cbc) -| (q_2, bc) -| (q_1, c) -| (q_2)

Example 1.11 : Design a Finite Automata that reads strings made up of letters in the Word 'CHARIOT' and recognizes those strings that contain the word 'CAT' as substring.

Solution :

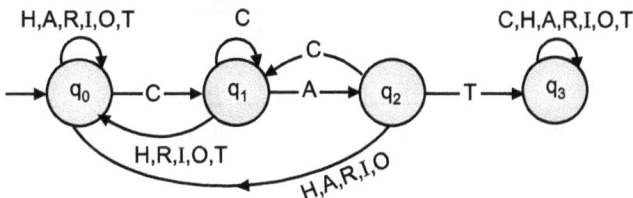

Fig. 1.29

Example 1.12 : Give a non-deterministic finite automata to accept the following language over $\{0,1\}^*$. The set of all strings containing either 101 or 110 as a substring.

Solution :

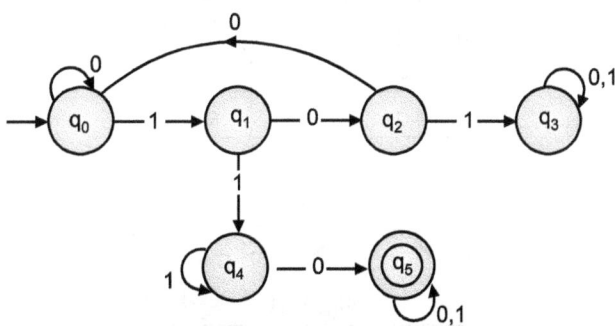

Fig. 1.30

1.3.2 Problems on Divisibility Testing

Follow the rules which are given below.

1. Write down the number of states vertically equal to the number for which you are testing the divisibility.

   e.g. Write down three states q_0, q_1, q_2 vertically in State Transition Table, if you are testing divisibility for '3'.

2. Write down all the inputs horizontally.

   e.g. For binary number, inputs are 0 and 1.

3. Then write down all the states horizontally in circular fashion row by row from initial state to final state.

e.g.

Q\Σ	0	1
→ q_0	q_0	q_1
q_1	q_2	q_0
q_2	q_1	q_2

4. Draw the abstract machine like above solved examples.
5. Repeat the remaining states which are mentioned in 'procedure to solve the problems on DFA'.

1. Divisibility by 3 :

Examples 1.13 : L = {0,1} | All strings when treated as binary number are congruent to 0 mod 3 (Accept the binary number divisible by 3).

Solution :

Q\Σ	0	1
→ q_0	q_0	q_1
q_1	q_2	q_0
q_2	q_1	q_2

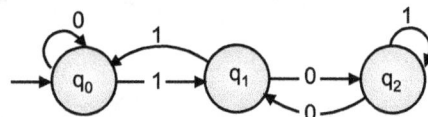

Fig. 1.31

Examples 1.14 : Construct a DFA for decimal number divisible by 3.

Solution: M = (Q, Σ, δ, q_0, F)

where,

Q = {q_0, q_1, q_2}
Σ = {0,1,2...9}
δ = Transitions are given in state transition table.
q_0 = initial state
F = { q_0 }

Transition table is as follows :

Q\Σ	0	1	2	3	4	5	6	7	8	9
→ q_0	q_0	q_1	q_2	q_0	q_1	q_2	q_0	q_1	q_2	q_0
q_1	q_1	q_2	q_0	q_1	q_2	q_0	q_1	q_2	q_0	q_1
q_2	q_2	q_0	q_1	q_2	q_0	q_1	q_2	q_0	q_1	q_2

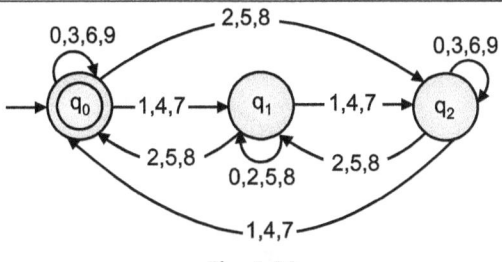

Fig. 1.32

Examples 1.15 : Construct a DFA for a ternary number divisible by 3.

Solution :

Q\Σ	0	1	2
→ q_0	q_0	q_1	q_2
q_1	q_0	q_1	q_2
q_2	q_0	q_1	q_2

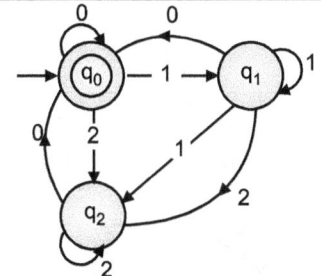

Fig. 1.33

For simulation first take any decimal number and convert it into ternary.

e.g. 1.14

3	12	0
3	4	1
3	1	1
	0	

$$12_{(10)} = 110_{(3)}$$

$(q_0, 110) \vdash (q_1, 10) \vdash q_0$ (final state)

2. Divisibility by 5 :

Example 1.16 : L = {0,1} | All strings when treated as binary number are congruent to 0 mod 5 (Accept the binary number divisible by 5).

Solution :

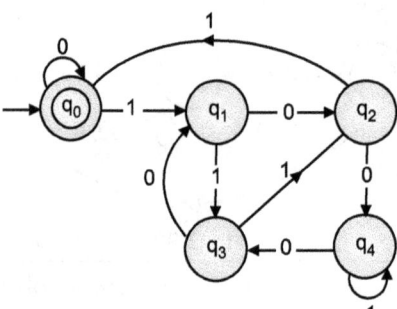

Fig. 1.34

Q\Σ	0	1
→q_0	q_0	q_1
q_1	q_2	q_3
q_2	q_4	q_0
q_3	q_1	q_2
q_4	q_3	q_4

Example 1.17 : L = {0,1,2} | All strings when treated as ternary number are congruent to 0 mod 5 (Accept the ternary number divisible by 5).

Solution :

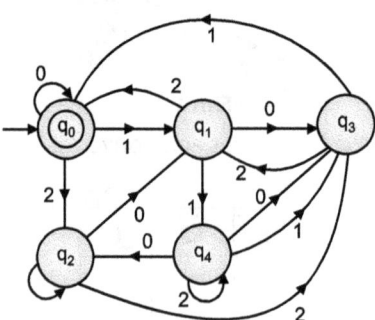

Fig. 1.35

Q\Σ	0	1	2
→q_0	q_0	q_1	q_2
q_1	q_3	q_4	q_0
q_2	q_1	q_2	q_3
q_3	q_4	q_0	q_1
q_4	q_2	q_3	q_4

Examples 1.18 : Design a FSM to check given decimal number is divisible by 4 or not.

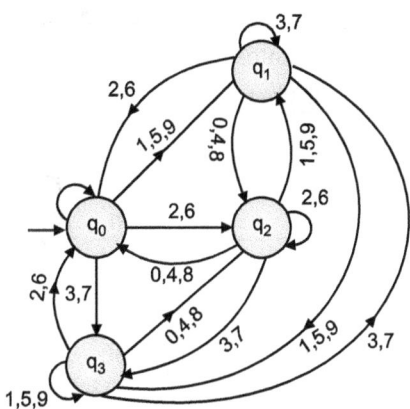

Fig. 1.36

Solution :

Q\Σ	0	1	2	3	4	5	6	7	8	9
→ q_0	q_0	q_1	q_2	q_3	q_0	q_1	q_2	q_3	q_0	q_1
q_1	q_2	q_3	q_0	q_1	q_2	q_3	q_0	q_1	q_2	q_3
q_2	q_0	q_1	q_2	q_3	q_0	q_1	q_2	q_3	q_0	q_1
q_3	q_2	q_3	q_0	q_1	q_2	q_3	q_0	q_1	q_2	q_3

1.3.3 NFA : Non-deterministic Finite Automata

Non-deterministic finite automata can reside in a multiple states at the same time.

Example 1.19 :

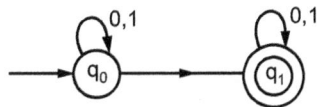

Fig. 1.37

Here on q_0, input is 1 then our machine will reside on two different states i.e. q_0 and q_1.

Definition of NFA :

Non-deterministic finite automata is a set of 5-tuples.

$$M = \{Q, \Sigma, \delta, q_0, F\}$$

where,
Q = A set of finite state
Σ = A set of input symbols

δ : Transition function
: $Q \times \Sigma \rightarrow 2^Q$ means power set of Q.
q_0 : Start state $q_0 \in Q$
F : Final state $F \subseteq Q$

Example 1.20 :

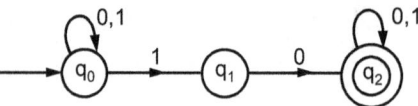

Fig. 1.38

State Transition Table

	0	1
→ q_0	q_0	{q_0 q_1}
q_1	q_2	φ
* q_2	q_2	q_2

See in Fig. 1.29, q_0 on 1, we are moving towards two different states as q_0 and q_1. In deterministic finite automata, we move towards only one state. But in NFA, we are getting different set of states.

Processing of String in NFA :

w is the string over an alphabet Σ^* and it is accepted in NFA. Let us see how the string is processed by NFA.

e.g. : w = 11100

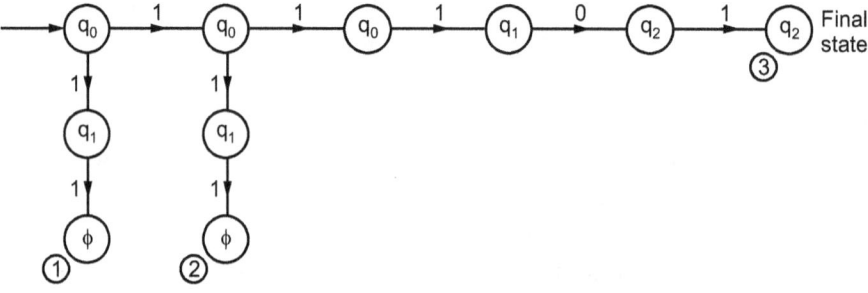

Fig. 1.39

We are getting 3 paths. But in (1) and (2) path the string is not accepted by FA, so that, we are using (3) path for accepting the string 11100 via path (5) 11100 is accepted by the machine.

Example 1.21 : Draw a non-deterministic automata to accept strings containing the substring 0101.

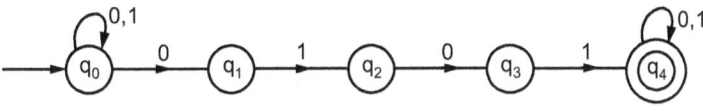

Fig. 1.40

Solution :

	0	1
→ q_0	{q_0, q_1}	{q_4}
q_1	φ	{q_2}
q_2	{q_3}	φ
q_3	φ	{q_4}
*q_4	{q_4}	{q_4}

Example 1.22 : Construct a NFA that accepts any positive number of occurrences of various strings from the following language L given by Fig. 1.32.

Solution :

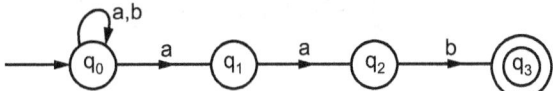

Fig. 1.41

State Transition Table

	a	b
→ q_0	{q_0, q_1}	q_0
q_1	q_2	–
q_2	–	q_3
*q_3	–	–

Example 1.23 : Construct the NFA and DFA for the following languages :
 (i) L = {x ∈ {a, b, c}* | x contains exactly one b immediately following c}
 (ii) L = {x ∈ {0, 1}* | x is starting with 1 and |x| is divisible by 3}
 (iii) L = {x ∈ {a, b}* | x consists any number of a's followed by at least one b}.

Solution : (i) L = {x ∈ {a, b, c}* | x contains exactly one b immediately following c}

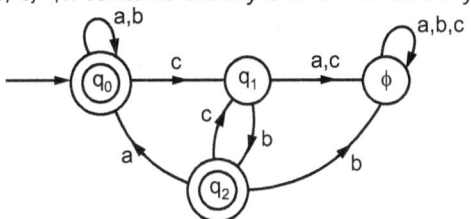

Fig. 1.42

(ii) L = {x ∈ {0, 1}* | x is starting with 1 and |x| is divisible by 3}

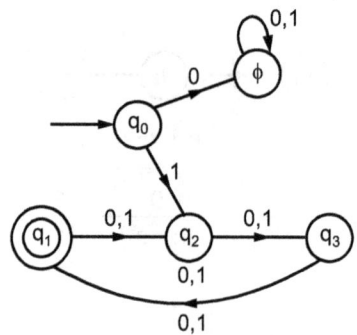

Fig. 1.43

(iii) L = {x ∈ {a, b}* | x consists any number of a's followed by at least one b}.

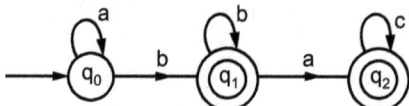

Fig. 1.44

Example 1.24 : Construct NFA for accepting L over {0, 1} such that each 1 is immediately preceded and immediately followed by 0.

Solution :

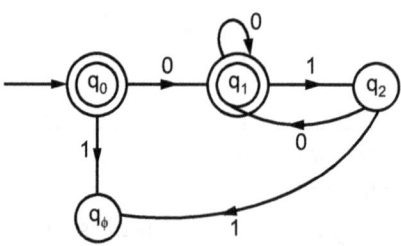

Fig. 1.45 : State transition diagram

State Transition Table

	0	1
→ q_0*	q_1	q_ϕ
q_1*	q_1	q_2
q_2	q_1	q_ϕ

Example 1.25 : Construct the NFA for binary number where the first and last digits are same.
Solution :

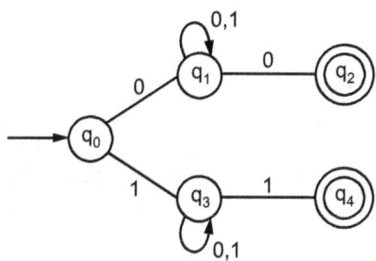

Fig. 1.46 : State transition diagram

State Transition Table

	0	1
→ q_0	q_1	q_3
q_1	{q_1, q_2}	q_1
* q_2	–	–
q_3	{q_3, q_4}	q_3
* q_4	–	–

Example 1.26 : Design a NFA for set of {0, 1}, the string start and end with 101 and end with 101.
Solution :

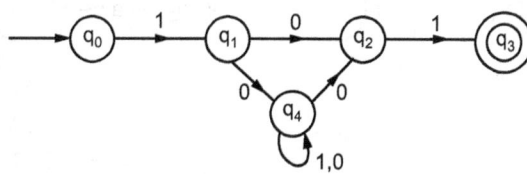

Fig. 1.47

The string start with 10 and end with 01 is possible in string of 101 – 101 string is also accepted by the above DFA.

Examples 1.27 : Draw the NFA for the language containing strings with either two consecutive 0's or consecutive 1's.
Solution :

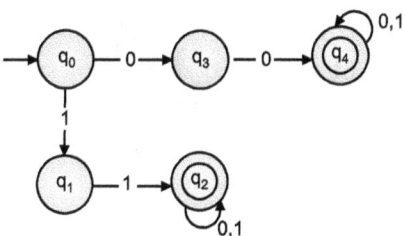

Fig. 1.48

Example 1.28 : L = {0, 1} accepts two 0's, which are separated by string of length 4i where i is an integer >=0.
Solution :

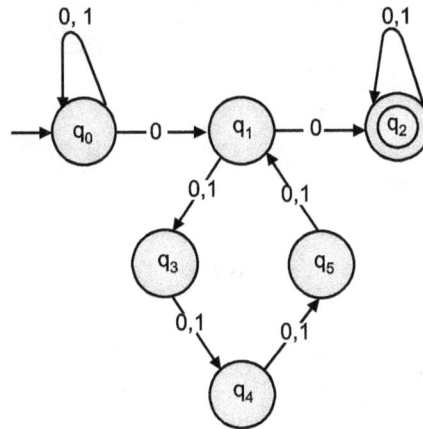

Fig. 1.49

Example 1.29 : L = {a, b} accept all strings in which sixth symbol from right is b.
Solution :

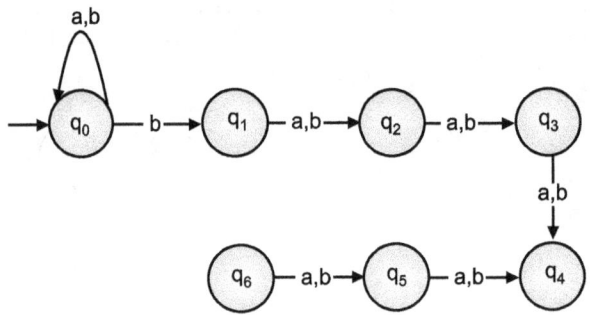

Fig. 1.50

1.3.4 ∈-NFA

∈ is nothing but empty symbol. By using this we can transits from one state to another without any input symbol.

Definition : ∈-NFA is the set of 5 tuples.

$$M = \{Q, \Sigma, q_0, \delta, F\}$$

where,
- Q = set of states
- Σ = set of input symbols
- q_0 = start states
- δ = transition function
- δ : Q × {Σ ∪ U} → 2a

Example 1.30 :

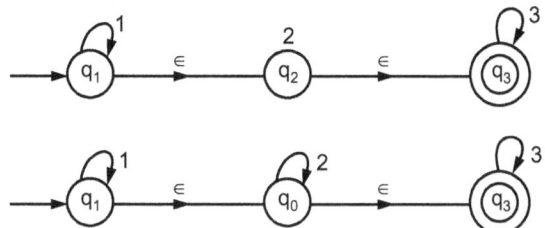

Fig. 1.51 : State transition diagram

Transition Table

	∈	1	2	2
→ q₁	{q₁}	{q₁}	φ	φ
q₂	{q₃}	φ	{q₂}	φ
q₃	φ	φ	φ	{q₃}

Examples of Divisibility :

Example 1.31 : Design a DFA which can accept a binary number divisible by 3.

Solution : Input in the binary form

$$\Sigma = \{0, 1\}$$

- When we divide any number by 3, possibilities for getting remainder is in either 0, 1, 2.
- 0, 1, 2 are in decimal form, so convert it into binary

    0 → 00, it is associated with q_0

    1 → 01, it is associated with q_1

    2 → 10, it is associated with q_2

- Required number of states are 3 because, we are required to handle 3 types of remainder.

The calculation of next remainder is as shown below.

Previous state	Next input	Calculation of remainder	Next state
00(q₀)	0	000%3 = 0	q₀
00(q₀)	1	001%3 = 1	q₁
01(q₁)	0	000%3 = 10	q₂
01(q₁)	1	011%3 = 0	q₀
11(q₂)	0	110%3 = 1	q₁
11(q₂)	1	111%3 = 10	q₂

Transition Table

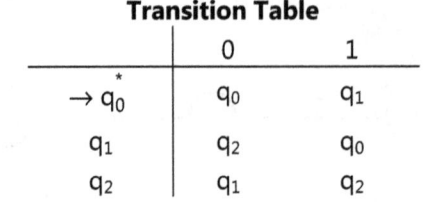

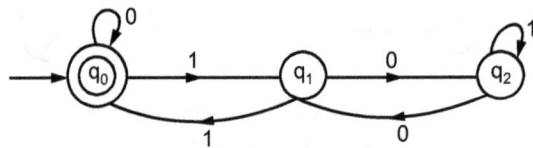

Fig. 1.52 : State transition diagram

Example 1.32 : Design DFA which can accept a binary number divisible by 4.

Solution : Possibilities for remainder.

$$0 \ (00) \to q_0$$
$$1 \ (01) \to q_1$$
$$2 \ (10) \to q_2$$
$$3 \ (11) \to q_3$$

Calculating the next state :

0(00)	0	000 % 4 = 00	it is associated with q_0
	1	001 % 4 = 01	it is associated with q_1
1(01)	0	010 % 4 = 10	it is associated with q_2
	1	011 % 4 = 11	it is associated with q_3
2(10)	0	100 % 4 = 00	it is associated with q_0
	1	101 % 4 = 01	it is associated with q_1
3(11)	0	110 % 4 = 10	it is associated with q_2
	1	111 % 4 = 11	it is associated with q_3

Transition Table

	0	1
$\to q_0^*$	q_0	q_1
q_1	q_2	q_0
q_2	q_0	q_1
q_3	q_2	q_3

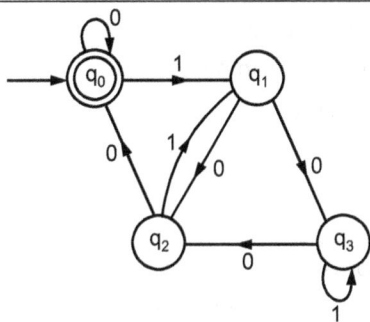

Fig. 1.53 : State transition diagram

1.3.5 Conversion of NFA to DFA

- In NFA, we resides in multiple state for each input in the machine and in DFA, we have only one transition path from the given path.
- The conversion steps for NFA to DFA is as follows :
  1. Tracing the various paths followed by the machine for the given string.
  2. Find the set of states from the start state of the machine for the each symbol of the string.
  3. If the set of states obtained from state 2 containing the final state then we conclude that the string is accepted by the NFA.

Example 1.33 : Convert following NFA to DFA.

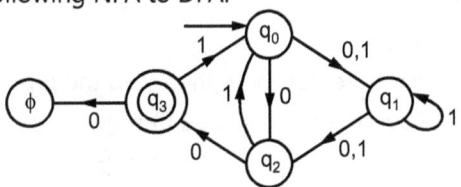

Fig. 1.54

Solution :

	0	1
→ q_0	{q_1, q_2}	{q_1}
q_1	{q_2}	{q_1, q_2}
q_2	{q_3}	{q_0}
* q_3	φ	{q_0}

Step - 1 : Take start state and find out 0 successor and 1 successor of the start state.

Start state is q_0,

$$0 \text{ successor of } q_0 = \delta(q_0, 0) = \{q_1, q_2\}$$
$$1 \text{ successor of } q_0 = \delta(q_0, 1) = \{q_1\}$$

{q_1, q_2} and {q_1} these are newly generated sets.

Take 0 and 1 successor of these sets in next state.

Step - 2 : (a)   0 successor of {q_1, q_2} = $\delta(\{q_1, q_2\}, 0)$
$$= \delta(q_1, 0) \cup \delta(q_2, 0)$$
$$= \{q_2\} \cup \{q_3\}$$
$$= \{q_2, q_3\}$$

1 successor of {q_1, q_2} = $\delta(\{q_1, q_2\}, 1)$
$$= \delta(q_1, 1) \cup \delta(q_2, 1)$$
$$= \{q_1, q_2\} \cup \{q_0\}$$
$$= \{q_0, q_1, q_2\}$$

(b)   0 successor of q_1 = {q_2}

1 successor of q_1 = {q_1, q_2}

Newly generated subsets are {q_2, q_3}, {q_0, q_1, q_2} and {q_2}.

Step - 3 :   0 successor of {q_2, q_3} = {q_3}

1 successor of {q_2, q_3} = {q_0}

0 successor of {q_0, q_1, q_2} = {q_1, q_2, q_3}

1 successor of {q_0, q_1, q_2} = {q_0, q_1, q_2}

0 successor of {q_2} = {q_3}

1 successor of {q_2} = {ϕ}

Newly generated subset is q_3 and {q_1, q_2, q_3}, that is why we are moving towards the next step, otherwise we will stop the process.

Note : If newly generated subsets are not there then stop the procedure.

Step - 4 :   0 successor q_3 = $\delta(q_3, 0)$ = ϕ

1 successor q_3 = $\delta(q_3, 1)$ = q_0

0 successor of {q_1, q_2, q_3} = {q_2, q_3}

1 successor of {q_1, q_2, q_3} = {q_1, q_2}

Collect all subsets generated in each step and draw transition table and diagram for the DFA.

	0	1
→ q_0	{q_1, q_2}	{q_1}
{q_1, q_2}	{q_2, q_3}	{q_1, q_2, q_0}
{q_1}*	{q_2}	{q_1, q_2}
{q_2, q_3}	{q_3}	{q_0}
{q_0, q_1, q_2}	{q_1, q_2, q_3}	{q_0, q_1, q_2}
{q_2}	{q_3}	ϕ
{q_3}*	ϕ	{q_0}
{q_1, q_2, q_3}*	{q_2, q_3}	{q_1, q_2}

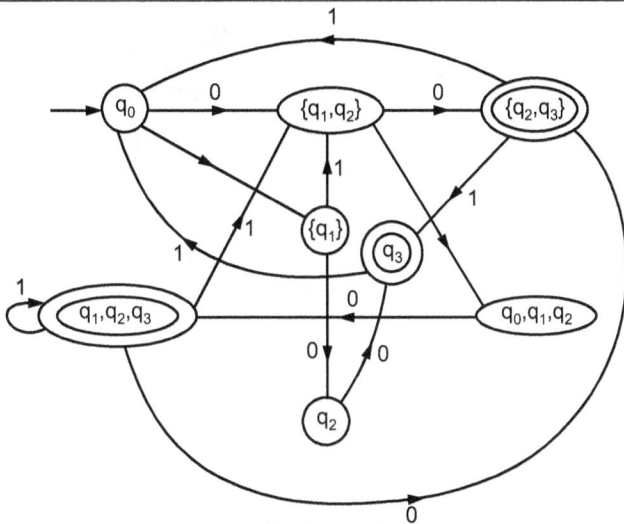

Fig. 1.55

In NFA, q_3 is the final state. So wherever q_3 is occurred in newly generated subset becomes the final state in DFA.

Example 1.34 : Convert to DFA the following NFA.

	0	1
{p}	{q, s}	q
q*	{r}	{q, r}
r	{s}	{p}
s*	φ	{p}

Solution :

Step - 1 : Start state p,

        0 successor of p = {q, s}
        1 successor of p = {q}

Take 0 and 1 successor of {q, s} and {q}.

Step - 2 :
        0 successor of {q} = {r}
        1 successor of {q} = {q, r}
        0 successor of {q, s} = {r}
        1 successor of {q, s) = {p, q, r}

Step - 3 :
        0 successor of r = {s}
        1 successor of s = {p}
        0 successor of {q, r} = {r, s}
        1 successor of {q, r} = {p, q, r}
        0 successor of {q, r} = {q, r, s}
        1 successor for {q, r} = {p, q, r}

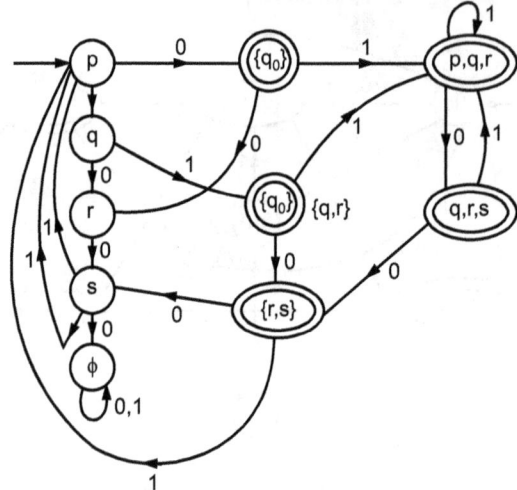

Fig. 1.56 : State transition diagram

Example 1.35 : Convert given NFA to DFA.

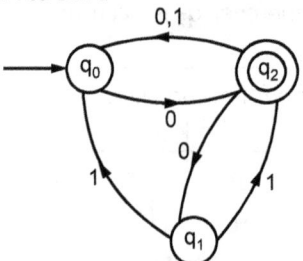

Fig. 1.57

Solution :

	0	1
→ q_0	$\{q_2\}$	ϕ
q_1	ϕ	$\{q_0, q_2\}$
*q_2	$\{q_0, q_1\}$	$\{q_0\}$

Step - 1 :   0 successor of q_0 = q_2
                    1 successor of q_ϕ = ϕ

  q_2 is newly generated state/subset.

Step - 2 :   0 successor of q_2 = $\{q_0, q_1\}$
                    1 successor of q_2 = $\{q_0\}$

  Newly generated state $\{q_0, q_1\}$

Step - 3 :   0 successor of $\{q_0, q_1\}$ = $\{q_2\}$
                    1 successor of $\{q_0, q_1\}$ = $\{q_0, q_2\}$

  Newly generated state $\{q_0, q_2\}$

Step - 4 :   0 successor of $\{q_0, q_2\} = \{q_0, q_1, q_2\}$
                 1 successor of $\{q_0, q_2\} = \{q_0\}$

Newly generated state $\{q_0, q_1, q_2\}$

Step - 5 :   0 successor of $\{q_0, q_1, q_2\} = \{q_0, q_1, q_2\}$
                 1 successor of $\{q_0, q_1, q_2\} = \{q_0, q_2\}$

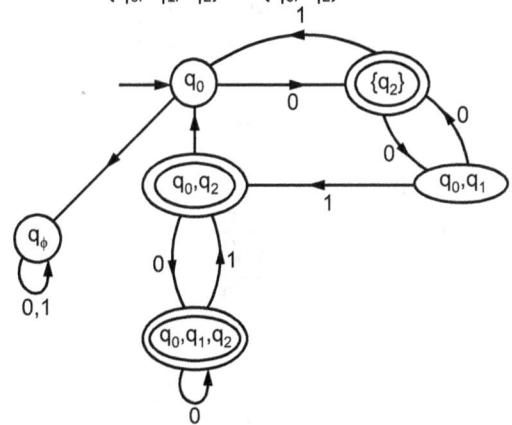

Fig. 1.58

Example 1.36 : Convert the following NFA to DFA.

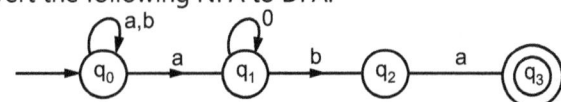

Fig. 1.59

Solution : Step - 1 :
                 a successor of $q_0 = \{q_0, q_1\}$
                 b successor of $q_1 = \{q_0\}$

Step - 2 :   a successor of $\{q_0, q_1\} = \{q_0, q_1\}$
               b successor of $\{q_0, q_1\} = \{q_0, q_2\}$

Step - 3 :   a successor of $\{q_0, q_2\} = \delta(\{q_0, q_2\}, a) = \{q_0, q_1, q_3\}$
               b successor of $\{q_0, q_2\} = \delta(\{q_0, q_2\}, b) = \{q_0\}$

Step - 4 :   0 successor of $\{q_0, q_1, q_3\} = \{q_0, q_1\}$
               1 successor of $\{q_0, q_1, q_3\} = \{q_0, q_2\}$

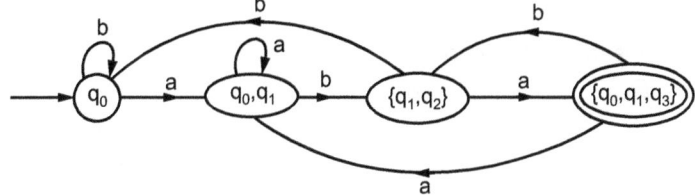

Fig. 1.60

1.3.6 Conversion of ∈-NFA to DFA

Example 1.37 : Convert ∈-NFA to DFA.

	∈	a	b	c
→p	φ	{p}	{q}	{r}
q	{p}	{q}	{r}	φ
r*	{q}	{r}	φ	{p}

Solution : Construct or draw a state transition diagram from the transition table.

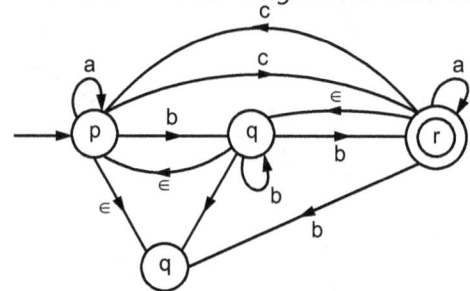

Fig. 1.61

Step - 1 : Find ∈-closure of each state present in the ∈-NFA

$$\epsilon\text{-closure } p = \{p\}$$
$$\epsilon\text{-closure } q = \{p, q\}$$
$$\epsilon\text{-closure } r = \{p, q, r\}$$

Step - 2 : Start state is p, so that find out a, b, c successor of p.

$$\text{successor of } p = \epsilon\ \delta(\{p\}, a)$$
$$= \epsilon\text{-closure } \delta(\{p\}, a)$$
$$= \epsilon\text{-closure } \{p\}$$
$$= p$$

$$\text{b successor of } p = \epsilon\text{-closure } (\delta(p, b))$$
$$= \epsilon\text{-closure } (q)$$
$$= \{p, q\}$$

$$\text{c successor of } p = \epsilon\text{-closure } (\delta(p, c))$$
$$= \epsilon\text{-closure } (r)$$
$$= \{p, q, r\}$$

Newly generated states {p, q} and {p, q, r}.

Step - 3 :

$$\text{a successor of } \{p, q\} = \epsilon\text{-closure } (\delta((p, q), q)))$$
$$= \epsilon\text{-closure } (\delta(p, a) \cup \delta(q, a))$$
$$= \epsilon\text{-closure } (p, q)$$
$$= \{p, q\}$$

b successor of {p, q} = ε-closure (δ({p, q}, b))
= ε-closure {q, r}
= {p, q, r}
c successor of {p, q} = ε-closure (δ((p, q), c)))
= ε-closure (r)
= {p, r, q}

Newly generated set {p, q, r}.

Step - 4 : a successor of (p, q, r) = ε-closure (δ(p, q, r), a))
= {p, q, r}
b successor of (p, q, r) = ε-closure (δ((p, q, r), b))
= ε-closure (δ(p, b) ∪ δ(q, b) ∪ δ(r, b))
= ε-closure (q, r)
= {q, r}
c successor of (p, q, r) = ε-closure (δ(p, q, r), c))
= ε-closure (δ(p, c) ∪ δ(q, c) ∪ δ(r, c))
= {p, q, r}

Now new subset is generated.

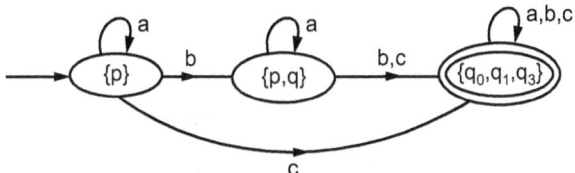

Fig. 1.62

Transition Table

	a	b
→ {p}	{p}	{p, q}
{p, q}	{p, q}	{p, q, r}
{p, q, r}*	{p, q, r}	{p₁, q, r}

Example 1.38 : Convert ε-NFA to DFA.

	ε	a	b	c
→ p	{q, r}	φ	{q}	{r}
q	φ	{p}	{r}	{p, q}
r	φ	φ	φ	φ

Solution : Step - 1 : ε-closure of each state.

p = {p, q, r}
q = {q}
r = {r}

Step - 2 : p is the start state

$$\epsilon\text{-closure }(p) = \{p, q, r\}$$
$$a \text{ successor of } (p, q, r) = \epsilon\text{-closure }(\delta(\{p, q, r\}, a))$$
$$= \epsilon\text{-closure }(\delta(p, a) \cup \delta(q, a) \cup \delta(q, r)\}$$
$$= \epsilon\text{-closure }(p)$$
$$= \{p, q, r\}$$
$$b \text{ successor of } (p, q, r) = \epsilon\text{-closure }(\delta(p, q, r), b))$$
$$= \{q, r\}$$
$$c \text{ successor of } (p, q, r) = \epsilon\text{-closure }(\delta((p, q, r), c))$$
$$= \epsilon\text{-closure }(\delta(p, c) \cup \delta(q, c) \cup \delta(r, c))$$
$$= \epsilon\text{-closure }(\{p, q, r\})$$
$$= \{p, q, r\}$$

Step - 3 : New subsets are $\{q, r\}$

$$a \text{ successor of } \{q, r\} = \epsilon\text{-closure }(\delta\{q, r\}, a\})$$
$$= \epsilon\text{-closure }(\delta(q, a) \cup \delta(r, a))$$
$$= \epsilon\text{-closure }(p)$$
$$= \{p, q, r\}$$
$$b \text{ successor of } \{q, r\} = \epsilon\text{-closure }(\delta\{q, r\}, b)$$
$$= \epsilon\text{-closure }(r)$$
$$= r$$
$$c \text{ successor of } \{q, r\} = \epsilon\text{-closure }(\delta\{q, r\}, c)$$
$$= \epsilon\text{-closure }(p, q)$$
$$= \{p, q, r\}$$

Step - 4 : Newly generated subset is $\{r\}$.

$$a \text{ successor of } \{r\} = \phi, b \text{ successor of } \{r\} = \phi, c \text{ successor of } \{\phi\} = \phi$$

Every subset containing r, is marked as a final state.

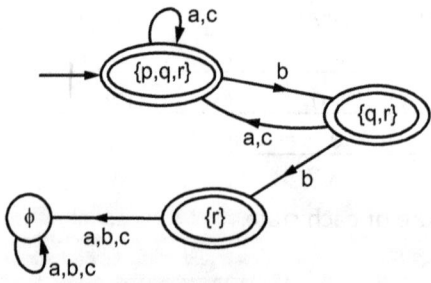

Fig. 1.63

Example 1.39 : Convert the following ϵ-NFA to DFA.

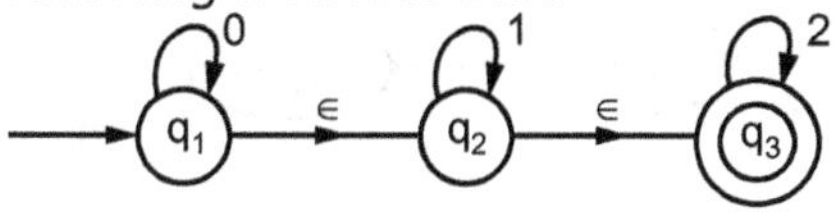

Fig. 1.64

Solution : Step - 1 :
ϵ-closure $(q_1) = \{q_1, q_2, q_3\}$
ϵ-closure $(q_2) = \{q_2, q_3\}$
ϵ-closure $(q_3) = \{q_3\}$

Step - 2 : Start state is q_1, so take ϵ-closure of q_1

ϵ-closure $(q_1) = \{q_1, q_2, q_3\}$

$$\begin{aligned}
\text{0 successor of } (q_1, q_2, q_3) &= \epsilon\text{-closure }(\delta(\{q_1, q_2, q_3\}, 0)) \\
&= \epsilon\text{-closure }(\delta(q_1, 0) \cup \delta(q_2, 0) \cup \delta(q_3, 0)) \\
&= \epsilon\text{-closure }(q_1) \\
&= \{q_1, q_2, q_3\}
\end{aligned}$$

$$\begin{aligned}
\text{1 successor of } (q_1, q_2, q_3) &= \epsilon\text{-closure }(\delta(q_1, q_2, q_3), 1) \\
&= \epsilon\text{-closure }(\delta(q_1, 1) \cup \delta(q_2, 1) \cup \delta(q_3, 1)) \\
&= \epsilon\text{-closure }(q_2) \\
&= \{q_2, q_3\}
\end{aligned}$$

$$\begin{aligned}
\text{2 successor of } (q_1, q_2, q_3) &= \epsilon\text{-closure }(\delta(\{q_1, q_2, q_3\})) \\
&= \{q_3\}
\end{aligned}$$

Newly generated states are $\{q_2, q_3\}$ and $\{q_3\}$.

Step - 3 :
0 successor of $\{q_3\} = \phi$
1 successor of $\{q_3\} = \phi$
2 successor of $\{q_3\} = \{q_3\}$

$$\begin{aligned}
\text{0 successor of } \{q_2, q_3\} &= \epsilon\text{-closure }(\delta(q_2, q_3), 0) \\
&= \epsilon\text{-closure }(\delta(q_2, 0) \cup \delta(q_3, 0)) \\
&= \epsilon\text{-closure }(\phi \cup \phi) \\
&= \phi
\end{aligned}$$

$$\begin{aligned}
\text{1 successor of } \{q_2, q_3\} &= \epsilon\text{-closure of }\{q_2\} \\
&= \{q_2, q_3\}
\end{aligned}$$

$$\begin{aligned}
\text{2 successor of } \{q_2, q_3\} &= \epsilon\text{-closure }(q_3) \\
&= (q_3)
\end{aligned}$$

Transition Table

	0	1	2
$\rightarrow \{q_1, q_2, q_3\}^*$	$\{q_1, q_2, q_3\}$	$\{q_2, q_3\}$	$\{q_3\}$
$\{q_3\}^*$	ϕ	ϕ	$\{q_3\}$
$\{q_2, q_3\}^*$	ϕ	$\{q_2, q_3\}$	$\{q_3\}$

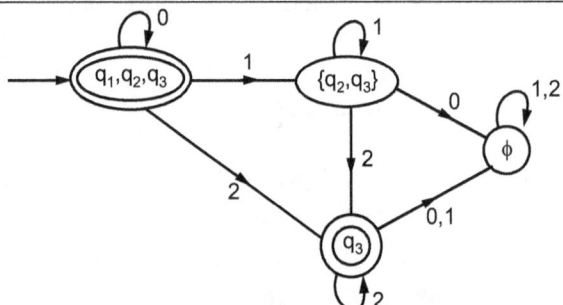

Fig. 1.65 : State transition diagram

1.4 FINITE AUTOMATA AS OUTPUT DEVICE

We have seen the finite automata. In that acceptance of the string was based on the reachability of a machine from starting state to the final state. A finite automata can also be used as an output device.

- In this machine generates output on every input.
- The value of output is a function of current state to the current input.
- This type of machine is having mainly two characteristic.
    1. State transition function (δ) – STF
    2. Output function (X) – MAF.

Alternative name for output machine is machine function Q.

$\delta : \Sigma \times Q \to Q$
$\lambda : \Sigma \times Q \to O$ this output function related to Mealy machine
$\lambda : Q \to O$ this output function related to Moore machine

Now we see the Moore and Mealy machine.

1.4.1 Mealy Machine

It is a machine with finite number of states and for which, the output symbol at a given time depends upon the present input symbol as well as the present state of the machine.

A Mealy machine is defined by a six-Tuple.

$M = \{Q, \Sigma, O, \delta, \lambda, q_0\}$

where,
- Q = set of states present in machine
- Σ = set of input symbols
- O = set of output symbols
- δ = transition function $\delta : Q \times \Sigma \to Q$
- λ = output function $\lambda : Q \times \Sigma \to O$
- q_0 = initial/start state

Characteristics :

- The output symbol depends on both current state and current input symbol.
- Concept of final state does not exist.

Example 1.40 :

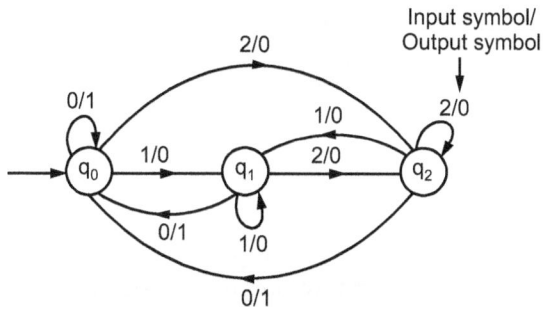

Fig. 1.66

First, we see how to draw the state transition table.

Solution :

	0	1	2
→ q_0	q_0	q_1	q_2
q_1	q_0	q_1	q_2
q_2	q_0	q_1	q_2

Output function or MAF (Machine Function)

	Inputs		
	0	1	2
→ q_0	1	0	0
q_1	1	0	0
q_2	1	0	0

Common STF and MAF function.

Current state	Inputs		
	0	1	2
→ q_0	q_0/1	q_1/0	q_2/0
q_1	q_0/1	q_1/0	q_2/0
q_2	q_0/1	q_1/0	q_2/0

So, definition of Mealy machine.

$$M = \{Q, \Sigma, O, \delta, \lambda, q_0\}$$
$$Q = \{q_0, q_1, q_2\}$$

Σ = {0, 1, 2}
O = {0, 1}
q_0 = initial state

δ, λ are represented in above table.

1.4.2 Moore Machine

It is the machine with finite number of states and for which, the output symbol at a given time depends only upon the present state of machine.

A Moore machine is defined by six-Tuples.

$$M = \{Q, \Sigma, O, \delta, \lambda, q_0\}$$

where,
- Q = set of states
- Σ = set of input symbols
- O = set of output symbols
- δ = transition function, $\delta : Q \times \Sigma \rightarrow Q$
- λ = output function, $\lambda : Q \rightarrow O$
- q_0 = start state

Characteristics :

1. Output symbol is associated with each state.
2. Concept of final state does not exist.

Example 1.44 :

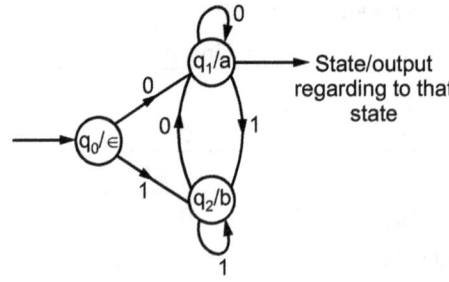

Fig. 1.67

Solution :

State Transition Table

	0	1
→ q_0	q_1	q_2
q_1	q_1	q_2
q_2	q_1	q_2

Machine Function

	Output
→ q_0	$\in$
q_1	a
q_2	b

Definition of Moore Machine:

$$M = \{Q, \Sigma, O, \delta, \lambda, q_0\}$$
$$Q = \{q_0, q_1, q_2\}$$
$$\Sigma = \{0, 1\}$$
$$O = \{a, b\}$$
$$q_0 = \text{start state}$$

Common STF and MAF function as follows:

	Inputs		Output
	0	1	
→ q_0	q_1	q_2	$\in$
q_1	q_1	q_2	a
q_2	q_1	q_2	b

Now we see more examples on Moore and Mealy machine.

Example 1.42: Design Moore and Mealy machine for 1's complement of binary number.

Solution: Input in binary form = {0, 1} set of input symbols

1's complement, that is why output is again in binary form = {0, 1}

Whenever 1 is input machine generate output 0 and whenever 0 is input machine generate output as 1.

First, we see Mealy machine.

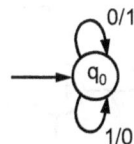

Fig. 1.68

STF and MAF function:

	0	1
→ q_0	$q_0/1$	$q_0/0$

Moore Machine:

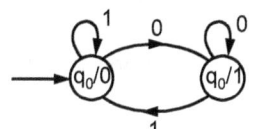

Fig. 1.69

Common STF and MAF function.

	0	1	Output
→ q_0	q_1	q_0	0
q_1	q_1	q_0	1

Example 1.43 : Design Moore and Mealy machine that gives an output of 1, if the input string ends in bab.

Solution : (a) Mealy Machine :

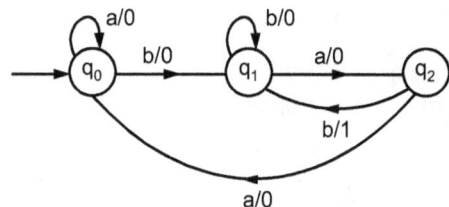

Fig. 1.70 : State transition diagram

Common STF and MAF function.

	a	b
→ q_0	q_2/0	q_1/0
q_1	q_2/0	q_1/0
q_2	q_2/0	q_1/1

(b) Moore Machine : In Moore machine, output is represented on states.

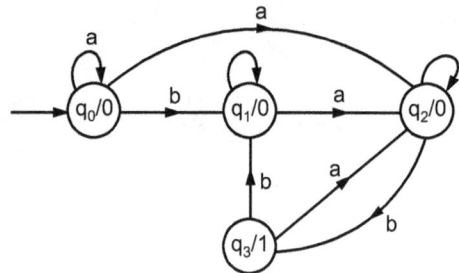

Fig. 1.71 : State transition diagram

Common STF and MAF function.

	Inputs		Output
	a	b	
→ q_0	q_0	q_1	0
q_1	q_2	q_1	0
q_2	q_0	q_3	0
q_3	q_2	q_1	1

Example 1.44 : Give Mealy and Moore machine for the following from input Σ^*, where $\Sigma = \{0, 1, 2\}$ print the residue modulo 5 of the input treated as ternary (base 3).

Solution : (a) Mealy Machine :

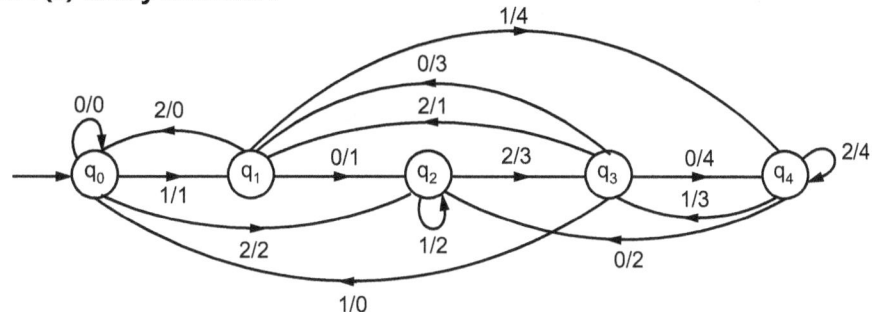

Fig. 1.72

q_0 – Running remainder 0
q_1 – Remainder 1
q_2 – Remainder 2
q_3 – Remainder 3 = (10) 3
q_4 – Remainder 4 = (11) 3

(b) Moore Machine :

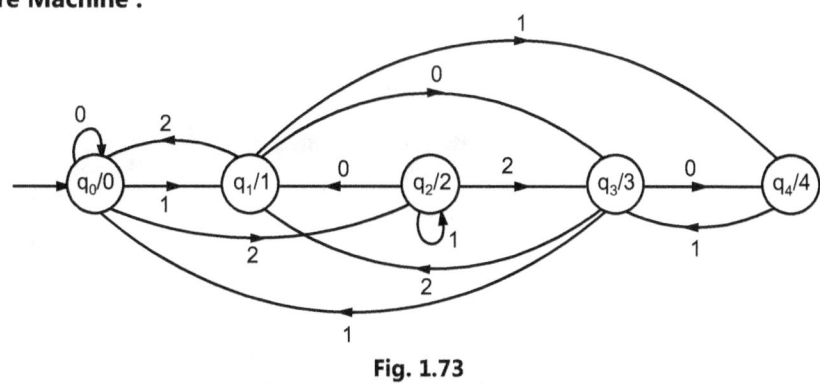

Fig. 1.73

Example 1.45 : Give the Mealy and Moore machine for the following processes. For input from $(0 + 1)^*$, if input ends in 101 output X, if input ends in 110 output Y, otherwise output Z.

Solution : Input symbols = {0, 1}
Output symbols = {X, Y, Z}

Conditions :

String ends in 101 output X
String ends in 110 output Y
Other than these two outputs Z.

(a) Mealy Machine :

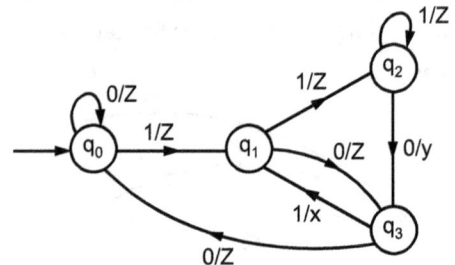

Fig. 1.74

(b) Moore Machine :

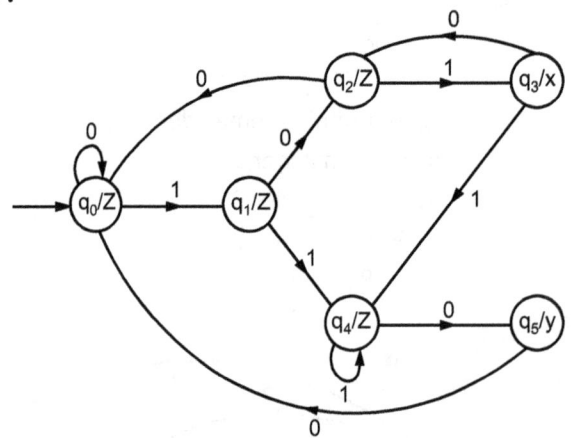

Fig. 1.75 : State transition diagram

Common STF and MAF function.

	Inputs		Output
	0	1	
→ q_0	q_1	q_0	Z
q_1	q_2	q_4	Z
q_2	q_0	q_3	Z
q_3	q_2	q_4	X
q_4	q_5	q_4	Z
q_5	q_0	ϕ	Y

Example 1.46 : Design Moore and Mealy machine for a binary input sequence, such that if it has a substring 110 the machine outputs A. If it has a substring 101 machine outputs B. Otherwise outputs C.

Solution : Given data :   Input = {0, 1}
                                 Output = {A, B, C}

Conditions :
- Substring as 110 – A output
- Substring as 101 – Generate output B
- Substring other than 110 and 101 – Generate output C

(a) Mealy Machine :

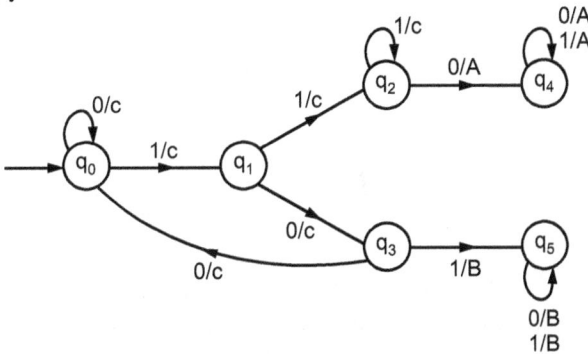

Fig. 1.76

(b) Moore Machine :

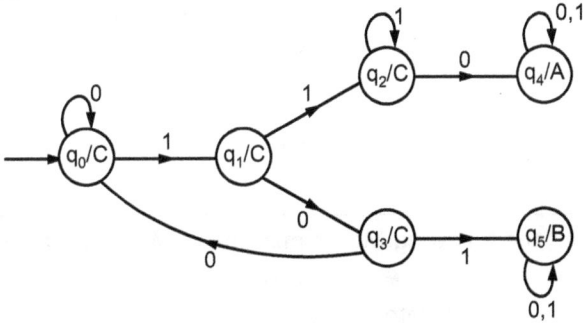

Fig. 1.78

1.4.3 Conversion of Moore Machine into Mealy Machine

In Moore machine output is associated with state and in Mealy machine output is on transition, so transfer output associated with state onto transition.

Example 1.47 : Consider the Moore machine described by the transition table given below. Construct corresponding Mealy machine.

Present state	Next state		Output
	0	1	
→ q_1	q_1	q_2	0
q_2	q_1	q_3	0
q_3	q_1	q_3	1

Solution : In Moore machine, q_1 generate output 0, so in transition wherever the q_1 present write it as $q_1/0$.

Present state	Next state	Output
	0	1
→ q_1	$q_1/0$	q_2
q_2	$q_1/0$	q_3
q_3	$q_1/0$	q_3

q_2 produce 0 and q_3 produce 1.

Present state	Next state	Output
	0	1
→ q_1	$q_1/0$	$q_2/0$
q_2	$q_1/0$	$q_3/1$
q_3	$q_1/0$	$q_3/1$

We are getting transition table for Mealy machine, so draw Mealy machine from the above table.

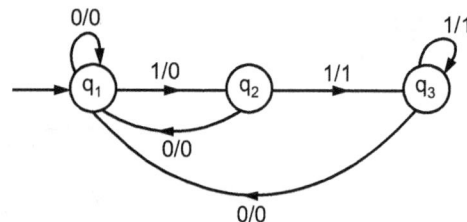

Fig. 1.79

Example 1.48 : Convert the following Moore machine to Mealy machine.

Present state	Next state		Output
	0	1	
→ p	s	q	0
q	q	r	1
r	r	s	0
s	s	p	0

Solution : (1) Moving the output associated with p to transition into state p. p generating output as 0, so transfer it on transition.

Present state	Next state	
	0	1
→ p	s	q
q	q	r
r	r	s
s	s	p/0

(2) q generating output as 1, so transfer it on transition into q.

Present state	Next state	
	0	1
→ p	s	q/1
q	q/1	r
r	r	s
s	s	p/0

(3) r generating output as 0 and also s generating output as 0, so transfer these outputs into its respective transition into r, s respectively.

Present state	Next state	
	0	1
→ p	s/0	q/1
q	q/1	r/0
r	r/0	s/0
s	s/0	p/0

We are getting common STF and MAF function for the Mealy machine, so draw the Mealy machine.

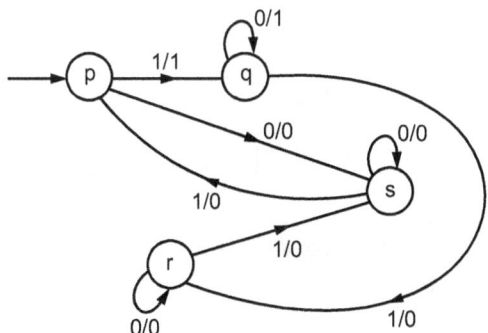

Fig. 1.80 : State transition diagram

1.4.4 Conversion of Mealy Machine to Moore Machine

Mealy machine can be transformed into its equivalent Moore machine, so that both machines giving the same output for any input given to that machine.

Conversion process of Mealy to Moore machine is as follows.

Check incoming transition for each state present in machine.

If we are getting same output on transition then splitting is not required.

Else, split the state on different output.

Example 1.49 :

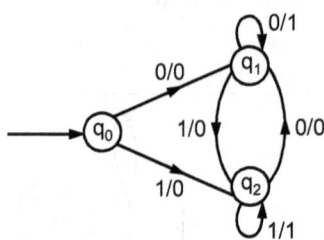

Fig. 1.81 : State transition diagram of Mealy machine

Solution : Step - 1 : Check incoming lines of each state.

- q_0 having no incoming lines and it is a start state, so q_0 producing output as ϵ.
  Here we are getting the state as – q_0/ϵ.
- q_1 having three incoming transitions and

Output	
q_0 to q_1 – 0	Same out as 0
q_2 to q_1 – 0	
q_1 to q_1 – 1 → 1	

Here different outputs are generated

Here we are getting different output, so splitting is required. Split q_1 state into two parts for generating 0 and 1 output. Here we are getting states as $q_{10}/0$ and $q_{11}/1$.

- q_2 having three incoming transitions.

	Outputs
q_0 to q_2	0
q_1 to q_2	0
q_2 to q_2	1

Different output, split the state

Split q_2 state for producing output as 0 and 1.
Here we are getting the state as
q_{20} for generating 0
q_{21} for generating 1.

Transition Table for Moore Machine

Present state	Inputs		Output
	0	1	
→ q_0/ϵ	q_{10}	q_{20}	ϵ
q_{10}	q_{11}	q_{20}	0
q_{21}	q_{11}	q_{20}	1
q_{20}	q_{10}	q_{21}	0
q_{21}	q_{10}	q_{21}	1

Step - 2 : Draw the state transition diagram of Moore machine.

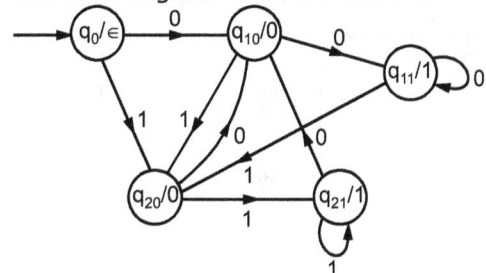

Fig. 1.82 : State transition diagram of Moore machine

Example 1.50 : Convert the following Mealy machine to Moore machine.

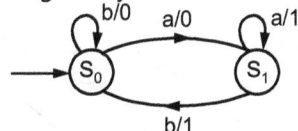

Fig. 1.83

Solution : Step - 1 : Check incoming transition of s_0 state.

	Output
s_0 to s_0	0
s_1 to s_0	1

Different outputs split the state

Here we are splitting the state as

s_{01} for output 0

s_{01} for output 1

Check incoming transition of s_1 state.

	Output
s_0 to s_1	1
s_0 to s_0	0

Different outputs, so split the state

Here we are splitting the state as

s_{10} for generating 0 output

s_{11} for generating 1 output

s_0 is the start state. So generating output as $\in$.

Finally, we are getting states as follows.

Output

$s_{0\in} \rightarrow \in$

$s_{00} \rightarrow 0$

$s_{01} \rightarrow 1$

$s_{10} \rightarrow 0$

$s_{11} \rightarrow 1$

Present state	Inputs a	b	Output
→ $S_{0\epsilon}$	S_{10}	S_{00}	ϵ
S_{00}	S_{10}	S_{00}	0
S_{01}	S_{10}	S_{00}	1
S_{10}	S_{01}	S_{11}	0
S_{11}	S_{01}	S_{11}	1

Step - 2 : Draw the state transition diagram for Moore machine.

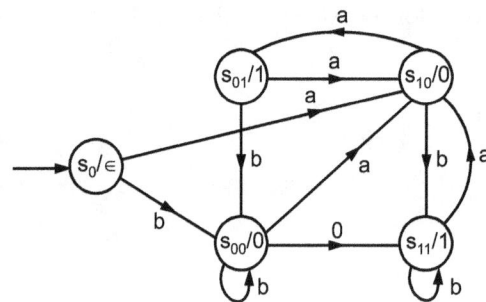

Fig. 1.84 : State transition diagram for the Moore machine

1.4.5 Minimization of Mealy Machine

- For minimization of Mealy machine, we are following the same process as the minimization of DFA. But one small change in grouping formation.
- In DFA, initial grouping is based on final states and non-final states present in DFA. But in minimization of Mealy machine, we are forming the grouping based on outputs.

Example 1.50 :

Present state	Next state/Output 0	1
→ q_0	$q_4/0$	$q_3/1$
q_1	$q_5/0$	$q_3/0$
q_2	$q_4/0$	$q_1/1$
q_3	$q_5/0$	$q_1/0$
q_4	$q_2/0$	$q_5/1$
q_5	$q_1/0$	$q_2/0$

Step - 1 : q_0, q_2, q_4 having same output behaviour and q_1, q_3, q_5 having the same output behaviour, so we form 1st group of q_0, q_2, q_4 and 2nd group of q_1, q_2, q_3.

$$p = \{q_0, q_2, q_4\} \{q_1, q_3, q_4\}$$

Step - 2 : Find 2 equivalent partitions based on the transition.

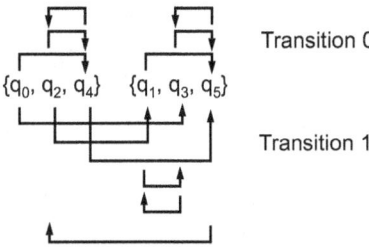

Fig. 1.85

On transition, 1 q_5 having different behaviour other than q_1, q_3. So that we are splitting $\{q_1, q_3, q_5\}$ group into two parts as $\{q_1, q_3\}$ and $\{q_5\}$.

Step - 3 : Find 3 equivalent partitions based on the transition.

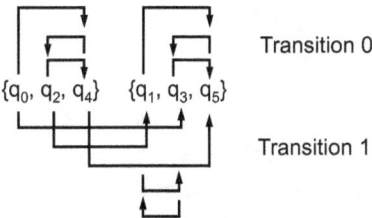

Fig. 1.86

Step - 4 : Finding 3 equivalent partitions p_3 based on transition.

    1 successor of q_0 and q_2 belongs to $\{q_1, q_3\}$

    1 successor of q_4 belongs to $\{q_5\}$

Behaviour of q_4 is different that q_0, q_2, so we are splitting that group into $\{q_0, q_2\}$ and $\{q_4\}$.

After that further division is not possible, the minimal machine is as follows.

Present state	Next state/Output	
	0	1
(q_0, q_2) as p_0	p_1, 0	p_2, 1
(q_4) as p_1	p_0, 0	p_3, 1
(q_1, q_3) as p_2	p_3, 0	p_2, 0
(q_5) as p_3	p_2, 0	p_0, 0

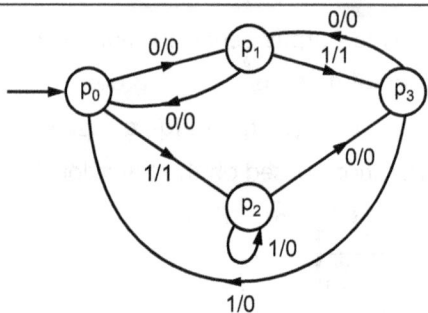

Fig. 1.87 : State transition diagram

1.5 MINIMIZATION OF DFA

DFA may have equivalent states or redundant states. These states can be eliminate from the DFA without changing the language accepted by DFA. This process is called as minimization of DFA.

Procedure to Minimize DFA :
1. Write down the state transition table for the given DFA. Sometimes state transition table is given in the example instead of state transition diagram.
2. Divide the number of states into two groups. This is called as 0-equivalence.
   (i) Non-final states into one group
   (ii) Final states into second group.
3. Then apply all inputs one by one on both blocks. Keep states in the group which are going into the same group. This is called as 1-equivalence.
4. Continue step 3 till new groups are formed and given next equivalence number.
5. Finally draw the state transition diagram for the groups. One group is considered as a one state.

Example 1.51 : Construct the minimum state automata for the following DFA.

	0	1
→q_0	q_1	q_0
q_1	q_0	q_2
q_2	q_3	q_1
(q_3)	q_3	q_0
q_4	q_3	q_5
q_5	q_6	q_4
q_6	q_5	q_6
q_7	q_6	q_3

Solution :

Step - 1 : 0 equivalence

Divide the states into two groups of non-final and final.

(q_0, q_1, q_2, q_4, q_5, q_6, q_7) (q_3)

Step - 2 : Apply input 0 and 1 and divide groups into subgroups (1-equivalence)
Input = 1

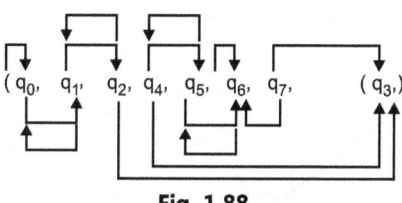

Fig. 1.88

Input = 0
For input 0 (q_2, q_4) group is formed.
For input 1 (q_7) group is formed.
Hence new groups are
(q_0, q_1, q_5, q_6) (q_2, q_4) (q_7) (q_3)

Step - 3 : 2-equivalence
Input = 1

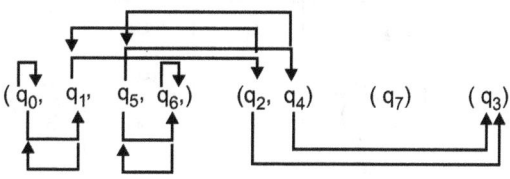

Fig. 1.89

For input 0, no new group is formed.
For input 1, (q_1, q_5) is formed from 1st group (q_2, q_4) group remain unchanged. Hence new groups are (q_0, q_6) (q_1, q_5), (q_2, q_4) (q_7) (q_3)

Step - 4 : 3-equivalence

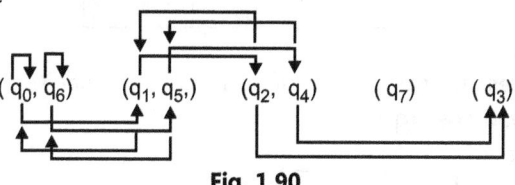

Fig. 1.90

All groups remain unchanged. Hence these groups are final.

Step - 5 : Draw DFA for that

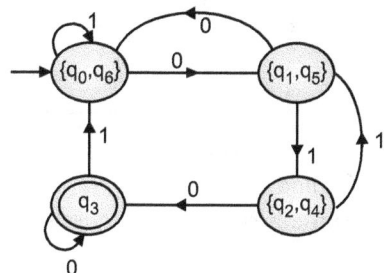

Fig. 1.91

Unit I | 1.63

Example 1.52 :

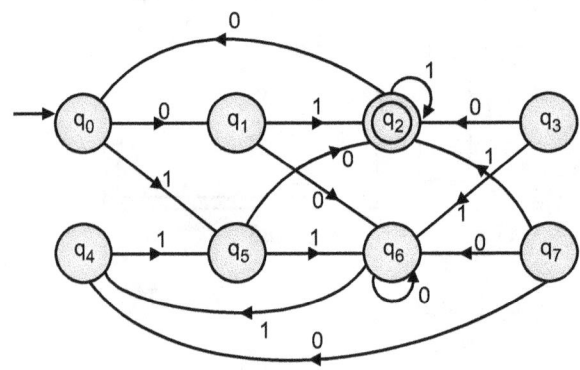

Fig. 1.92

Solution : Step - 1 : Draw state transition table

	0	1
→q_0	q_1	q_5
q_1	q_6	q_2
(q_2)	q_0	q_2
q_3	q_2	q_6
q_4	q_7	q_5
q_5	q_2	q_6
q_6	q_6	q_4
q_7	q_6	q_2

Step - 2 : 0 equivalence

Divide total states into two groups of non-final and final.

(q_0, q_1, q_3, q_4, q_5, q_6, q_7) (q_2)

Step - 3 : 1-equivalence

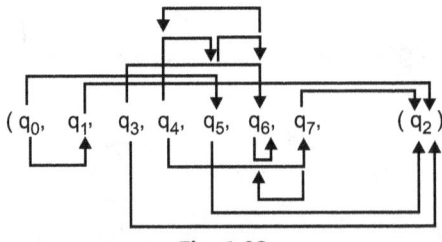

Fig. 1.93

For input 0, {q_3, q_5} group is formed.
For input 1, {q_1, q_7} group is formed. Remaining group is {q_0, q_4, q_6}.
Hence new groups are
{q_0, q_4, q_6} {q_3, q_5}, {q_1, q_7} {q_2}

Step - 4 : 2-equivalence

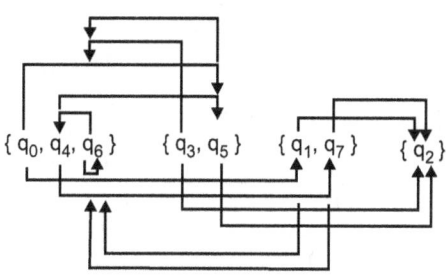

Fig. 1.94

- For input 0 and 1, group $\{q_0, q_4, q_6\}$ is divided into two groups $\{q_0, q_4\}$ and $\{q_6\}$.
- Remaining groups are unchanged.

Step - 5 : 3-equivalence

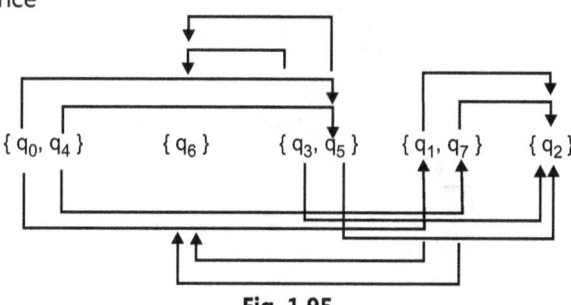

Fig. 1.95

Hence all groups are unchanged.

Hence final groups are $\{q_0, q_4\}, \{q_6\}, \{q_3, q_5\} \{q_1, q_7\} \{q_2\}$

Step - 6 : Hence draw the minimized DFA as

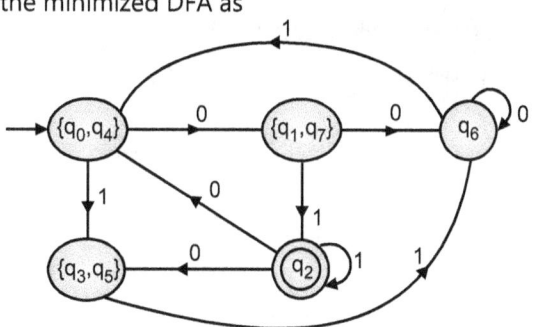

Fig. 1.96

Example 1.53 : Construct the minimized DFA for the following

	0	1
q_0	q_1	q_4
q_1	q_2	q_5
(q_2)	q_3	q_7

q_3	q_4	q_7
q_4	q_5	q_7
ⓠ$_5$	q_6	q_1
q_6	q_7	q_1
q_7	q_8	q_2
ⓠ$_8$	q_0	q_4

Solution : Step - 1 : 0-equivalence

Divide total number of states into two groups of non-final and final.

$\{q_0, q_1, q_3, q_4, q_6, q_7\} \{q_2, q_5, q_8\}$

Step - 2 : 1-equivalence

Note : In this step, apply input on only first group. From next step, apply input on all groups.

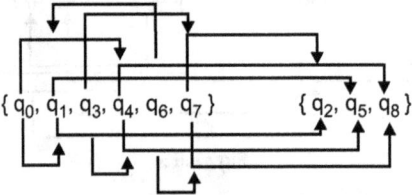

Fig. 1.97

For input 0 and 1 new group formed is $\{q_1, q_4, q_7\}$.

Hence groups are $\{q_0, q_3, q_6\} \{q, q_4, q_3\}$ and $\{q_2, q_5, q_5\}$

Step - 3 : 2-equivalence

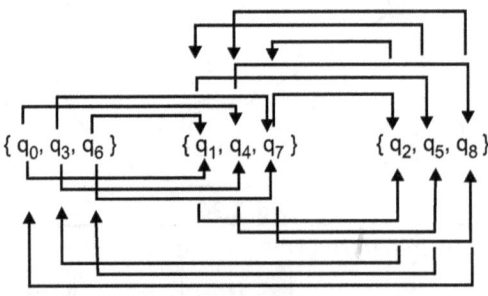

Fig. 1.98

Hence all groups are unchanged.

Hence final groups are $\{q_0, q_3, q_6\}, \{q_1, q_4, q_7\}$ and $\{q_2, q_5, q_8\}$

Step - 4 : Hence minimized DFA is

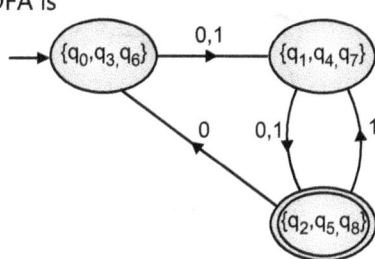

Fig. 1.99

1.6 EQUIVALENCE OF DFAS

Two finite automata M_1 and M_2 are said to be equivalent if they accept the same language i.e. $L(M_1) = L(M_2)$

Testing Equivalence of DFAs :

(1) Construct a combined DFA for two DFAs

Let,

$$M_1 = \{ S, \Sigma, \delta_1, S_0, F_7 \}$$
$$M_2 = \{ Q, \Sigma, \delta_2, q_0, F \}$$
then $M_3 = \{ S * Q, \Sigma, \delta_3, <S_0, q_0>, F_3 \}$

where, $\delta_3(< S_i, q_i >, a) = < \delta_1(S_i, a), \delta_2(q_i, a) >$

Construction of M_3 :

(a) Add the state $<S_0, q_0>$ to M_3

(b) Expand $<S_0, q_0>$ on all inputs

(c) Repeat state (b), still new state is created.

(d) Stop the process, if no new process is created.

(2) M_1 and M_2 are equivalent if for every state of M_3 i.e. $<S_i, q_i>$

$S_i, q_i \in F_3$ or $S_i, q_i \notin F_3$

(3) It is not equivalent if

$S_i \in F$ and $q_i \notin F$ or $S_i \notin F$ and $q_i \in F$

Examples 1.54 :

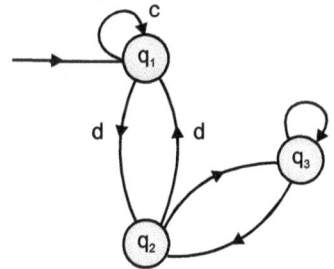
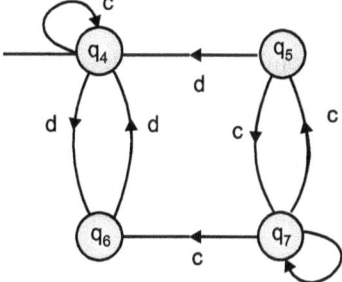

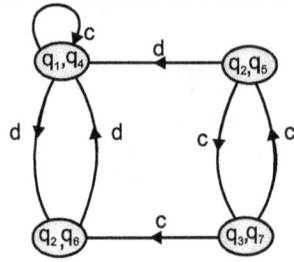

Fig. 1.100

Solution :

Here $<q_1,q_4>$ – Both are final

$<q_2,q_5>$ – Both are non–final

$<q_2,q_6>$ – Both are non–final

$<q_3,q_7>$ – Both are non–final

Hence Two DFAs M_1 and M_2 are equivalent

Closure property of language accepted by a DFA :

(1) Union – $L(M_1) \cup L(M_2)$

(2) Intersection – $L(M_1) \cap L(M_2)$

(3) Difference – $L(M_1) - L(M_2)$ or $L(M_2) - L(M_1)$

1.7 LIMITATIONS OF FINITE AUTOMATA

- Finite Automata have limited memory. Hence it cannot be used for general problems.
- Finite Automata can read the input string only in forward direction.
- Finite Automata can recognize only regular language.
- Finite Automate cannot generate any output for the given input string. It can only accept or reject the input string.
- Due to above limitation, it cannot be used for computation.
- FA have limited number of states.

QUESTIONS

1. Explain the Mathematical Preliminaries.
2. Explain graph and tree in detail.
3. Define finite state machine with suitable example ?
4. How we can accept a string by FA ? Explain with suitable example ?
5. Define DFSM and NDFSM. Also differentiate between them.
6. Explain the different output device of FA.
7. Find the transitive closure and the symmetric closure of the relation.
   {(1, 2) (2, 3), (3, 4), (5, 4)}
8. Prove for any set A, B and C if $A \cap B = \phi$ and $C \subseteq B$, then $A \cap C = \phi$.
9. Consider a relation R = {(1, 1), (2, 2), (3, 4), (4, 3)}, defined on set A = {1, 2, 3, 4} obtain R* (Relative and transitive closure of R)
10. Construct DFA for given NFA

State	0	1
p	p, q	p
q	r	r
r	s	-
s*	s	s

11. Consider the Moore machine described by the transition table given below, construct corresponding Mealy machine.

Present state	Next state		Output
	a = 0	a = 1	
→ q_1	q_1	q_2	0
q_2	q_1	q_3	0
q_3	q_1	q_3	1

12. Write and explain all the steps required for conversion of NFA to DFA with suitable example ?

13. An NFA with states 1-5 and input alphabet {a, b} has the following transitions.

q	δ (q, a)	δ (a, b)
1	{1, 2}	{1}
2	{3}	{3}
3	{4}	{4}
4	{5}	{φ}
5	φ	{5}

(a) Draw a transition diagram
(b) Calculate δ* (1, ab)
(c) Calculate 0* (1, abaa b)

14. Explain Moore machine and Mealy machine with suitable example. How do we construct equivalent Mealy machine for given Moore machine ? Given the suitable example.

Unit - II
REGULAR EXPRESSIONS

2.1 INTRODUCTION

- The set of strings accepted by the finite automata is known as regular language.
- For representing the language, we are using mainly three operators :
  (a) + - union operator.
  (b) • - concatenation operator.
  (c) * - star operator or closure operator.

2.2 REGULAR EXPRESSION

- In regular language, we are using set of operators for representing/describing the expression.
- The class of regular expression over Σ is defined recursively as follows :
  (1) The letter ϕ (null set) and Σ (empty string of length 0) are regular expression over 'Σ'.
  (2) Every letter 'a' E Σ is regular expression over Σ.
  (3) If 'R_1' and 'R_2' are regular expression over Σ, then '($R_1 + R_2$)', ($R_1 \cdot R_2$) and (R_1)* where '+' indicates alteration (parallel path) '.' Indicates concatenation (series) and '*' denotes iteration (closure).
  (4) The regular expressions are those that are obtained using rule (1) to (3)
- Following are some examples on regular expressions.

	Language	Automata	Regular Expression (R.E.)
1.	{∈}		R.E. = ∈
2.	{a}		R.E. = a
3.	{a,b}		R.E. = a + b

	Language	Automata	Regular Expression (R.E.)
4.	{ab}	→○--a-→○--b-→((q_1))	R.E. = a • b
5.	φ	→○←a--(q_1)	R.E. = φ
6.	{a,aa,aaa....}	→○--a-→(($\circ$))↺a	R.E. = a • a* = a^+
7.	{ab}	→○--a-→○--b-→(($\circ$))	R.E. = a • b •
8.	(a + b)*	→(($\circ$))↺a,b	R.E. = (a + b)*
9.	{ab, ba}	→○ (a→○→b / b→○→a) (($\circ$))	R.E. = (ab + ba)

Example 2.1 :

Write down the regular expressions for the following languages.

Solution :

1. L = {10, 1010, 101010 ... }
    R · E = 10 (10)*
    = $(10)^+$
2. L = {1010}
    R · E = 1010
3. L = {10, 1010}
    R · E = 10 + 1010
4. L = {∈, 0, 00, 000 ... }
    R · E = 0^*
5. L = {0, 00, 000, 0000 ... }
    R · E = 0^+

6. The set of strings starting with a over an alphabet {a, b}
   L = {a, ab, abb, aaa, abab ... }
   R · E = a(a + b)*
7. The set of strings ending with ab over an alphabet {a, b}
   L = {ab, aab, bab, abab, aabbab ... }
   R · E = (a + b)* ab

Example 2.2 :
Language over Σ = (a,b) with all strings starting and ending with 'a' and any number of 'b' in between.
Solution :

$$a.b^*.a$$

Example 2.3 :
Σ = (0,1) with at least two consecutive '0' using regular expression
Solution : $(0 + 1)^* . 0 . 0 (0 + 1)^*$

Example 2.4 :
L = Σ = (0,1,2) with at least one '0' followed by at least one '1' followed by at least one '2' is there, find regular expression 'r' representing this language.
Solution :
$$r = 0.0^* \cdot 1.1^* \cdot 2.2^*$$
$$r = 0^+ \cdot 1^+ \cdot 2^+$$

Example 2.5 :
If L(r) = { aaa ,aba, abb, baa ,bab, bba, bbb}
find out regular expression r which represent above set.
Solution : Each word of L(r) of length three and all possible combinations of '0' and 'b'.
At first position we can have 'a' or b, similarly at 2nd and 3rd.
∴ Σ = (a + b) . (a + b) . (a + b)

Example 2.6 :
Represent set of all words over Σ = (a, b) containing at least one 'a'.
Solution : $(a +b)^* \cdot a \cdot (a+b)^*$

Example 2.7 :
Let r = $(a +b)^* . a . (a +b)^* . a . (a +b)^*$
Describe the language L(r) represented by regular expression r using simple English.
Solution : L = Σ (a,b) containing at least two 'a's.

Example 2.8 : ϵ = $(1 + 10)^*$ L = Σ (0,1)
Solution : With strings beginning with '1' and not having two consecutive '0's

2.2.1 Identies for Regular Expression

Following are some identifies for Regular expressions. Let consider P, Q and R are regular expression.

$$\phi + R = R$$
$$\phi^* = \epsilon$$
$$\phi \cdot R = R \cdot \phi = \phi$$
$$\epsilon \cdot R = R \cdot \epsilon = R$$
$$\epsilon^* = \epsilon$$
$$\epsilon + RR^* = R^*$$
$$R + R = R$$
$$PQ + PR = P(Q + R)$$
$$QP + RP = (Q + R)P$$
$$R^* + R^* = R^*$$
$$(R^*)^* = R^*$$
$$RR^* = R^*R$$
$$(PQ)^* P = P(QP)^*$$
$$(P + Q)^* = (P^*Q^*)^* = (P^* + Q^*)^*$$
$$(P^* Q^*) = \epsilon + (P + Q)^* Q$$

Now we will see proofs for some basic identities.

Step 1 : $\phi + R = R$

Firstly construct transition diagram for $\phi + R$

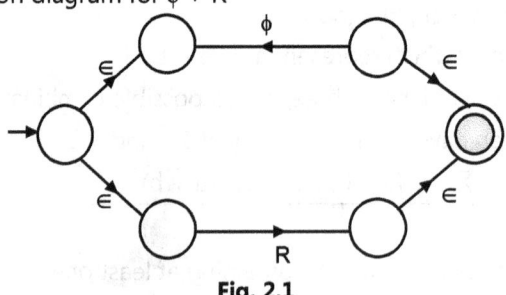

Fig. 2.1

Here is only one path from start state to final state.

$$\epsilon \cdot R \cdot \epsilon = R$$

Hence $\phi + R = R$

Step 2 : $\phi \cdot R = \phi$

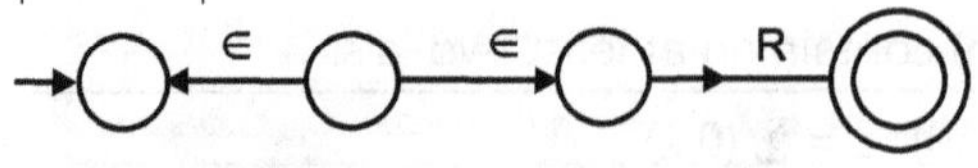

Fig. 2.2

We cannot reach to final state from initial state.

∴ $\phi \cdot R = \phi$

Step 3 : $\epsilon \cdot R = R$

Transition diagram for ϵ is

Fig. 2.3

Transition diagram for R is

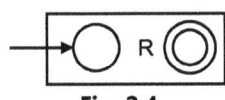

Fig. 2.4

∴ Transition diagram for $\epsilon \cdot R$ is

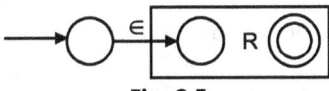

Fig. 2.5

∴ This machine accepts only R

∴ $\epsilon \cdot R = R$

Step 4 : $\epsilon + RR^* = R^*$

$$L \cdot H \cdot S = \epsilon + RR^*$$
$$= \epsilon + R\{\epsilon + R + RR + RRR + \ldots\}$$
$$= \epsilon + R + RR + RRR + \ldots$$
$$= R^*$$
$$= RHS$$

Step 5 : $(PQ)^* P = P(QP)^*$

$$L \cdot H \cdot S = (PQ)^* P$$
$$= \{\epsilon + PQ + (PQ)^2 + \ldots\} P$$
$$= \{G + PQ + PQPQ + \ldots\} P$$
$$= \{P + \{PQP + PQPQP + \ldots\}$$
$$= P\{\epsilon + QP + QPQP + \ldots\}$$
$$= P(QP)^*$$
$$= R \cdot H \cdot S$$

Step 6 : $(P^* Q)^* = \epsilon + (P + Q)^* Q$

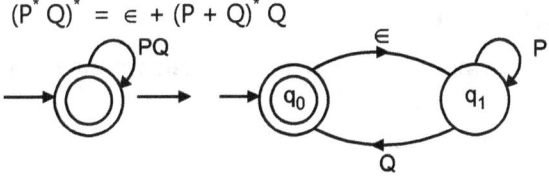

Fig. 2.6

Remove ∈-move by amplicating transition of q_1 on q_0.

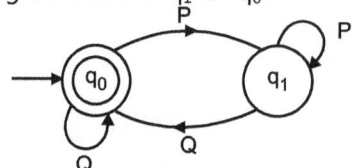

Fig. 2.7 FA for (P* Q)*

∴ FA for ∈ + (P + Q)* Q

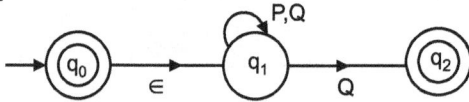

Fig. 2.8

Now we will construct equivalent DFA by direct method.

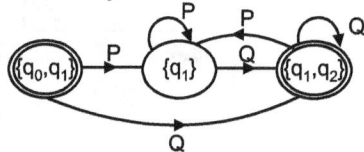

Fig. 2.9

Here {q_0, q_1} and {q_1, q_2} both are identical so we will these two states and we will say q_0 state.

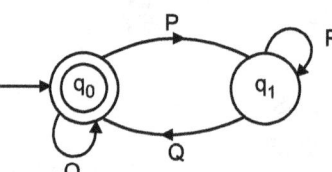

Fig. 2.10 : FA for G + (P + Q)* Q

Fig. (a) and Fig. (b) both are same FA.

∴ (P* Q)* = ∈ + (P + Q)* Q

2.3 FINITE AUTOMATA AND REGULAR EXPRESSION

2.3.1 NDFAs with ∈ - moves

∈ is nothing but empty symbol. By using this we can transit from one state to another without any input symbol.

Definition : ∈-NFA is the set of 5 tuples.

$$M = \{Q, \Sigma, q_0, \delta, F\}$$

where, Q = set of states

Σ = set of input symbols
q_0 = start states
δ = transition function
δ : $Q \times \{\Sigma \cup U\} \to 2a$

Example 2.9 :

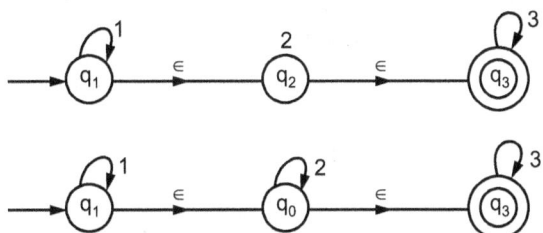

Fig. 2.11 : State transition diagram

Transition Table

	∈	1	2	2
→ q_1	{q_1}	{q_1}	φ	φ
q_2	{q_3}	φ	{q_2}	φ
q_3	φ	φ	φ	{q_3}

Examples of Divisibility :

Example 2.10 :

Design a DFA which can accept a binary number divisible by 3.

Solution : Input in the binary form

$$\Sigma = \{0, 1\}$$

- When we divide any number by 3, possibilities for getting remainder is in either 0, 1, 2.
- 0, 1, 2 are in decimal form, so convert it into binary

    $0 \to 00$, it is associated with q_0

    $1 \to 01$, it is associated with q_1

    $2 \to 10$, it is associated with q_2

- Required number of states are 3 because, we are required to handle 3 types of remainder.

The calculation of next remainder is as shown below.

Previous state	Next input	Calculation of remainder	Next state
00(q_0)	0	000%3 = 0	q_0
00(q_0)	1	001%3 = 1	q_1
01(q_1)	0	000%3 = 10	q_2
01(q_1)	1	011%3 = 0	q_0
11(q_2)	0	110%3 = 1	q_1
11(q_2)	1	111%3 = 10	q_2

Transition Table

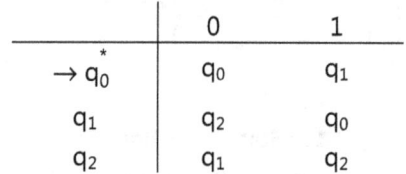

	0	1
→* q_0	q_0	q_1
q_1	q_2	q_0
q_2	q_1	q_2

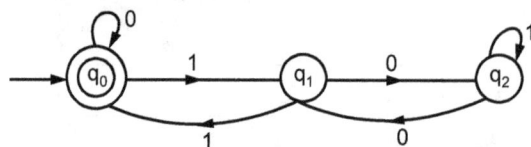

Fig. 2.12 : State transition diagram

Example 2.11 : Design DFA which can accept a binary number divisible by 4.

Solution : Possibilities for remainder.

$$0\ (00) \rightarrow q_0$$
$$1\ (01) \rightarrow q_1$$
$$2\ (10) \rightarrow q_2$$
$$3\ (11) \rightarrow q_3$$

Calculating the next state :

0(00) 0   000 % 4 = 00 it is associated with q_0
       1   001 % 4 = 01 it is associated with q_1
1(01) 0   010 % 4 = 10 it is associated with q_2
       1   011 % 4 = 11 it is associated with q_3
2(10) 0   100 % 4 = 00 it is associated with q_0
       1   101 % 4 = 01 it is associated with q_1

3(11) 0   110 % 4 = 10 it is associated with q_2
       1   111 % 4 = 11 it is associated with q_3

Transition Table

	0	1
$\rightarrow q_0^*$	q_0	q_1
q_1	q_2	q_0
q_2	q_0	q_1
q_3	q_2	q_3

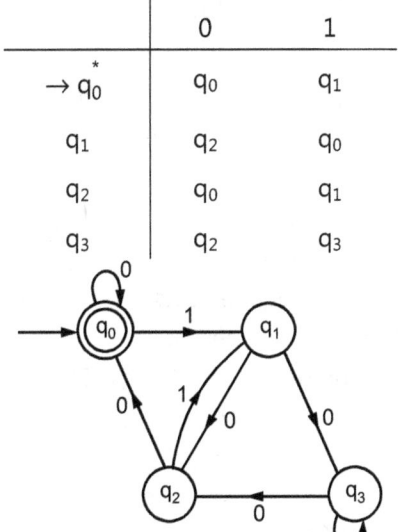

Fig. 2.13 : State transition diagram

2.3.2 Conversion of NFA to DFA

- In NFA, we resides in multiple state for each input in the machine and in DFA, we have only one transition path from the given path.
- The conversion steps for NFA to DFA is as follows :
  1. Tracing the various paths followed by the machine for the given string.
  2. Find the set of states from the start state of the machine for the each symbol of the string.
  3. If the set of states obtained from state 2 containing the final state then we conclude that the string is accepted by the NFA.

Example 2.12 : Convert following NFA to DFA.

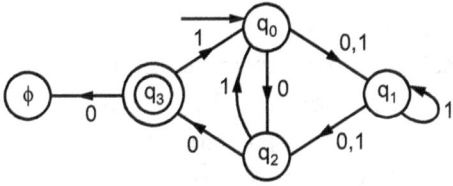

Fig. 2.14

Solution :

	0	1
$\to q_0$	$\{q_1, q_2\}$	$\{q_1\}$
q_1	$\{q_2\}$	$\{q_1, q_2\}$
q_2	$\{q_3\}$	$\{q_0\}$
q_3 *	ϕ	$\{q_0\}$

Step - 1 : Take start state and find out 0 successor and 1 successor of the start state.
Start state is q_0,

$$0 \text{ successor of } q_0 = \delta(q_0, 0) = \{q_1, q_2\}$$
$$1 \text{ successor of } q_0 = \delta(q_0, 1) = \{q_1\}$$

$\{q_1, q_2\}$ and $\{q_1\}$ these are newly generated sets.
Take 0 and 1 successor of these sets in next state.

Step - 2 : (a)
$$0 \text{ successor of } \{q_1, q_2\} = \delta(\{q_1, q_2\}, 0)$$
$$= \delta(q_1, 0) \cup \delta(q_2, 0)$$
$$= \{q_2\} \cup \{q_3\}$$
$$= \{q_2, q_3\}$$
$$1 \text{ successor of } \{q_1, q_2\} = \delta(\{q_1, q_2\}, 1)$$
$$= \delta(q_1, 1) \cup \delta(q_2, 1)$$
$$= \{q_1, q_2\} \cup \{q_0\}$$
$$= \{q_0, q_1, q_2\}$$

(b)
$$0 \text{ successor of } q_1 = \{q_2\}$$
$$1 \text{ successor of } q_1 = \{q_1, q_2\}$$

Newly generated subsets are $\{q_2, q_3\}$, $\{q_0, q_1, q_2\}$ and $\{q_2\}$.

Step - 3 :
$$0 \text{ successor of } \{q_2, q_3\} = \{q_3\}$$
$$1 \text{ successor of } \{q_2, q_3\} = \{q_0\}$$
$$0 \text{ successor of } \{q_0, q_1, q_2\} = \{q_1, q_2, q_3\}$$
$$1 \text{ successor of } \{q_0, q_1, q_2\} = \{q_0, q_1, q_2\}$$
$$0 \text{ successor of } \{q_2\} = \{q_3\}$$
$$1 \text{ successor of } \{q_2\} = \{\phi\}$$

Newly generated subset is q_3 and $\{q_1, q_2, q_3\}$, that is why we are moving towards the next step, otherwise we will stop the process.

Note : If newly generated subsets are not there then stop the procedure.

Step - 4 :
$$0 \text{ successor } q_3 = \delta(q_3, 0) = \phi$$
$$1 \text{ successor } q_3 = \delta(q_3, 1) = q_0$$
$$0 \text{ successor of } \{q_1, q_2, q_3\} = \{q_2, q_3\}$$
$$1 \text{ successor of } \{q_1, q_2, q_3\} = \{q_1, q_2\}$$

Collect all subsets generated in each step and draw transition table and diagram for the DFA.

	0	1
$\rightarrow q_0$	$\{q_1, q_2\}$	$\{q_1\}$
$\{q_1, q_2\}$	$\{q_2, q_3\}$	$\{q_1, q_2, q_0\}$
$\{q_1\}^*$	$\{q_2\}$	$\{q_1, q_2\}$
$\{q_2, q_3\}$	$\{q_3\}$	$\{q_0\}$
$\{q_0, q_1, q_2\}$	$\{q_1, q_2, q_3\}$	$\{q_0, q_1, q_2\}$
$\{q_2\}$	$\{q_3\}$	ϕ
$\{q_3\}^*$	ϕ	$\{q_0\}$
$\{q_1, q_2, q_3\}^*$	$\{q_2, q_3\}$	$\{q_1, q_2\}$

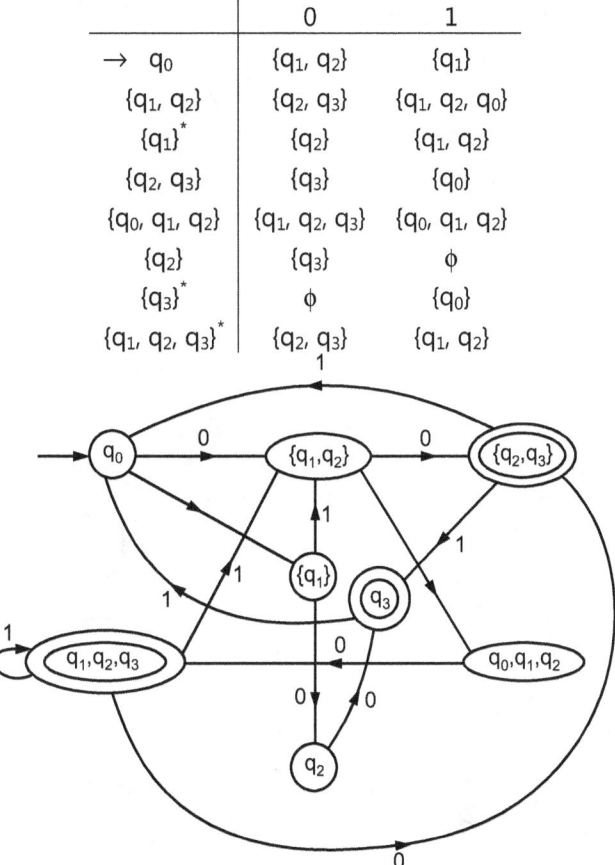

Fig. 2.15

In NFA, q_3 is the final state. So wherever q_3 is occurred in newly generated subset becomes the final state in DFA.

Example 2.13 :

Convert to DFA the following NFA.

	0	1
$\{p\}$	$\{q, s\}$	q
q^*	$\{r\}$	$\{q, r\}$
r	$\{s\}$	$\{p\}$
s^*	ϕ	$\{p\}$

Solution : Step - 1 : Start state p,

0 successor of p = {q, s}

1 successor of p = {q}
Take 0 and 1 successor of {q, s} and {q}.
Step - 2 :
0 successor of {q} = {r}
1 successor of {q} = {q, r}
0 successor of {q, s} = {r}
1 successor of {q, s} = {p, q, r}
Step - 3 :
0 successor of r = {s}
1 successor of s = {p}
0 successor of {q, r} = {r, s}
1 successor of {q, r} = {p, q, r}
0 successor of {q, r} = {q, r, s}
1 successor for {q, r} = {p, q, r}

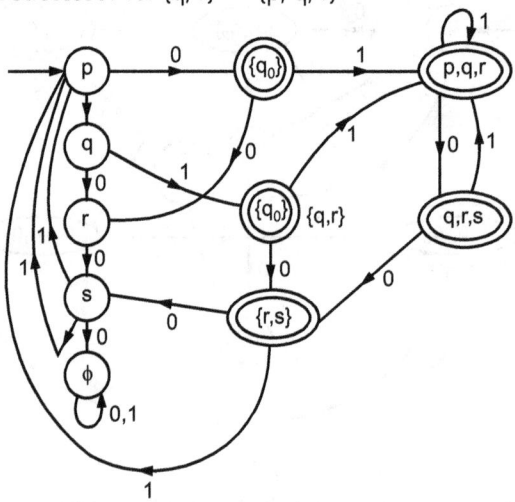

Fig. 2.16 : State transition diagram

Example 2.14 :
Convert given NFA to DFA.

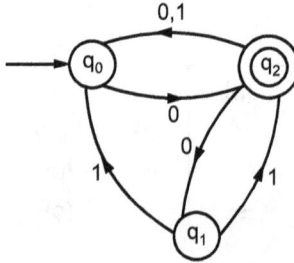

Fig. 2.17

Solution :

	0	1
→ q_0	{q_2}	φ
q_1	φ	{q_0, q_2}
*q_2	{q_0, q_1}	{q_0}

Step - 1 :   0 successor of q_0 = q_2
              1 successor of q_ϕ = φ

q_2 is newly generated state/subset.

Step - 2 :   0 successor of q_2 = {q_0, q_1}
              1 successor of q_2 = {q_0}

Newly generated state {q_0, q_1}

Step - 3 :   0 successor of {q_0, q_1} = {q_2}
              1 successor of {q_0, q_1} = {q_0, q_2}

Newly generated state {q_0, q_2}

Step - 4 :   0 successor of {q_0, q_2} = {q_0, q_1, q_2}
              1 successor of {q_0, q_2} = {q_0}

Newly generated state {q_0, q_1, q_2}

Step - 5 :   0 successor of {q_0, q_1, q_2} = {q_0, q_1, q_2}
              1 successor of {q_0, q_1, q_2} = {q_0, q_2}

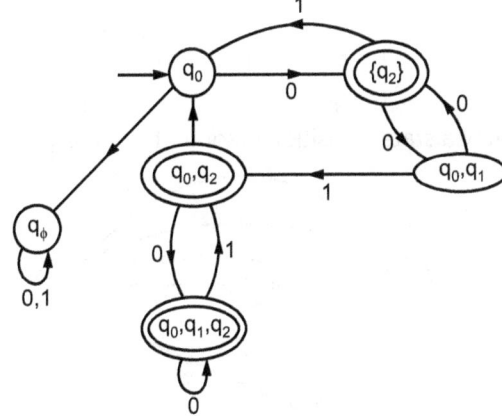

Fig. 2.18

Example 2.15 :
Convert the following NFA to DFA.

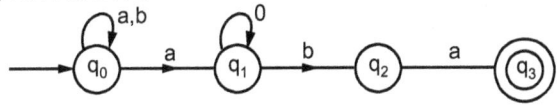

Fig. 2.19

Solution :

Step - 1 :   a successor of q_0 = $\{q_0, q_1\}$
                b successor of q_1 = $\{q_0\}$

Step - 2 :   a successor of $\{q_0, q_1\}$ = $\{q_0, q_1\}$
                b successor of $\{q_0, q_1\}$ = $\{q_0, q_2\}$

Step - 3 :   a successor of $\{q_0, q_2\}$ = $\delta(\{q_0, q_2\}, a)$ = $\{q_0, q_1, q_3\}$
                b successor of $\{q_0, q_2\}$ = $\delta(\{q_0, q_2\}, b)$ = $\{q_0\}$

Step - 4 :   0 successor of $\{q_0, q_1, q_3\}$ = $\{q_0, q_1\}$
                1 successor of $\{q_0, q_1, q_3\}$ = $\{q_0, q_2\}$

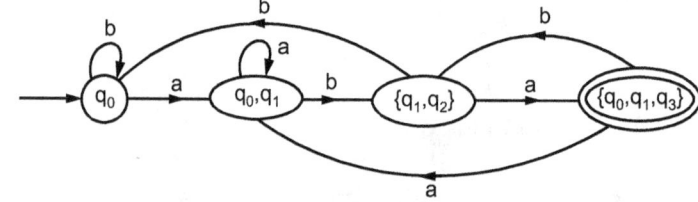

Fig. 2.20

2.3.3 Conversion of ϵ-NFA to DFA

Example 2.16 : Convert ϵ-NFA to DFA.

	ϵ	a	b	c
$\rightarrow$ p	ϕ	{p}	{q}	{r}
q	{p}	{q}	{r}	ϕ
r*	{q}	{r}	ϕ	{p}

Solution : Construct or draw a state transition diagram from the transition table.

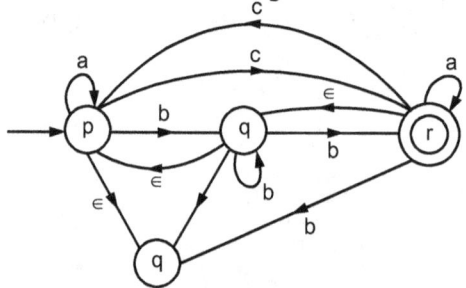

Fig. 2.21

Step - 1 : Find ϵ-closure of each state present in the ϵ-NFA

         ϵ-closure p = {p}

         ϵ-closure q = {p, q}

         ϵ-closure r = {p, q, r}

Step - 2 : Start state is p, so that find out a, b, c successor of p.

$$\text{successor of } p = \epsilon\, \delta(\{p\}, a)$$
$$= \epsilon\text{-closure } \delta(\{p\}, a)$$
$$= \epsilon\text{-closure } \{p\}$$
$$= p$$
$$\text{b successor of } p = \epsilon\text{-closure } (\delta(p, b))$$
$$= \epsilon\text{-closure } (q)$$
$$= \{p, q\}$$
$$\text{c successor of } p = \epsilon\text{-closure } (\delta(p, c))$$
$$= \epsilon\text{-closure } (r)$$
$$= \{p, q, r\}$$

Newly generated states {p, q} and {p, q, r}.

Step - 3 :
$$\text{a successor of } \{p, q\} = \epsilon\text{-closure } (\delta((p, q), q)))$$
$$= \epsilon\text{-closure } (\delta(p, a) \cup \delta(q, a))$$
$$= \epsilon\text{-closure } (p, q)$$
$$= \{p, q\}$$
$$\text{b successor of } \{p, q\} = \epsilon\text{-closure } (\delta(\{p, q\}, b))$$
$$= \epsilon\text{-closure } \{q, r\}$$
$$= \{p, q, r\}$$
$$\text{c successor of } \{p, q\} = \epsilon\text{-closure } (\delta((p, q), c)))$$
$$= \epsilon\text{-closure } (r)$$
$$= \{p, r, q\}$$

Newly generated set {p, q, r}.

Step - 4 :
$$\text{a successor of } (p, q, r) = \epsilon\text{-closure } (\delta(p, q, r), a))$$
$$= \{p, q, r\}$$
$$\text{b successor of } (p, q, r) = \epsilon\text{-closure } (\delta((p, q, r), b))$$
$$= \epsilon\text{-closure } (\delta(p, b) \cup \delta(q, b) \cup \delta(r, b))$$
$$= \epsilon\text{-closure } (q, r)$$
$$= \{q, r\}$$
$$\text{c successor of } (p, q, r) = \epsilon\text{-closure } (\delta(p, q, r), c))$$
$$= \epsilon\text{-closure } (\delta(p, c) \cup \delta(q, c) \cup \delta(r, c))$$
$$= \{p, q, r\}$$

Now new subset is generated.

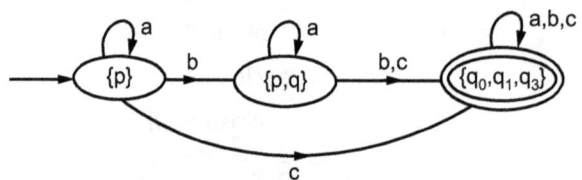

Fig. 2.22

Transition Table

	a	b
→ {p}	{p}	{p, q}
{p, q}	{p, q}	{p, q, r}
{p, q, r}*	{p, q, r}	{p₁, q, r}

Example 2.17 : Convert ϵ-NFA to DFA.

	ϵ	a	b	c
→ p	{q, r}	φ	{q}	{r}
q	φ	{p}	{r}	{p, q}
r	φ	φ	φ	φ

Solution : Step - 1 : ϵ-closure of each state.

p = {p, q, r}
q = {q}
r = {r}

Step - 2 : p is the start state

$$\epsilon\text{-closure }(p) = \{p, q, r\}$$
$$a \text{ successor of } (p, q, r) = \epsilon\text{-closure }(\delta(\{p, q, r\}, a))$$
$$= \epsilon\text{-closure }(\delta(p, a) \cup \delta(q, a) \cup \delta(q, r)\}$$
$$= \epsilon\text{-closure }(p)$$
$$= \{p, q, r\}$$
$$b \text{ successor of } (p, q, r) = \epsilon\text{-closure }(\delta(p, q, r), b))$$
$$= \{q, r\}$$
$$c \text{ successor of } (p, q, r) = \epsilon\text{-closure }(\delta((p, q, r), c))$$
$$= \epsilon\text{-closure }(\delta(p, c) \cup \delta(q, c) \cup \delta(r, c))$$
$$= \epsilon\text{-closure }(\{p, q, r\})$$
$$= \{p, q, r\}$$

Step - 3 : New subsets are {q, r}

$$a \text{ successor of } \{q, r\} = \epsilon\text{-closure }(\delta\{q, r\}, a\})$$
$$= \epsilon\text{-closure }(\delta(q, a) \cup \delta(r, a))$$

$= \epsilon\text{-closure}(p)$

$= \{p, q, r\}$

b successor of $\{q, r\}$ $= \epsilon\text{-closure}(\delta\{q, r\}, b)$

$= \epsilon\text{-closure}(r)$

$= r$

c successor of $\{q, r\}$ $= \epsilon\text{-closure}(\delta\{q, r\}, c)$

$= \epsilon\text{-closure}(p, q)$

$= \{p, q, r\}$

Step - 4 : Newly generated subset is $\{r\}$.

a successor of $\{r\} = \phi$, b successor of $\{r\} = \phi$, c successor of $\{\phi\} = \phi$

Every subset containing r, is marked as a final state.

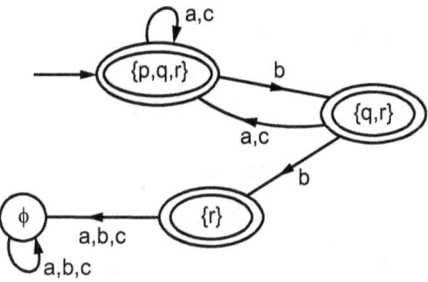

Fig. 2.23

Example 2.18 :

Convert the following ϵ-NFA to DFA.

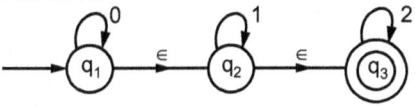

Fig. 2.24

Solution : Step - 1 : $\epsilon\text{-closure}(q_1) = \{q_1, q_2, q_3\}$

$\epsilon\text{-closure}(q_2) = \{q_2, q_3\}$

$\epsilon\text{-closure}(q_3) = \{q_3\}$

Step - 2 : Start state is q_1, so take ϵ-closure of q_1

$\epsilon\text{-closure}(q_1) = \{q_1, q_2, q_3\}$

0 successor of (q_1, q_2, q_3) $= \epsilon\text{-closure}(\delta(\{q_1, q_2, q_3\}, 0))$

$= \epsilon\text{-closure}(\delta(q_1, 0) \cup \delta(q_2, 0) \cup \delta(q_3, 0))$

$= \epsilon\text{-closure}(q_1)$

$= \{q_1, q_2, q_3\}$

1 successor of (q_1, q_2, q_3) = ϵ-closure $(\delta(q_1, q_2, q_3), 1)$
= ϵ-closure $(\delta(q_1, 1) \cup \delta(q_2, 1) \cup \delta(q_3, 1))$
= ϵ-closure (q_2)
= $\{q_2, q_3\}$

2 successor of (q_1, q_2, q_3) = ϵ-closure $(\delta(\{q_1, q_2, q_3\}))$
= $\{q_3\}$

Newly generated states are $\{q_2, q_3\}$ and $\{q_3\}$.

Step - 3 :

0 successor of $\{q_3\}$ = ϕ
1 successor of $\{q_3\}$ = ϕ
2 successor of $\{q_3\}$ = $\{q_3\}$

0 successor of $\{q_2, q_3\}$ = ϵ-closure $(\delta(q_2, q_3), 0)$
= ϵ-closure $(\delta(q_2, 0) \cup \delta(q_3, 0))$
= ϵ-closure $(\phi \cup \phi)$
= ϕ

1 successor of $\{q_2, q_3\}$ = ϵ-closure of $\{q_2\}$
= $\{q_2, q_3\}$

2 successor of $\{q_2, q_3\}$ = ϵ-closure (q_3)
= (q_3)

Transition Table

	0	1	2
$\rightarrow \{q_1, q_2, q_3\}^*$	$\{q_1, q_2, q_3\}$	$\{q_2, q_3\}$	$\{q_3\}$
$\{q_3\}^*$	ϕ	ϕ	$\{q_3\}$
$\{q_2, q_3\}^*$	ϕ	$\{q_2, q_3\}$	$\{q_3\}$

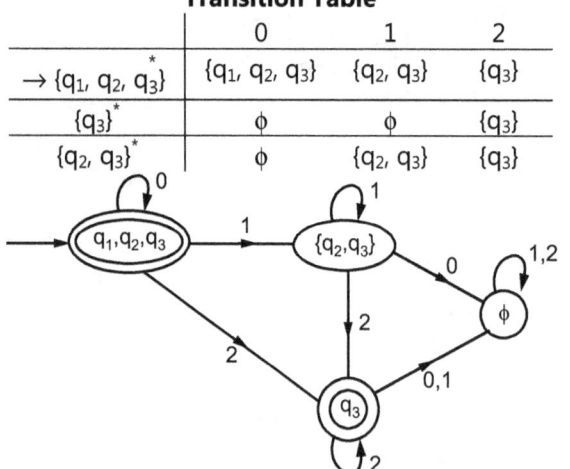

Fig. 2.25 : State transition diagram

2.4 BUILDING REGULAR EXPRESSIONS

- We can always construct an ϵ-NFA for recognizing the set of strings represented by a regular expression.
- For representing regular expressions, we are using the ϵ-NFA.
- Then convert ϵ-NFA to NFA and NFA to DFA.

2.4.1 Construction of Finite Automata Equivalent to a Regular Expression

Example 2.19 : Suppose, R_1 and R_2 are two regular expressions then construct the FA for regular expressions.

Solution : $R_1 + R_2$

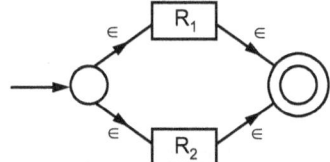

Fig. 2.26 (a)

$R_1 R_2$

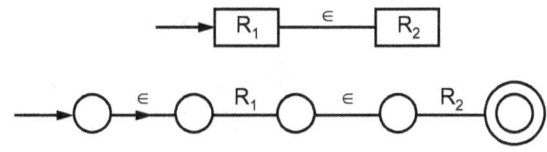

Fig. 2.26 (b)

R_1^*

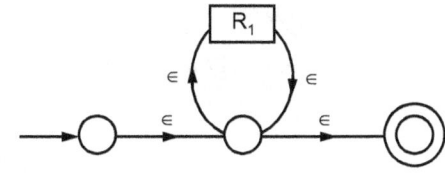

Fig. 2.26 (c)

Now we see some examples for constructing the FA for the regular expression.

$R \cdot E = a^*$

Fig. 2.26 (d)

$R \cdot E = a \cdot b$

Fig. 2.26 (e)

R · E = ε

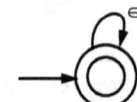

Fig. 2.26 (f)

R · E = a + b

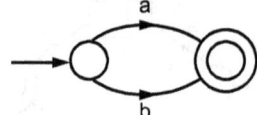

Fig. 2.26 (g)

Example 2.20 :
Construct the finite automata for the following regular expressions.

1. **(A + B)***

   A finite automata for recognizing (A + B)* is given by

   Ans. :

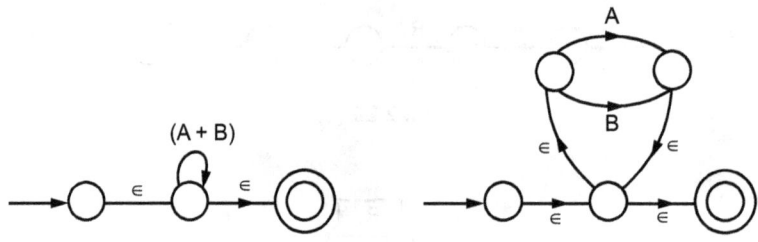

Fig. 2.27 (a)

2. **(A · B)***

   Ans. :

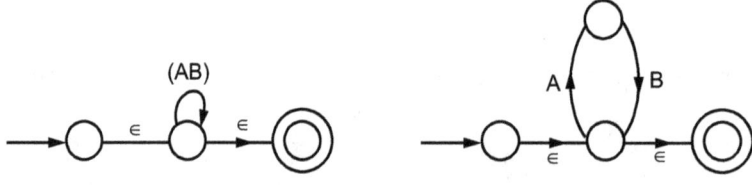

Fig. 2.27 (b)

3. **R = (A + B(AB)*)***

   Ans. :

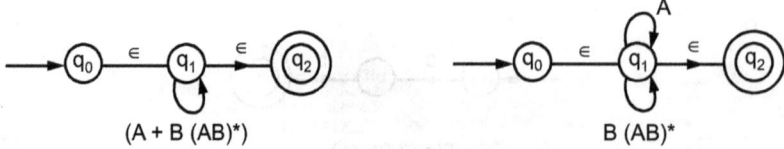

Fig. 2.27 (c)

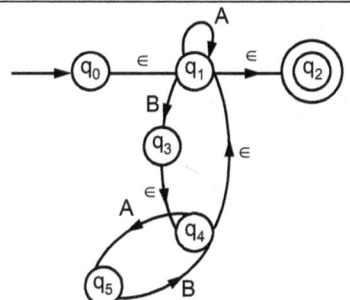

Fig. 2.27 (d)

4. R · E = $(0 + 1(01)^+)^*$

Ans. :

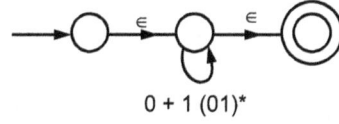

Fig. 2.27 (e)

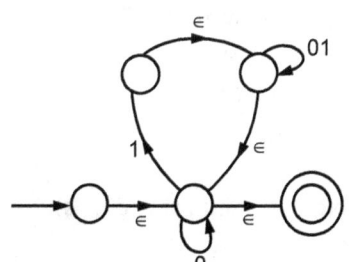

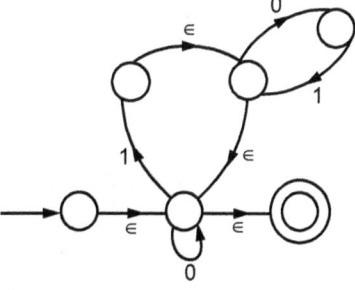

Fig. 2.27 (g)

5. R · E = $(a^* b^*)^*$

Ans. :

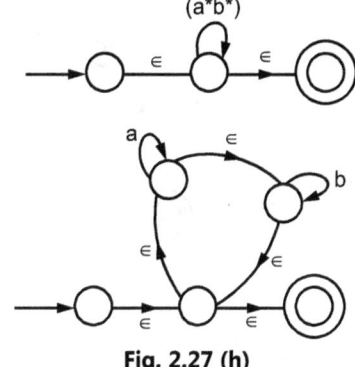

Fig. 2.27 (h)

Example 2.21 : Prove that following is the R · E.

$$(r^* s^*)^* = (r + s)^*$$

Solution : (1) Draw ϵ-NFA for $(r^* s^*)^*$

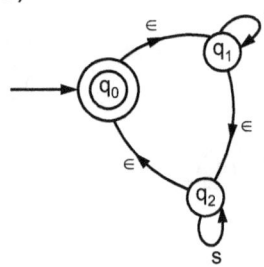

Fig. 2.28 (a)

(2) Convert ϵ-NFA to DFA

$$\epsilon\text{-closure of } q_0 = \{q_0, q_1, q_2\}$$
$$\epsilon\text{-closure of } q_1 = \{q_0, q_1, q_2\}$$
$$\epsilon\text{-closure of } q_2 = \{q_0, q_1, q_2\}$$

$$\begin{aligned}
r \text{ equivalent of } \{q_0, q_1, q_2\} &= \epsilon(\delta(q_0, q_1, q_2), r) \\
&= \epsilon(\delta(q_0, r) \cup \delta(q_1, r) \cup \delta(q_2, r)) \\
&= \epsilon(\phi \cup q_1 \cup \phi) \\
&= \epsilon\text{-closure of } (q_1) \\
&= \{q_0, q_1, q_2\}
\end{aligned}$$

$$\begin{aligned}
s \text{ equivalent of } \{q_0, q_1, q_2\} &= \epsilon(\delta(q_0, q_1, q_2), s) \\
&= \epsilon(\delta(q_0, s) \cup \delta(q_1, s) \cup \delta(q_2, s)) \\
&= \epsilon(q_2) \\
&= \epsilon\text{-closure }(q_2) \\
&= \{q_0, q_1, q_2\}
\end{aligned}$$

Final DFA

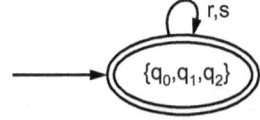

Fig. 2.28 (b)

Renaming the state from $\{q_0, q_1, q_2\}$ to A.

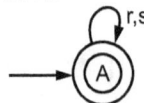

Fig. 2.28 (c)

$$R \cdot E = (r + s)^*$$
$$= \text{R.H.S. Hence proved}$$

Example 2.22: Prove that $\epsilon + 1^*(011)^* (1^*(011)^*)^* = (1 + 011)^*$

Solution: L.H.S. $= \epsilon + 1^*(011)^* (1^*(011)^*)^*$

So $1^*(011)^*$ is the common part, so replace that part by A.

$= \epsilon + A(A)^*$ $(A(A)^* = A^+)$
$= \epsilon + A^+$ $(\epsilon + A^+ = A^*)$
$= A^*$ (Replace $A = 1^*(011)^*$)
$= (1^*(011)^*)^*$
$= (1 + 011)^*$
$=$ R.H.S. Hence proved

Example 2.23: If S = {a, b} write all strings in S^* which are having length 2 or less, also say the following is true or false.

(i) $(S^+)^* = (S^*)^*$
(ii) $(S^+)^+ = S^+$
(iii) $(S^*)^+ = (S^+)^*$

Solution: Given data: S = {a, b}

Form the set of strings which is having the length 2 over an alphabet {a, b}

Set of strings of length 0 = {ϵ}
Set of strings of length 1 = {a, b}
Set of strings of length 2 = {ab, bb, ba, aa}
Final set of strings = {ϵ, a, b, aa, bb, ab, ba}

(i) $(S^+)^* = (S^*)^*$

True, both sides containing the ϵ symbol is present.

(ii) $(S^+)^+ = S^+$

True, because on both sides ϵ symbol is absent.

(iii) $(S^*)^+ = (S^+)^*$

True, both $(S^*)^+$ and $(S^*)^*$ contain the ϵ symbols.

Example 2.24: Find all possible RE $L \subseteq \{0, 1\}^*$

(a) The set of all strings ending with 0.
(b) The set of all strings ending with 01.
(c) The set of all strings ending neither in 0 nor in 01.
(d) The set of all strings start with 01.
(e) The set of all strings containing 011 as a substring.

Solution : We are using the symbol $\{0, 1\}^*$ for constructing the language.

(a) The set of all strings ending with 0.
$$R \cdot E = (0 + 1)^* 0$$

(b) The set of all strings ending with 01.
$$R \cdot E = (0 + 1)^* 01$$

(c) The set of all strings ending neither in 0 nor in 01.
$$R \cdot E = \epsilon + 1 + (0 + 1)^* 00 + (0 + 1)^* 11$$

(d) The set of all strings start with 01.
$$R \cdot E = 01 (0 + 1)^*$$

(e) The set of all strings containing 011 as a substring.
$$R \cdot E = (0 + 1)^* 011 (0 + 1)^*$$

Example 2.25 :
Find regular expression corresponding to each of the following subsets of $\{0, 1\}^*$.

Solution : (1) The language of all strings containing exactly two 0's.

So find $R \cdot E$ for the language of all strings containing exactly two zero's.

Here we are forming the language in which the set of strings containing exactly two zero's. Those strings which are containing less than or more than 2 zero's are not allowed in the regular language.

So regular expression for above language is
$$R \cdot E = 1^* 0 1^* 0 1^*$$

(2) The language of all strings containing at least two 0's.
$$R \cdot E = (0 + 1)^* 0 (1 + 0)^* 0 (1 + 0)^*$$
$$= (0 + 1)^* 0 (1 + 0)^* 0 (1 + 0)^*$$

(3) The language of all strings that do not end with 01.
$$R \cdot E = (1 + 0)^* (00 + 11 + 10)$$
$$= (1 + 0)^* 00 + (1 + 0)^* 11 + (1 + 0)^* 10$$
$$= (1 + 0)^* (00 + 11 + 10)^*$$
$$= (1 + 0)^* (00 + 11 + 10)$$

2.4.2 Conversion of Regular Expression to Finite Automata

Example 2.26 :
For each of the following draw DFA of following regular expressions :

1. $(11 + 00)^*$
2. $(111 + 100)^* 0$
3. $(0 + 1(01)^*)^*$
4. $[00 + 11 + (01 + 10)(00 + 11)^* (01 + 10)]^*$

Solution : (1) $(11 + 00)^*$

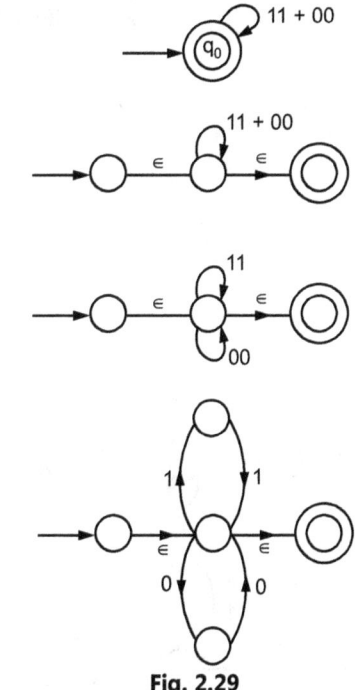

Fig. 2.29

(2) $(111 + 100)^* 0$

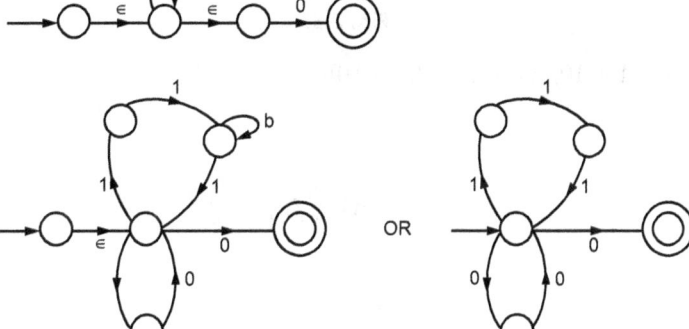

Fig. 2.30 (a)

Here $(111 + 100)^*$ is present, so we require loop.

Fig. 2.30 (b)

(3) $((0 + 1(01)^*)^*$

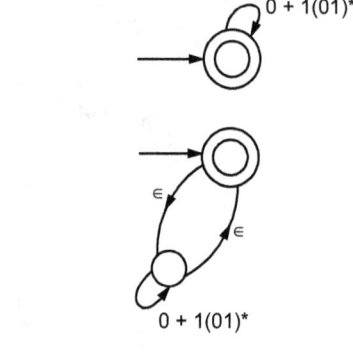

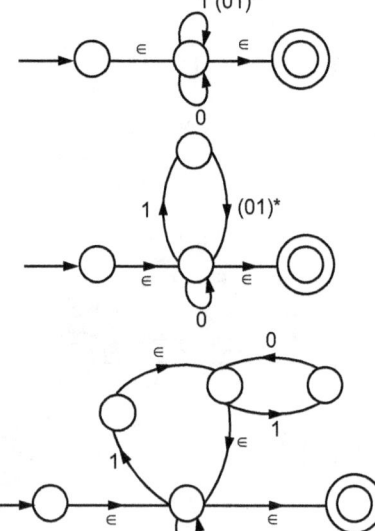

Fig. 2.31

(4) $[00 + 11 + (01 + 10)(00 + 11)^* (01 + 10)]^*$

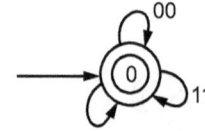

Fig. 2.32 (a)

$(01 + 10)(00 + 11)^* (01 + 10)$

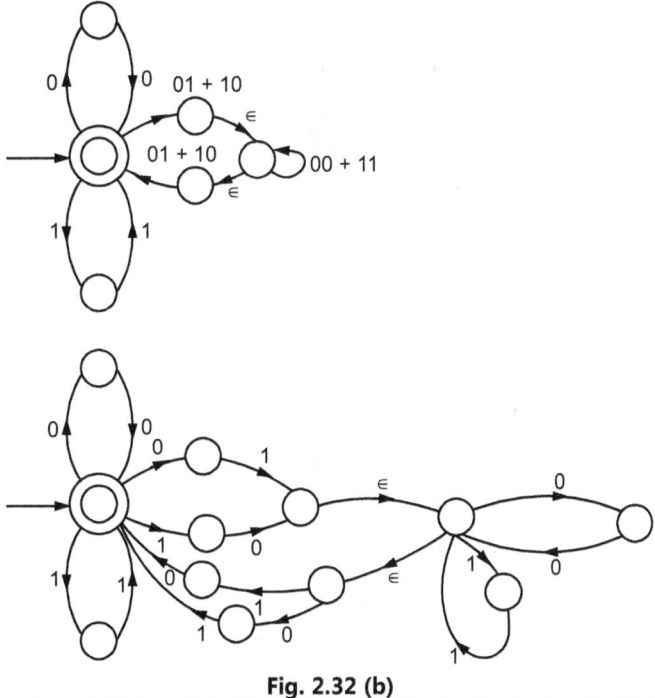

Example 2.27 : For each of the following regular expressions, draw a finite automata recognizing the corresponding language.

1. $(1 + 10 + 110)^* 0$
2. $1(01 + 10)^* + 0(11 + 10)^*$
3. $(010 + 00)^* (10)$
4. $1(1 + 10)^* + 10(0 + 01)^*$

Solution : (1) Finite Automata for $(1 + 10 + 110)^* 0$

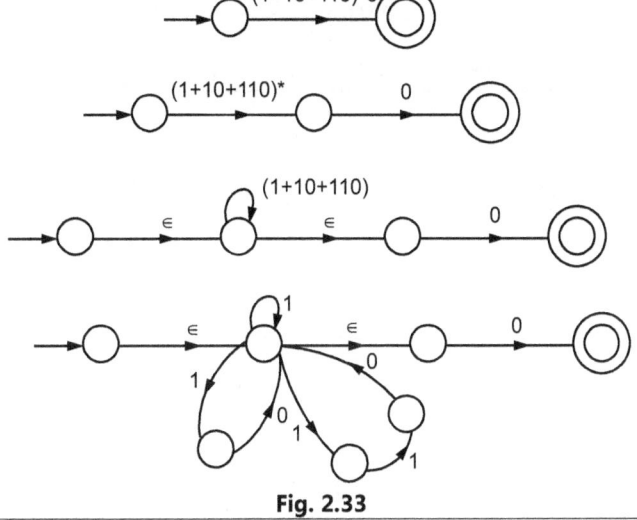

Fig. 2.33

(2) Finite Automata for $1(01 + 10)^* + 0(11 + 10)^*$

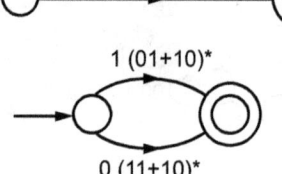

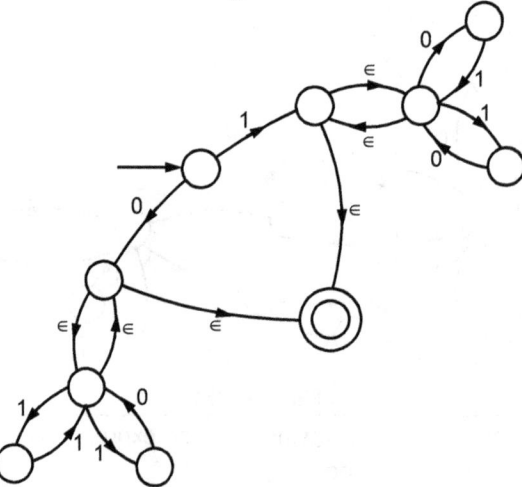

Fig. 2.35

(3) Finite Automata for $(010 + 00)^* (10)$

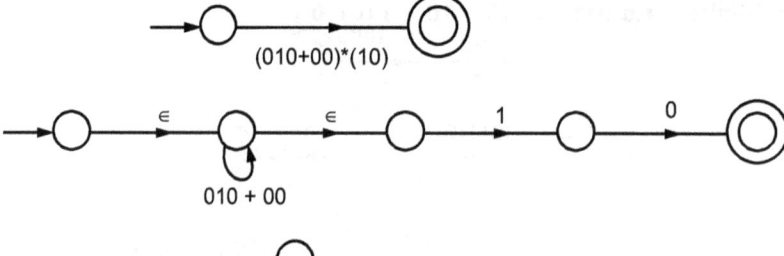

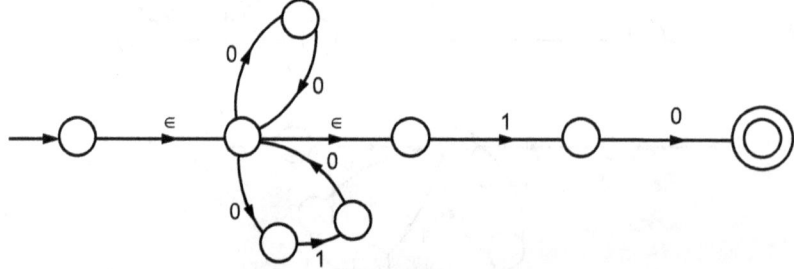

Fig. 2.36

(4) Finite Automata for $1(1 + 10)^* + 10(0 + 01)^*$

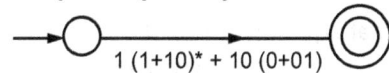

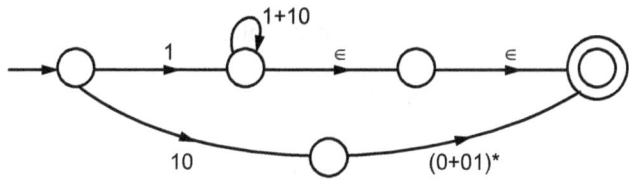

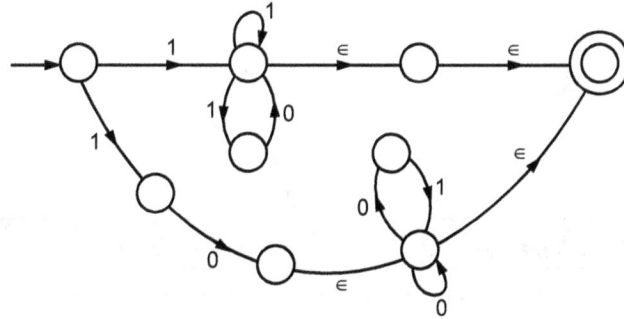

Fig. 2.37

Example 2.28 :

Let $\Sigma = \{0, 1\}$. Construct NFA and regular expressions for each of the following :

1. $L_1 = \{w \in \Sigma^* \mid w$ has at least one pair of consecutive 0's$\}$
2. $L_2 = \{w \in \Sigma^* \mid w$ has no pair of consecutive zero$\}$
3. $L_3 = \{w \in \Sigma^* \mid w$ consists of an even number of 0's followed by odd number of 1's$\}$

Solution : (1) $L_1 = \{w \in \Sigma^* \mid w$ has at least one pair of consecutive 0's$\}$

Our problem statement is w has at least one pair of consecutive 0's.

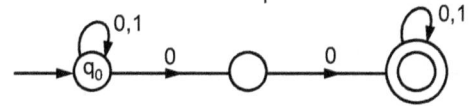

Fig. 2.38 (a)

$$R \cdot E = (0 + 1)^* 00 (0 + 1)^*$$

(2) $L_2 = \{w \in \Sigma^* \mid w$ has no pair of consecutive zero$\}$

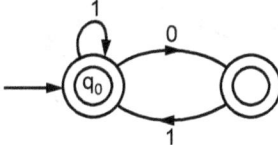

Fig. 2.38 (b)

$$\text{R.E. for } q_0 = (1+01)^*$$
$$\text{R} \cdot \text{E for state } q_1 = (1+01)^* 0$$
$$\text{The final R} \cdot \text{E} = (1+01)^* + (1+01)^* 0$$
$$= (1+01)^* [\epsilon + 0]$$

(3) $L_3 = \{w \in \Sigma^* \mid w$ consists of an even number of 0's followed by an odd number of 1's$\}$

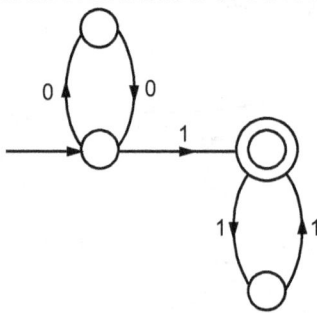

Fig. 2.38 (c)

$$\text{R} \cdot \text{E} = (00)^* 1(11)^*$$

2.5 FINITE AUTOMATA TO REGULAR EXPRESSION

There are mainly two methods for constructing RE from the finite automata as :

1. Through state/loop elimination.
2. Arden's theorem.

So first, we see the first method as a state/loop elimination method.

2.5.1 Through State/Loop Elimination

In this method, we are removing the state and loop from the FA.

Example 2.29 :
For eliminating state from FA.
Solution :

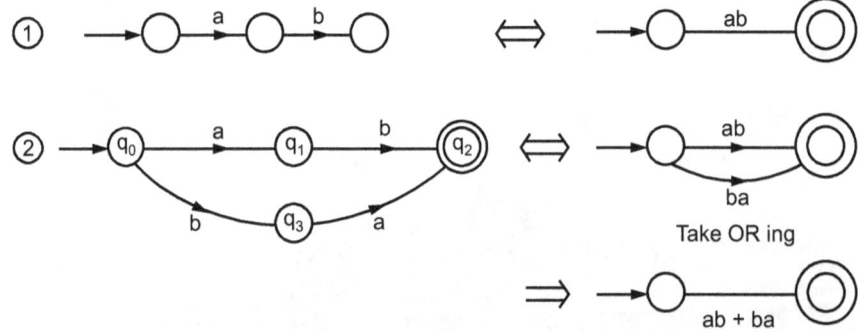

Fig. 2.39 (a)

For eliminating loop.

1.

Fig. 2.39 (b)

$$R \cdot E = R^*$$

2.

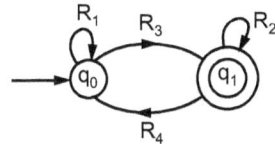

Fig. 2.39 (c)

First removing loop in between q_0, q_1, so transfer the effect of loop on either q_0 or q_1. After eliminating loop maintain the path from q_0 to q_1 and write the regular expressions.

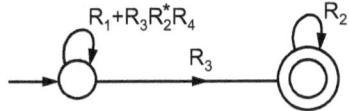

Fig. 2.39 (d)

$$R \cdot E = (R_1 + R_3 R_2^* R_4)^* R_3 R_2^*$$

3.

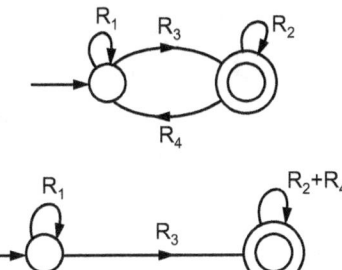

Fig. 2.39 (e)

$$R \cdot E = R_1^* R_3 (R_2 + R_4 R_1^* R_3)$$
$$= R_1^* \cdot R_3 (R_2 + R_4 R_1^* R_3)$$

Example 2.30 : Find the regular expression for the following DFA.

Solution : (1)

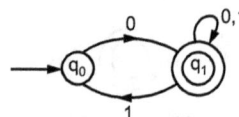

Fig. 2.40 (a)

R · E for this machine is first transfer loop either on q_0 or q_1

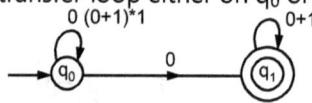

Fig. 2.40 (b)

R · E = $(0(0 + 1)^* 1)^* 0(0 + 1)^*$

(2)

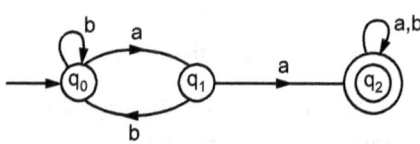

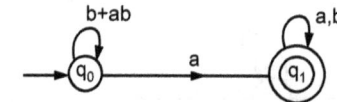

Fig. 2.40 (c)

R · E = $(b + ab)^* a(a + b)^*$

(3)

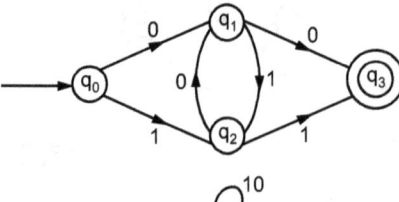

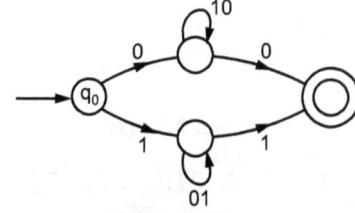

Fig. 2.40 (d)

R · E = $0(10)^* 0 + 1(01)^* 1$

2.5.2 Arden's Theorem

(1) It is used to find RE recognized by NFA.

(2) Following assumptions are made about NFA.

  (i) The NFA doesn't have ϵ-transitions

  (ii) It has only one initial state say V_1.

  (iii) The vertices are $V_1, V_2..... V_n$

  (iv) To get the RE, we have to take unions of V_1's corresponding to final states.

  (v) Important Formula

   If $R = P + RQ$ or

   $RQ + P$, then $\Rightarrow R = PQ^*$

Example 2.31 :

Find regular expression by using Arden's theorem.

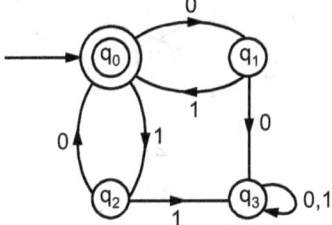

Fig. 2.41

Solution : Step 1 : Find out the incoming transition for each state and write the equation of each state.

(a) For q_0 incoming transitions are

q_1 to q_0 → q_1 1

ϵ to q_0 → ϵ ($\because q_0$ is the start state)

q_2 to q_0 → q_2 0

Equation of $q_0 = \epsilon + q_1 1 + q_2 0$ ... (1)

(b) Incoming transition for q_1,

q_0 to q_1 → q_0 0   ... (2)

(c) Incoming transition for q_2,

q_0 to q_2 → q_0 1   ... (3)

(d) q_3 is a dead state, so there is no need to find the equation for state q_3.

From equations (2) and (3) we are getting the value of q_1 and q_2, so put value of q_1 and q_2 in equation (1).

$$q_0 = \epsilon + q_0\,01 + q_0\,10$$
$$q_0 = \epsilon + q_0\,01 + q_0\,10$$
$$= \epsilon + q_0\,(01 + 10)$$

The equation is in the form of
$$R = Q + RP \quad \text{(By Arden's theorem)}$$
$Q = \epsilon$, $R = q_0$, $P = (01 + 10)$

and its solution is given by
$$R = QP^*$$
$$q_0 = \epsilon\,(01 + 10)^*$$
$$q_0 = (01 + 10)^*$$
$$R \cdot E = (01 + 10)^* \text{ because } q_0 \text{ is a final state}$$

Example 2.32 :

Find $R \cdot E$ by using Arden's theorem.

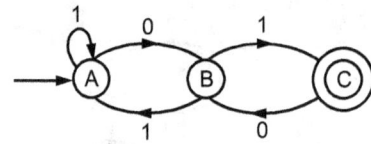

Fig. 2.42

Solution : In Arden's theorem, we require equation in $R = Q + RP$ form.
So first find out the equation for each state.

$$A = \epsilon + A1 + B1 \quad \ldots (1)$$
$$B = A0 + C0 \quad \ldots (2)$$
$$C = B1 \quad \ldots (3)$$

As C is a final state, find out the regular expression for C.
$$C = B1$$

Replace value of B by equation (2)
$$C = A0 + C0$$

Replace A by,
$$A = (\epsilon + B1)\,1^*$$
$$B = (\epsilon + B1)\,1^*0 + B10$$
$$= 1^*0 + B11^*0 + B10$$
$$\underset{R}{B} = \underset{Q}{1^*0} + \underset{R}{B}\underset{P}{(11^*0 + 10)} \quad (\because R = QP^*)$$

By Arden's theorem,
$$B = 1^*0\,(11^*0 + 10)^*$$

Put value of B in equation (3), we will get

$$C = 1^* 0 (11^* 0 + 10)^* 1$$
$$R \cdot E = 1^* 0 (11^* 0 + 10)^* 1$$

Example 2.33 : Find RE by using Arden's theorem.

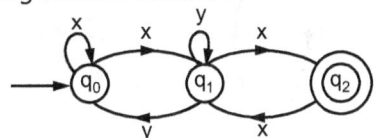

Fig. 2.43

Find out the equation for q_0, q_1, q_2.

Solution :

$$q_0 = q_0 x + q_1 y + \epsilon \qquad \ldots (1)$$
$$q_1 = q_0 x + q_1 y + q_2 x \qquad \ldots (2)$$
$$q_2 = q_1 x \qquad \ldots (3)$$

Find the value of q_0, q_1, q_2 by using Arden's theorem.

1.
$$q_1 = q_0 x + q_1 y + q_2 x$$
$$= q_0 x + q_1 y + q_1 xx$$
$$\underset{R}{q_1} = \underset{Q}{q_0 x} + \underset{R}{q_1} \underset{P}{(y + xx)}$$

By Arden's theorem, $R = QP^*$

$$\boxed{q_1 = q_0 x (y + xx)^*} \qquad \ldots (4)$$

2.
$$q_0 = q_0 x + q_1 y + \epsilon$$
$$q_0 = q_0 x + q_0 x(y + xx)^* y + \epsilon$$
$$\underset{R}{q_0} = \underset{R}{q_0} \underset{P}{(x + x(y + xx)^* y)} + \underset{Q}{\epsilon}$$

This is in $R = Q + RP$ form, use Arden's theorem.

$$q_0 = \epsilon (x + x(y + xx)^* y)^*$$
$$q_0 = (x + x(y + xx)^* y)^*$$

3.
$$q_1 = (x + x(y + xx)^* y)^* x(y + xx)^*$$

[∵ Put value of q_0 in equation (4)]

$$q_2 = (x + x(y + xx)^* y)^* x(y + xx)^* a$$
$$R \cdot E = (x + x(y + xx)^* y)^* x(y + xx)^* a$$

Example 2.34 : Find RE by using Arden's theorem.

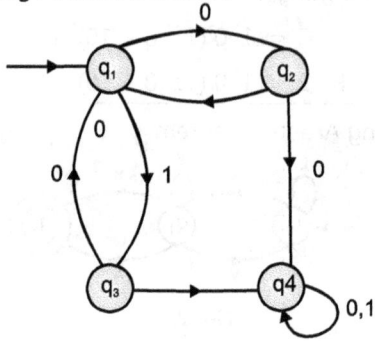

Fig. 2.44

Solution :

$q_1 = q_2 1 + q_3 0 + \epsilon$
$q_2 = q_1 0$
$q_3 = q_1 1$
$q_4 = q_2 0 + q_4 0 + q_4 1$

Now, observe that q_1 is the only final state, and its equation involves q_2 and q_3.
∴ q_4 becomes redundant and hence neglected.
Now, substitute the value of q_2 and q_3 in the equation of q_1.

∴
$$q_1 = q_1 01 + q_1 10 + \epsilon$$
$$\underset{R}{q_1} = \underset{R}{q_1} \underset{Q}{(01 + 10)} + \underset{P}{\frac{\epsilon}{}}$$

∴
$$q_1 = E (01 + 10)*$$
$$q_1 = (01 + 10)*$$

RE is $\boxed{(01 + 10)^*}$

Example 2.35 : Find RE by using Arden's theorem.

Fig. 2.45

Solution :

$q_1 = q_1 0 + E$
$q_2 = q_1 1 + q_2 1$
$q_3 = q_2 0 + q_3 0 + q_3 1$

(i) $q_1 = q_1 0 + \epsilon$
∴ $q_1 = \epsilon 0^*$
i.e. $q_1 = 0^*$

(ii) $q_2 = q_1 1 + q_2 1$

Substitute the value of q_1

$$\underset{R}{q_2} = \underset{P}{\frac{0^* 1}{}} + \underset{Q}{\frac{q_2 1}{}}$$

$$q_2 = 0^*1.1^*$$
$$= 0^*1^+$$

Resultant RE is union of q_1 and q_2

$$\therefore q_1 + q_2 = 0^* + 0^* 1^+$$

Hence RE is

$$\boxed{0^* + 0^* 1^+}$$

2.6 CLOSURE PROPERTIES OF REGULAR LANGUAGES

Regular grammar generates the regular language then we say that regular language is closed under following operations:

1. Union
2. Concatenation
3. Kleene star
4. Intersection
5. Difference
6. Reversal

2.6.1 Union

Take two machine as M_{01} and M_{02}

$$M_{01} = \{M_1, \delta_1, \Sigma, m_1, F\}$$
$$M_{02} = \{M_2, \delta_2, \Sigma, m_2, G\}$$

Take another machine m_{03} which accepts the every string generated by M_{01} and M_{02}.

$$L(M_{03}) = L(M_{01}) \cup L(M_{02})$$

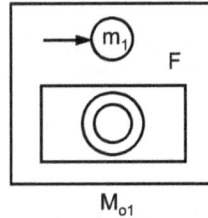
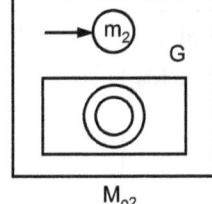
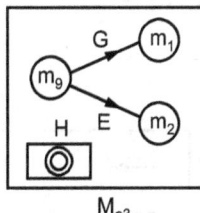

Fig. 2.46

Machine, $M_{03} = \{M_3, \delta_3, \Sigma, m_3, H\}$

$$M_{03} = \{M_3, \delta_3, \Sigma, m_3, H\}$$

where,
$$M_{03} = M_{01} \cup M_{02} \cup r_0 \quad (\because r_0 \text{ is the start state of } M_{03})$$
$$H = F \cup G$$
$$\delta_3 = \delta_1 \cup \delta_3 \cup \{(M_3, \in, s_0), (M_3, \in, q_0)\}$$

In this we are taking the language accepted by either M_{01} or M_{02}

$$\boxed{L(M_{03}) = L(M_0) \cup L(M_{02})}$$

2.6.2 Concatenation

Let,
$$M_{01} = \{M_1, \Sigma, \delta_1, m_1, F\}$$
$$M_{02} = \{M_2, \Sigma, \delta_2, m_2, G\}$$

Take machine M_{03} such that, language accepted by M_{03} is language accepted by the machine M_{01} and machine M_{02}.

Means $\qquad L(M_{03}) = L(M_{03}) \cdot L(M_{02})$

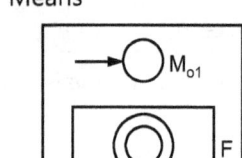  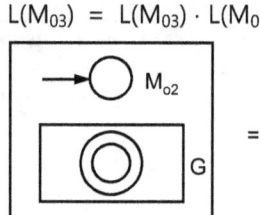 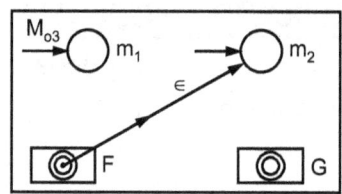

Fig. 2.47

$$M_{03} = \{M_3, \Sigma, \delta_3, m_3, H\}$$
$$M_{03} = M_2 \cup M_1$$
$$\delta_3 = \delta_1 \cup \delta_2 \cup \{\text{take transition from final state of } M_{01} \text{ to start state of machine } M_{02} \text{ on } \epsilon\}$$

2.6.3 KLeene Star

Let, $M_{01} = \{M_1, \Sigma, \delta_1, m_1, F\}$ is the automata, we can construct M_2 in such a way that
$$L(M_{02}) = L(M_{01})^*$$

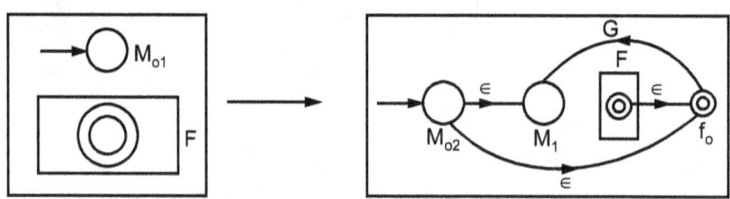

Fig. 2.48

M_{02} is constructed as follows :

1. A new start state is added M_{02} on ϵ moves from M_{02} to M_{01}.

2. A new final state f_0 is added with ϵ-moves from F to f_0. An ϵ-move is added from M_{02} to f_0 as ϵ is a member of $L(M_{01})^*$.

$$M_{02} = \{M_2, \Sigma, \delta_1, m_2, f_0\}$$

$$M_{02} = M_{01} \cup M_{02} \cup f_0$$

Machine can accept string $\in L(M_{01})$ and resume back from the start state M_{01} through the ϵ-machine from M_{02} to f_0 as ϵ is a member of $2(M_{01})^*$.

Machine can accept a string $\in L(M_{01})$ and resume back from the start state M_1 through the ϵ-move from f_0 to M_{01}.

Thus, accepting $L(M_1)^*$.

2.6.4 Intersection

L_1 and L_2 are two regular languages, take intersection of L_1 and L_2.

$$\begin{aligned} L_1 \cap L_2 &= ((L_1 \cap L_2)')' \\ &= (\overline{L_1} \cup \overline{L_2})' \\ &= \Sigma^* - \{(\Sigma^* - L_1) \cup (\Sigma^* - L_2)\} \end{aligned}$$

2.6.5 Difference

Let L_1 and L_2 are two regular languages. Take a difference between two set of languages $L_2 - L_1$.

Meaning of $L_2 - L_1$ is the set of strings that are in languages L_1 but not in L_2.

2.6.6 Reversal

Reversal of a language L is obtained by reversing every string in L.

Reversal of any language L is represented by the symbol L^R.

If, L = {baa, abb, aba} then
L^R = {aab, bba, aba}

2.7 THE PUMPING LEMMA FOR REGULAR LANGUAGES

Every regular language can be accepted by a finite automata (FA), a recognizing device with finite set of states and no auxiliary memory. A language that does not have this property is not regular language.

2.7.1 Pumping Lemma

Suppose L is a regular language recognized by a finite automata with n states. For any $x \in L$ with $|x| \geq n$, x is written as x = uvw for some strings u, v and w so that,

$$x = uvw$$
$$|uv| \leq n$$
$$|v| > 0$$

For any $i \geq 0, uv^iw \in L$.

In order to use the pumping lemma to show that a language L is not regular, we must show that L fails to have the property described in the Lemma. We can show this by assuming that the property is satisfied and deriving a contradiction.

We try to find out a specific string x with $|x| \geq n$, so that the statements involving x in the theorem will lead to contradiction.

We don't know what is n, therefore, we must show that for any n, we can find $x \in L$ with $|x| \geq n$, so that statement about x the theorem lead to contradiction. So it is important to choose x carefully in order to obtain the contradiction. We are free to choose any x.

2.7.2 Applications of Pumping Lemma

- Pumping Lemma should be used to prove that given set is not regular.
- Pumping Lemma is used to show that given language is not regular.

For above proof, use following steps.

1. Initially make the assumption that given language L is regular.
2. Now, choose the string x such that $x \in L$ and $|x| \geq n$.
3. Rewrite x = uvw such that $|uv| \leq n$ and $|v| > 0$.

Then, pump the string such that $x = uv^i w$, where $i > 0$, show that for any i, $uv^i w \in L$.

Here given language L is not regular.

Example 2.36 :

Show that $L = \{0^n 1^n \mid n \geq 0\}$ is not regular.

Solution : Step - 1 : Consider given language L is regular.

Step - 2 : Choose the string x such that

$|x| \geq n$ and rewrite it as

$$x = uvw \text{ such that}$$
$$|uv| \leq n \text{ and } |v| > 0$$

Hence, $0^n 1^n$ is written as

$$x = \underbrace{0^m}_{u} \underbrace{0^k}_{v} \underbrace{0^{n-m-k} 1^n}_{w}$$

Step - 3 :
Check for

$$x = uv^i w \text{ where } i > 0$$
$$i = 2$$
$$x = 0^m (0^k)^2 0^{n-m-k} 1^n = 0^{m+k+k+n-m-k} 1^n$$
$$= 0^{n+k} 1^n$$

Since $|v| > n$ means $k > 0$, hence number of 0's are more than number of 1s. Hence $uv^2 w \in L$. Hence given language L is not regular.

Example 2.37 :

Prove that L $\{0^n \mid n$ is prime is not regular$\}$.

Solution : Step - 1 : Assume that given x such that

Step - 2 : Consider the string x such that $x = 0^P$. Hence $|x| = |G^P| = P \geq n$

Step - 3 : Now consider the string $x = uv^iw$

$$|uv| \leq n \text{ and } |v| > 0$$

Consider $\quad v = a^m$ for $m > 0$

i.e. $\quad |v| = |a^m| = m > 0$

Now, consider $\quad uv^iw = uvw + y^{i-1}$

Hence $\quad |uv^iw| = |uvw| + |v^{i-1}|$

Hence total length is $p + mq$ where $q > 0$, and $p \geq 0$ $\qquad [\because |v| = |a^m|]$

Now, let us check $p + mq$ is prime or not.

If we choose, $m = p$

Then, $\quad p \mid mq = p + pq = p(1 + q)$

If we choose $\quad m = p + 2q + 2$, then

$$p + mq = p + (p + 2q + 2)q$$
$$= (p + 2q) + (p + 2q)q$$
$$= (p + 2q) + (1 + q)$$

It is having factors as $(p + 2q)$ and $(1 + q)$.

Hence it is not prime.

Hence $x \notin L$. Hence given language is not regular.

Example 2.38 :

Using pumping lemma for regular sets, prove that the language

$$L = \{ww \mid w \in (0, 1)^*\} \text{ is not regular.}$$

Solution : Step - 1 : Consider given language L is regular.

Step - 2 : Consider the string

$$x = \frac{0^n q^n}{w} \frac{0^n q^n}{w}$$

$\therefore \quad |x| = 2n + 2n \geq n$

Step - 3 : According to pumping lemma,

$$|v| > 0 \text{ and } |uv| \leq n$$

Now consider $x = uv^iw$ such that

$$x = 0^n 1^n \, 0^n \, q^n = \underbrace{0^m \, 0^k}_{u \quad v} \underbrace{0^{n-m-k} \, 1^n \, 0^n \, q^n}_{w} \text{ where } k > 0$$

Consider $\quad i = 2$

$$x = 0^m \, 0^{2k} \, 0^{n-m-k} \, 0^n \, q^n$$

$$= \underbrace{0^{n+k} 1^n}_{w} \, \underbrace{0^n q^n}_{w}$$

Here $k > 0$ here first half of the string have more number of 0's than second half.

Hence $x \notin L$. Hence given language is not regular.

Example 2.39 :

Prove that the language L = {0, 1^v| all the strings are palindrome} OR

$$L = \{ww^R \mid w \in (0, 1)^*\}$$

Solution : Step - 1 : Consider given language L is regular.

Step - 2 : Consider the string x such that

$$x = \underbrace{0^n 1}_{w} \, \underbrace{1 0^n}_{w^R}$$

Where $\quad |x| = n + 1 + n + 1 = 2n + 2 \geq n$

Step - 3 : Consider the string

$$x = uv^i w \text{ such that}$$

$$|uv| \leq n \text{ and } |v| > 0$$

Now, $\quad x = 0^m \, 0^k \, 0^{n-m-k} \, 1 \, 1 \, 0^n$ such that $k > 0$

Now for $i = 2$, $\quad x = 0^m \, 0^{2k} \, 0^{n-m-k} \, 1 \, 1 \, 0^n$

$$= \underbrace{0^{n+k} 1}_{w} \, \underbrace{1 \, 0^n}_{wR}$$

Hence as the first half number of 0s are more than 2nd half, hence $w \neq w^R$. Hence $x \notin L$. Hence given language is not regular.

Example 2.40 :

Using pumping lemma for regular sets, prove that the language

$$L \{a^m \, b^n \mid m > n\} \text{ is not regular.}$$

Solution : Step - 1 : Consider that the language L is regular.

Step - 2 : Let's consider the string

$$x = a^p \, b^q \text{ where } p > q$$

$$p + q > n$$

Step - 3 : Consider the string $x = uv^iw$ such that $|v| > 0$ and $|uv| \leq n$.

Consider the string x such that

$$x = \underbrace{a^{p-i}}_{u} \underbrace{(a^i b^j)}_{v} \underbrace{b^{q-j}}_{w}$$

Consider i = 2

$$\begin{aligned} x = uv^2w &= a^{p-i} (a^i b^j)^2 b^{q-j} \\ &= a^{p-i} a^i b^j a^i b^j b^{q-j} \\ &= a^{p-i+i} b^j a^i b^{j+q-j} \\ &= a^p b^j a^i b^q \end{aligned}$$

Here, first a come, then b and then a. Hence $x \notin L$. Hence given language is not regular.

Example 2.41 :

Prove that the language $L = \{0^m 1^n 0^{m+n} | m \geq 1 \text{ and } n \geq 1\}$ is not regular.

Solution : Step - 1 : Consider the given language is regular.

Step - 2 : Consider the string

$$x = 0^m 1^n 0^{m+n}$$
$$|x| = 2(m+n) \geq n$$

Step - 3 : Now consider the string $x = uv^iw$ such that $|uv| \leq n$ and $|v| > 0$

$$\therefore \quad x = \underbrace{0^p}_{u} \underbrace{0^q}_{v} \underbrace{0^{m-p-q} q^n 0^{m+n}}_{2}$$

Now consider $\quad i = 2$

$$\therefore \quad x = 0^p 0^{2q} 0^{m-p-q} 1^n 0^{m+n}$$
$$= 0^{m+q} 1^n 0^{m+n}$$

Hence $x \notin L$. Hence given language is not regular.

QUESTIONS

1. Define Regular Expression ?
2. Explain the property of pumping lemma of regular set. Where do we apply this property? Give the example ?
3. Prove or disprove the following regular expression
   (i) (a* ab + ba)* a* = (a + ab + ba)*   (ii) (rs + r)* = r (sr + r)*

4. What are the applications of pumping lemma ?
5. Construct FA equivalent to the following regular set and describe in English set denoted by following regular set.
   (a) 10 + (0 + 11) 0* 1
   (b) 01 [1 (10)* + 1(1)* + 0]* 1
   (c) [00 + 11 + (01 + 10) (00 + 11)* (01 + 10)]*
6. Use the pumping lemma to show that each of these languages is not regular.
   (a) L = {ww | w ∈ {0, 1)*}
   (b) L = {xy | x, y ∈ {0, 1}* and y is x*}
7. Consider the following transition diagram, convert it to equivalent regular expression using Arden's theorem ?

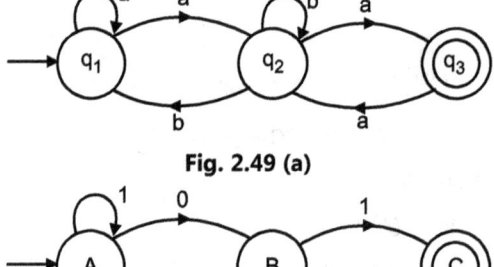

Fig. 2.49 (a)

Fig. 2.49 (b)

8. Using pumping lemma for regular sets prove that which of the following languages are regular sets.
   (i) $\{0^m 1^n 0^{m+n}\}\ m \geq 1$ and $n \geq 1\}$
   (ii) $\{0^n\ |\ n$ is a prime$\}$
9. Prove that L = {wwR | w is (0 +1)* and w^R is reverse of w} is not regular.
10. Explain the closure properties of regular set.

◈ ◈ ◈

Unit - III

GRAMMARS

3.1 INTRODUCTION

In previous units, we have seen that finite automata is used for accepting the language L and for describing the language, we are using regular expressions, but there are several languages which are not regular. For representing the non-regular languages, we are using the concept of grammar.

First we see some languages which are non-regular.

Examples

1. $L_1 = \{ww^R \mid w \in \{a, b\}^*\}$ is non-regular language.
2. $L_2 = \{a^p \mid p \text{ is a prime}\}$ is non-regular language.
3. $L_3 = \{a^n b^n \mid n \geq 0\}$ is non-regular language.
4. $L_4 = \{ww \mid w \in \{a, b\}^*\}$ is again non-regular language.

These are some examples of non-regular languages. For representing non-regular languages, we are using grammar.

Grammar :

Grammar is nothing but set of rules for representing the language. In this we are using equations to generate the language and equations are recursive in nature.

In finite automata, we are using number of states, number of input symbols, transition for accepting the language. But in grammar we are using terminals for constructing the language and equations are also used in grammar.

3.1.1 Difference between FA and Grammar

Table 3.1 : Difference between FA and Grammar

FA	Grammar
1. Finite automata is defined over an alphabet.	1. In grammar we are using set of terminals.
2. In FA, we are using set of transitions.	2. A grammar has set of equations for producing the language.

... (Contd.)

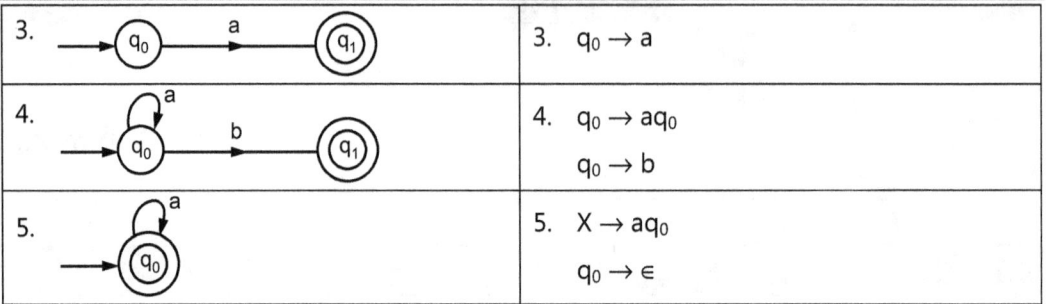

3.	3. $q_0 \to a$
4.	4. $q_0 \to aq_0$ $q_0 \to b$
5.	5. $X \to aq_0$ $q_0 \to \epsilon$

In DFA, if we want to produce $\{\epsilon, a, aa, aaa \ldots\}$, we have to add loop on start state and mark state as a final state. But in a context free grammar, we use production rules for generating the language. 1st rule is,

$$q_0 \to aq_0$$
$$q_0 \to \epsilon$$

Take string as aaaaa

$$q_0 \to aq_0$$

Replace q_0 by aq_0

$$q_0 \to aaq_0$$
$$\to aaaq_0$$
$$\to aaaaq_0$$
$$\to aaaaaq_0$$
$$\to aaaaa\epsilon$$
$$\to aaaaa$$

aaaaa is generated by aaaaa.

Parse Tree for above String :

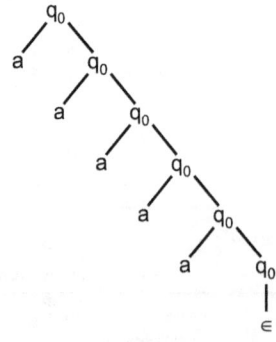

Fig. 3.1

3.2 CONTEXT FREE GRAMMAR

It is a set of four tuples {V, T, P, S}

where,
- V = set of variables
- T = set of terminals
- P = set of production rule
- S = Special symbol or start state and it is S ∈ V

- Terminals are represented in lower case letters.
- Non-terminals are represented in upper case letters.
- Sentential form is string of terminals and variables and it is denoted by α, β, γ etc.

3.2.1 The Language Generated by the Grammar

- Every grammar generates the language.
- A word of a language is generated by applying production of a finite number of times.
- Every derivation have the start state.
- The final string generated from the grammar should only contain the terminal symbols.

Example : If G is a grammar with start symbol as s, we are using set of terminals T. Then language of G is

$$L(G) = \{w \mid w \in T^* \text{ and } s \xrightarrow[G]{} w\}$$

It means w is a string which belongs to set of terminals. For generating w, we are using the start state along with production rule.

There are two ways for representing the grammar :
1. Sentential form.
2. Parse tree form.

First, we see the sentential form for representing the grammar.

1. **Sentential Form :** Let us consider a grammar given below.

$$s \rightarrow A1B$$
$$A \rightarrow 0A \mid \epsilon$$
$$B \rightarrow 0B \mid 1B \mid \epsilon$$

G is nothing but set of quadraples {V, T, P, S}

- V = {S, A, B}
- T = {0, 1, ∈}
- S = Start state
- P = S → A1B
  - A → 0A | ∈
  - B → 0B | 1B | ∈

Consider one string as 00101 and show this string is generated from the above grammar.

$$S \rightarrow \underline{A}1B$$
$$\rightarrow 0\underline{A}1B$$
$$\rightarrow 00\underline{A}1B$$
$$\rightarrow 00\epsilon 1B$$
$$\rightarrow 001\underline{B}$$
$$\rightarrow 0010\underline{B}$$
$$\rightarrow 00101\underline{B}$$
$$\rightarrow 00101\epsilon$$
$$\rightarrow 00101$$

It means string is generated from the above grammar.

$$00101 \in L(G)$$

There are two ways for deriving the string :

(i) Leftmost derivation.

(ii) Rightmost derivation.

(i) Leftmost Derivation : In this we are taking leftmost variable or symbol for expansion.

(ii) Rightmost Derivation : In this we are taking rightmost variable or symbol for expansion.

Example 3.1 : See the grammar given below,

$$S \rightarrow A1B$$
$$A \rightarrow 0A \mid \epsilon$$
$$B \rightarrow 0B \mid 1B \mid \epsilon$$

Find leftmost derivation and rightmost derivation for 10011.

Solution : Start from $S \rightarrow A1B$

Leftmost Derivation :

$S \rightarrow \underline{A}1B$
$\rightarrow \epsilon 1B$ ($\because$ left symbol is A, replace A = ϵ)
$\rightarrow 1\underline{B}$
$\rightarrow 10\underline{B}$ ($\because$ leftmost symbol is B. Replace B = 0B, because we want 0 after 1)
$\rightarrow 100B$
$\rightarrow 1001B$
$\rightarrow 10011\underline{B}$
$\rightarrow 10011\epsilon$
$\rightarrow 10011$

Rightmost Derivation :

$$S \to A1B$$

Rightmost symbol is B, so take expansion of B, for generating the string

→ A10B	Replace B = 0B
→ A100B	∵ B = 0B
→ A1001B	∵ B = 1B
→ A10011B	∵ B = 1B
→ A10011ε	∵ B = ε
→ ε10011	∵ A = ε
→ 10011	

2. Parse Tree Form :

A representation of derivation by using tree is nothing but a parse tree.

Parse tree is constructed with the following conditions.

- Root represents start symbol.
- Leaf node represents the terminal symbol and ε.
- Internal node represents the non-terminal symbol.

Example 3.2 : Construct parse tree for the following grammar.

$$S \to 0S1 \mid 01$$ for the string 00001111

Solution : $S \to 0S1$ replace S by 0S1

→ 00S11

→ 000S111 replace S by S = 01

→ 00001111

→ 00001111

Parse tree for generating above string.

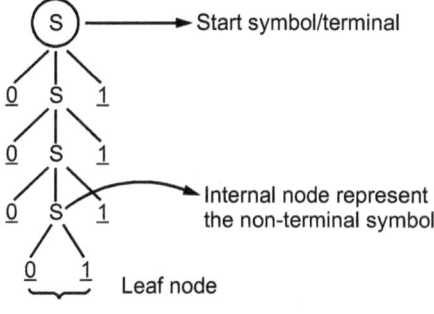

Fig. 3.2

Example 3.3 : The grammar given below.

$$E \rightarrow E + T \mid T$$
$$T \rightarrow T * F \mid F$$
$$F \rightarrow (E) \mid a/b$$

Give the derivation of (a + b) * a + b.

Solution : Definition of grammar : It is a set of quadruple.

$$G = \{V, T, P, S\}$$

where,
$$V = \{E, T, F\}$$
$$T = \{a, b, (\,,\,), +, *\}$$
$$P = E \rightarrow E + T \mid T$$
$$T \rightarrow T * F \mid F$$
$$F \rightarrow (E) \mid a \mid b$$
$$S = E \quad \text{start symbol.}$$

Derivation in Sentential Form :

$$E \rightarrow \underline{E} + T \qquad \qquad \because E \rightarrow T$$
$$\rightarrow \underline{T} + T$$
$$\rightarrow \underline{T} * F + T \qquad \qquad \because T \rightarrow T * F$$
$$\rightarrow \underline{F} * F + T \qquad \qquad \because T \rightarrow F$$
$$\rightarrow \underline{(E)} * F + T \qquad \qquad \because F \rightarrow (E)$$
$$\rightarrow (E + T) * F + T \qquad \because E \rightarrow E + T$$
$$\rightarrow (T + T) * F + T \qquad \because E \rightarrow T$$
$$\rightarrow (F + F) * F + T \qquad \because T \rightarrow F$$
$$\rightarrow (a + b) * a + F \qquad \because F \rightarrow a \text{ or } F \rightarrow b$$
$$\rightarrow (a + b) * a + b$$

By using parse tree :

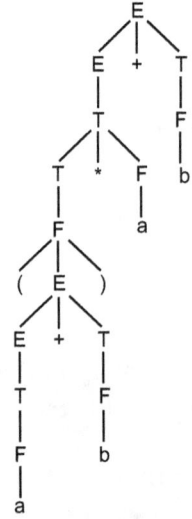

Fig. 3.3

Example 3.4 : Construct parse tree for the following strings by using

$$G = (\{S, A, B\}, \{a, b\}, P, \{S\})$$
$$P = \{S \to aB$$
$$S \to bA$$
$$A \to a$$
$$A \to aS$$
$$A \to bAA$$
$$B \to b$$
$$B \to bS$$
$$B \to aBB\}$$

1. Strings aaabbb.
2. abababba

Solution : (1) aaabbb :

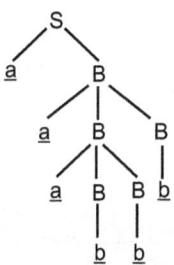

Fig. 3.4 (a)

We are getting the string as 000111 by this grammar.

(2) abababba :

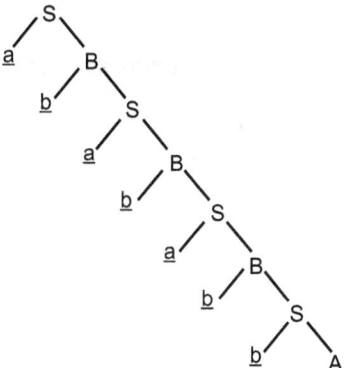

Fig. 3.4 (b)

Example 3.5 : Consider the following grammar

$$S \rightarrow aAS \mid a$$
$$A \rightarrow SbA \mid S$$
$$A \rightarrow ba$$

Derive the string aabbaa using :
1. Leftmost derivation and
2. Rightmost derivation.

Solution : (1) Leftmost derivation for string aaabbaa

S → aAS	(∵ S → aAS
→ aSb<u>A</u>S	A → SbA
→ aabAS	S → a
→ aabbaS	A → ba
→ aabbaa	S → a)

(2) Rightmost derivation :

S → aAS	(∵ S → aAS
→ aAa	∴ S → a
→ aSbAa	∴ S → SbA
→ aSbbaa	∵ A → ba
→ aabbaa	∵ S → a)

3.3 WRITING GRAMMAR FOR A LANGUAGE

Recursive Production : If left side variable is occurred in its right side variable, then we called that production as recursive production.

For example : (1) S → aS | ∈

S is the variable which is present in left side of production as well as right side of the production part.

Recursive production is used for generating infinite language.

(2) S → bS | ∈ L = {∈, b, bb, bbb, ... }

Generate bbbb from the above production rule.

S → b<u>S</u>	Replace S → bS
→ bb<u>S</u>	∵ S → bS
→ bbb<u>S</u>	∵ S → bS
→ bbbb<u>S</u>	∵ S → ∈
→ bbbb∈	
→ bbbb	

Parse Tree :

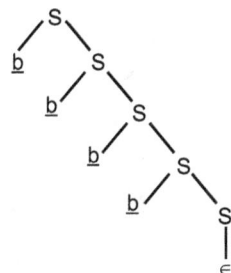

Fig. 3.5

Example 3.6 : L = {a, aa, aaa, ... } generate grammar using this language.

Solution : Production rules :

e.g. S → aS
     S → a

     S → a<u>S</u>
       → aa<u>S</u>   Sentential form
       → aaa

Three times of aaa is generated by the above grammar.

Parse tree for generating aaa

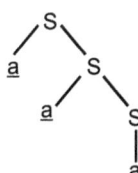

Fig. 3.6

Example 3.7 : Language L = {ab, b, aab, aaab ... } which production rules are required to generate the above language

Solution : S → aS
              S → b

The production S → aS can generate one or more a'S.
The production S → b is for termination of the string.
For example : Generate the string aaaab.
By using sentential form.

     S → a<u>S</u>
       → aa<u>S</u>
       → aaa<u>S</u>
       → aaaa<u>S</u>
       → aaaab

Parse Tree :

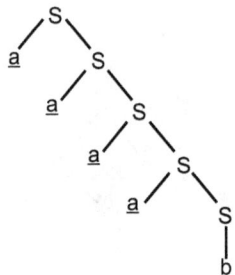

Fig. 3.7

Example 3.8 : L = {∈, a, b, aa, bb, ab, ba, ... } generate grammar for this language.

Solution :

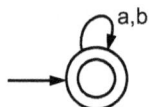

Fig. 3.8

$$R \cdot E = (a + b)^*$$
$$S \rightarrow aS$$
$$S \rightarrow bS$$
$$S \rightarrow \epsilon$$

e.g. Generate abab by using above grammar

(1) Sentential Form :

$$S \rightarrow aS$$
$$\rightarrow abS$$
$$\rightarrow abaS$$
$$\rightarrow ababS$$
$$\rightarrow abab\epsilon$$
$$\rightarrow abab$$

(2) Parse Tree Form :

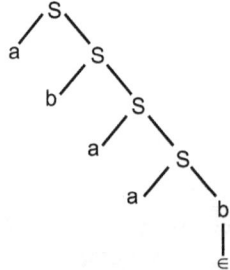

Fig. 3.8 (a)

Example 3.9 : Construct the grammar for the language.

L = {ϵ, ab, aabb, aaabbb, aaaabbbb, ... $a^n b^n$}

Solution : Number of a's followed by equal number of b.

$$S \rightarrow aSb$$
$$S \rightarrow \epsilon$$

Generate aaabbb by using sentential form and parse tree.

(1) Sentential Form :

$$S \rightarrow a\underline{S}b$$
$$\rightarrow aa\underline{S}bb$$
$$\rightarrow aaa\underline{S}bbb$$
$$\rightarrow aaa\epsilon\, bbb$$
$$\rightarrow aaabbb$$

(2) Parse Tree :

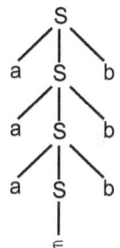

Fig. 3.9

3.3.1 Concatenation Rule for Grammar

If the language L_1 is generated by S_1 and language L_2 is generated by grammar with start symbol S_2. Then concatenation of language is $L_1 \cdot L_2$ and this is generated by another start symbol S.

$$S \rightarrow S_1 \cdot S_2$$
$$L_1 = \{a^n \mid n > 0\}$$
$$L_2 = \{b^n \mid b > 0\}$$

Grammar for L_1 are
$$S_1 \rightarrow aS_1$$
$$S_1 \rightarrow a$$

Grammar for L_2 are
$$S_2 \rightarrow bS_2$$
$$S_2 \rightarrow b$$

Then concatenation of these two grammar is as follows.

$$S \rightarrow S_1 S_2$$
$$S_1 \rightarrow aS \mid a$$
$$S_2 \rightarrow bS \mid b$$

3.3.2 Union for the Grammar

L_1 is generated by start symbol S_1 and L_2 is generated by start symbol S_2, then union of languages $L_1 \cup L_2$ can be generated with start symbol S, where

$$S \to S_1 | S_2$$

Let the languages L_1 and L_2 are given as below.

$$L_1 = \{a^n | n > 0\} \quad S_1 \to aS_1 | a$$
$$L_2 = \{b^n | n > 0\} \quad S_2 \to bS_2 | b$$

Production $L = L_1 \cup L_2$ can be written as follows

$$S \to S_1 | S_2$$
$$S_1 \to aS | a$$
$$S_2 \to bS | b$$

Generate the grammar for following R.E.

1. $(0 + 1)^*$

$$P = \begin{Bmatrix} S_1 \to 0S_1 | 1S_1 | \epsilon \\ S_1 \to 0S_1 | 1S_1 | \epsilon \end{Bmatrix}$$

2. $(01)^*$

$$P = \{S \to 01S | \epsilon\}$$

3. $(1 + (01)^*)^*$

$$P = \begin{Bmatrix} S_1 \to 1S_1 | S_2 S_1 | \epsilon \\ S_2 \to 01S_2 | \epsilon \end{Bmatrix}$$

4. $(1 + (01)^*)$

$$S = \begin{Bmatrix} S \to 1 | S_1 \\ S_1 \to 01S_1 | \epsilon \end{Bmatrix}$$

5. $0(0 + 1)^* 01 (0 + 1)^* 1$

$$S_1 \to 0S_1 | 1S_1 | \epsilon$$
$$S_1 \to 0S_1 | 1S_1 | \epsilon$$

$$P = \begin{Bmatrix} S \to 0S_1 0 | S_1 \\ S_1 \to 0S_1 | 1S_1 | \epsilon \end{Bmatrix} \text{ (this is a grammar generated for the R.E.)}$$

6. Construct the CFG for the following regular expression.

$$R = \underset{S_1}{(0 + 1)} \underset{S_2}{1^*} \underset{S_2}{(1 + (01)^*)}$$

For generating S_1, $S_1 \to 0 | 1$ ... (1)

Generate S_2, $S_2 \to S_2 | \epsilon$

Generate G_3, $S_3 \to 1 | S_4$

$S_4 \to 01S_4 | \epsilon$

Use concatenation rule, we can write a set of productions.

$$P = \begin{cases} S \to S_1 \cdot S_2 \cdot S_3 \\ S_1 \to 0 \mid 1 \\ S_2 \to S_2 \mid \epsilon \\ S_3 \to 1 \mid S_4 \\ S_4 \to 01S_4 \mid \epsilon \end{cases}$$ These are production rules for generating RE as a $(0 + 1)^* 1^* (1 + (01)^*)$

Example 3.10 : Construct the grammar for L which consists of strings over $\{0, 1\}^*$ with at least one occurrence of 000.

Solution : First construct the RE which contains at least one occurrence of 000.

$$R \cdot E = \underbrace{(0 + 1)^*}_{S_1} 000 \underbrace{(0 + 1)^*}_{S_1}$$

$$S_1 \to 0S_1 \mid 1S_1 \mid \epsilon$$

Use concatenation rule for generating the grammar.

$$P = \begin{cases} S \to S_1 000 S_1 \\ S_1 \to 1S_1 \mid 0S_1 \mid \epsilon \end{cases}$$

Example 3.11 : Construct CFG to represent a language defined by the regular expressions $a^* b^*$.

Solution : $R \cdot E = \underbrace{a^*}_{S_1} \underbrace{b^*}_{S_2}$ Find the grammar for S_1 and S_2

$$S_1 \to aS_1 \mid \epsilon$$
$$S_2 \to bS_2 \mid \epsilon$$

$$P = \begin{cases} S \to S_1 \cdot S_2 \mid \epsilon \\ S_1 \to aS_1 \mid \epsilon \\ S_2 \to bS_2 \mid \epsilon \end{cases}$$

$V = \{S, S_1, S_2\}$

$T \to \{a, b, \epsilon\}$

$S \to S$

Example 3.12 : Give CFG for all strings which contain at least two 0's.

Solution : $R \cdot E = \underbrace{(0 + 1)^*}_{S_1} 0 \underbrace{(0 + 1)^*}_{S_1} 0 \underbrace{(0 + 1)^*}_{S_1}$

$$S_1 \to 0S_1 \mid 1S_1 \mid \epsilon$$

$$P = \begin{cases} S \to S_1 0 S_1 0 S_1 \\ S_1 \to 0S_1 \mid 1S_1 \mid \epsilon \end{cases}$$

Example 3.13 : Give CFG for strings in ab^*.

Solution : $R \cdot E = \dfrac{ab^*}{S_1}$ Generate the grammar for S_1

$$S_1 \to bS_1 | \epsilon$$

Take concatenation of aS_1.

$$P = \begin{cases} S \to aS_1 \\ S_1 \to bS_1 | \epsilon \end{cases}$$

Example 3.14 : Give the CFG for strings in $a^* b^*$.

Solution : $R \cdot E = \dfrac{a^*}{S_1} \dfrac{b^*}{S_2}$

$$S_1 = aS_1 | \epsilon$$
$$S_2 \to bS_2 | \epsilon$$

$$P = \begin{cases} S = S_1 S_2 \\ S_1 = aS_1 | \epsilon \\ S_2 = bS_2 | \epsilon \end{cases}$$

Example 3.15 : Write the CFG which generates the language L defined by the regular expression $(a + b)^* aba(a + b)^*$.

Solution : $R \cdot E = \dfrac{(a + b)^*}{S_1} bbb \dfrac{(a + b)^*}{S_1}$

$$S_1 \to aS_1 | bS_1 | \epsilon$$

$$P = \begin{cases} S \to S_1 bbb S_1 \\ S_1 \to aS_1 | bS_1 | \epsilon \end{cases}$$

Example 3.16 : Write CFG for the language, $\Sigma = \{a, b\}$. Number of a's is multiple of 3.

Solution :

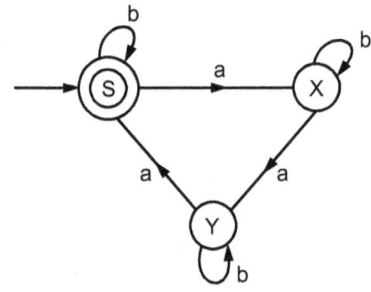

Fig. 3.10

$$P = \begin{cases} S = bS | aX | \epsilon \\ X \to bX | aY \\ Y \to aS | aY \end{cases}$$

FORMAL LANGUAGE & AUTOMATA THEORY (TE COMP. SEM-V NMU)   GRAMMARS

3.4 REGULAR GRAMMAR AND FINITE AUTOMATA

Finite automata accepts a language and that language can also be described by using a set of productions, which is known as regular grammar.

Production Rules :

where,
- A → a
- A → Aa
- A → aA
- A → ∈
- A = Non-terminal symbol
- a = Terminal symbol

There are two forms of regular grammar :
1. Right linear form.
2. Left linear form.

First we see the right linear form.

(1) Right Linear Form : In right linear grammar, production rules are in the given form.

- A → a
- A → aA
- A → ∈

(2) Left Linear Form : A left linear regular grammar will have production rules as given below.

- A → a
- A → Ba
- A → ∈

3.4.1 Convert DFA to Right Linear Regular Grammar (RLG)

1. (B) —a→ (C)

   Production rule for above DFA : B → aC

2. (B) —a→ ((C))

   Production rule for above DFA : B → aC, B → a

3. → ((B))

   Production rule for above DFA : B → ∈.

Example 3.17 : Give the right linear grammar for following DFA.

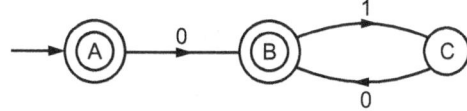

Fig. 3.11

Solution : Step - 1 : The set of production rules are as given below.

P = A → ε   Start state is final state
    A → 0B | 0   Transition from A to B on input 0
    B → 1C   Transition from B to C on input 1
    C → 0B | 0   Transition from C to B on input 0

where,   V = {A, B, C}
         T = {0, 1}
         S = A

Step - 2 :

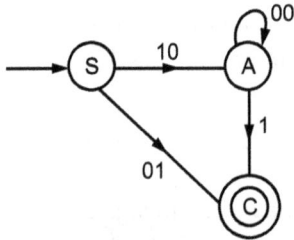

Fig. 3.12

P = S → 10A
    S → 01C | 01
    A → 00A | 1C | 1
    C → ε

where,   V = {S, A, C}
         T = {0, 1}
         S = start symbol

3.4.2 Right Linear Grammar (RLG) to DFA

Every right linear grammar can be represented using a DFA.
A production of the form A → aB.

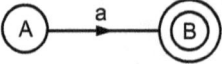

A production of the form A → aB | a

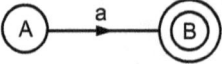

A production of the form A → ε

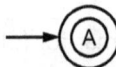

Example 3.18 : Convert the following right linear grammar to an equivalent DFA.

S → bB
B → bC | aB | b
C → a

Solution :

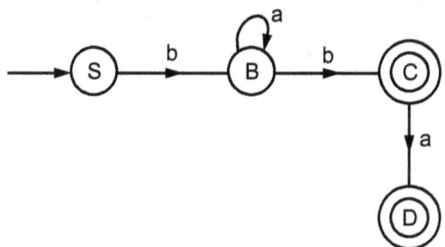

Fig. 3.13

Add another state as φ state to handle dead transition.

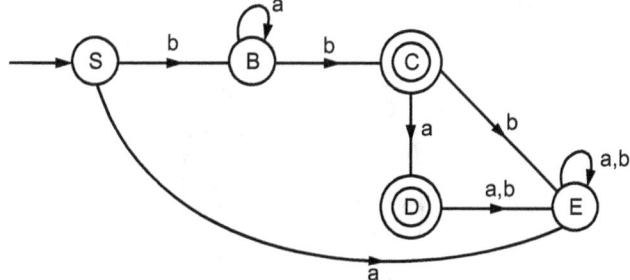

Fig. 3.14

Example 3.19 : Convert following RG to deterministic finite automata.

S → 0A | 1B
A → 0C | 1A | 0
B → 1B | 1A | 1
C → 0 | 0A

Solution :

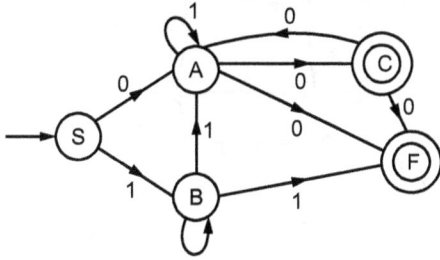

Fig. 3.15

But it is NFA, so convert NFA to DFA, we are getting following DFA.

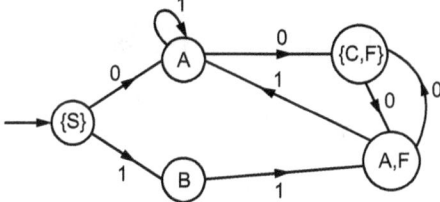

Fig. 3.15 (a)

3.4.3 Convert DFA to Left Linear Grammar (LLG)

Steps for converting DFA to left linear grammar are as follows :
1. Interchange start and final state.
2. Reverse the directions of each transition.
3. Write the grammar from the state transition diagram in linear form.

If DFA is in following form then we see the related LLG.
1.   A → Ba
2.   A → Ba
           A → a
3.   A → ∈

Example 3.20 : Give a left linear grammar for the following DFA.

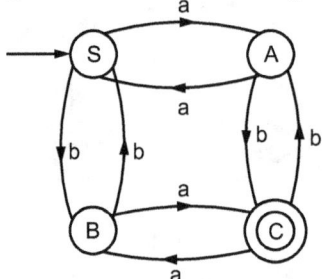

Fig. 3.16

Solution : 1. Interchange start state and final state.

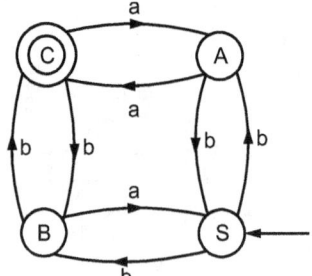

Fig. 3.16 (a)

2. Reverse the direction of all transitions.

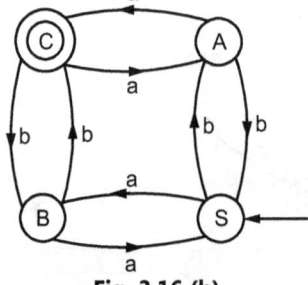

Fig. 3.16 (b)

3. Production rules : S → Ba | Ab
   A → Sb | Ca | a
   B → Sa | Cb | b
   C → Bb | Aa

Example 3.21 : Give a left linear grammar for the following DFA.

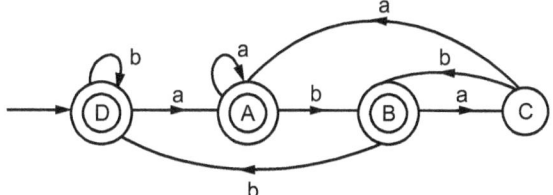

Fig. 3.17

Solution : Step - 1 : DFA contains three final states S, A and B. An equivalent DFA with a single state D by adding ∈-transitions from S to D, A to D and B to D.

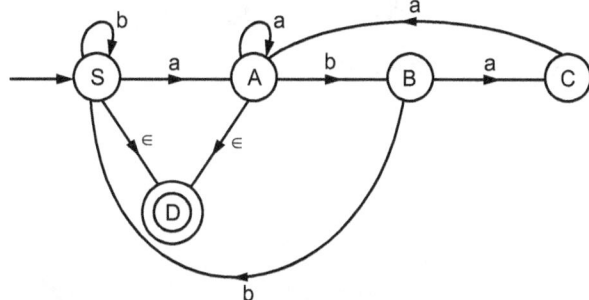

Fig. 3.17 (a)

Step - 2 : Interchanging starting and final state and reversing the direction of transitions.

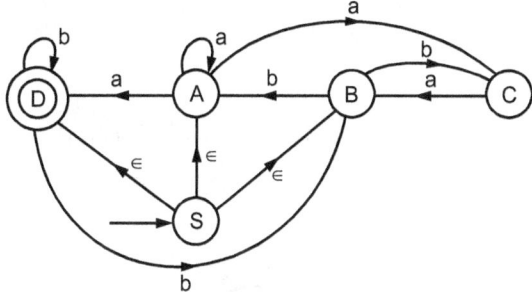

Fig. 3.17 (b)

Step - 3 : An equivalent left linear grammar is

S → D
S → A

Unit III | 3.19

S → B
C → Ba
B → Cb | Ab
A → Aa | Da | Ca | a
D → Bb | Db | b

Step - 4 : By removing unit productions, the resulting productions are :

S → Cb | Ab | Aa | Da | Ca | a | Bb | Db | b
C → Ba
B → Cb | Ab
A → Aa | Da | Ca | a
D → Ba | Db | b

3.4.4 Conversion of Left Linear Grammar (LLG) to DFA

Steps for converting left linear grammar to DFA are as follows :

1. Draw transition graph from the given LLG.
2. Interchange start and final state and reverse the direction of each transition.
3. Convert the FA to DFA.

Example 3.22: Construct DFA for the following grammar.

S → B1 | A0 | C0
A → A1 | B1 | C0 | 0
B → B1 | 1
C → A0

Solution : (1) Construct transition graph.

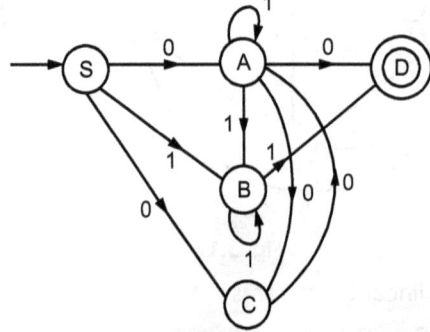

Fig. 3.18

(2) Apply second step, reverse the direction of each transition and interchange the start and final state.

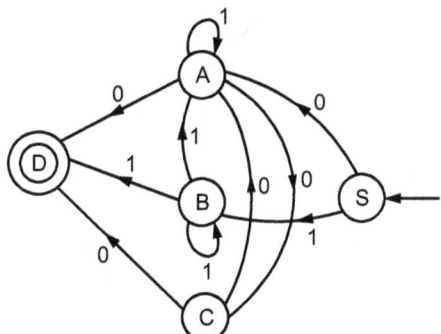

Fig. 3.18 (a)

(3) Above transition graph is not a DFA, so first convert it into DFA.

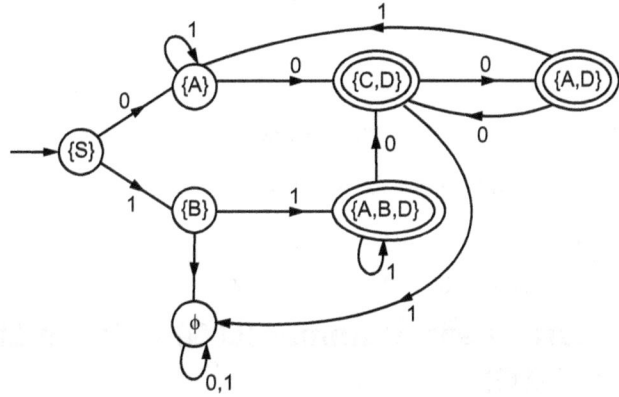

Fig. 3.18 (b)

3.4.5 Conversion of Right Linear Grammar (RLG) to Left Linear Grammar (LLG)

Conversion steps for RLG to LLG are as follows :

1. Construct transition graph from right linear grammar.
2. Interchange start and final state and reverse the direction of each transition.
3. Write left linear grammar.

Example 3.23 : For right linear grammar given below, obtain an equivalent left linear grammar.

$$S \rightarrow 10A \mid 01$$
$$A \rightarrow 00A \mid 1$$

Solution : (1) Construct transition graph from production rule.

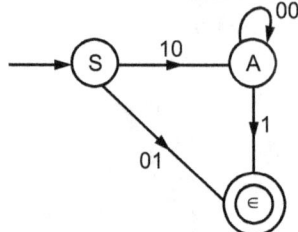

Fig. 3.19

(2) Reverse the direction of each transition and interchange the start and final state.

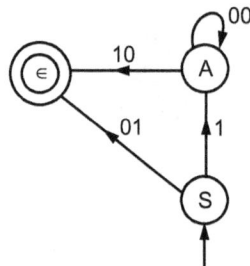

Fig. 3.19 (a)

(3) LLG from above transition graph is as follows.

$$S \rightarrow A1 \mid 01$$
$$A \rightarrow A00 \mid 10$$

3.4.6 Convert Left Linear Grammar (LLG) to Right Linear Grammar (RLG)

Conversion steps for LLG to RLG :

1. Construct transition graph from left linear grammar.
2. Interchange the start state and final state and reverse the direction of all transitions.
3. Write right linear grammar from the transition graph.

Example 3.24 : Write an equivalent right linear grammar from the given left linear grammar.

$$S \rightarrow C0 \mid A0 \mid B1$$
$$A \rightarrow A1 \mid C0 \mid B1 \mid 0$$
$$B \rightarrow B1 \mid 1$$
$$C \rightarrow A0 \mid$$

Solution : (1) Construct transition graph for the given left linear grammar.

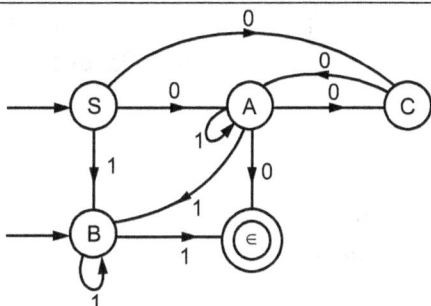

Fig. 3.20

(2) Interchange start and final state and reverse the direction of each transition.

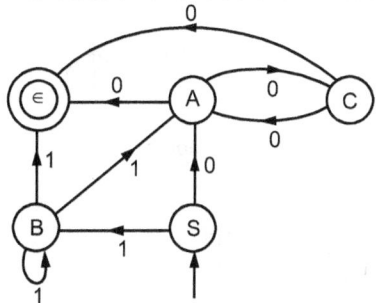

Fig. 3.20 (a)

(3) Write the right linear grammar from the above transition graph.

$$S \rightarrow 1B \mid 0A$$
$$A \rightarrow 0C \mid 1A \mid 0$$
$$B \rightarrow 1A \mid 1B \mid 1$$
$$C \rightarrow 0 \mid 0C$$

Example 3.25 : Describe the language generated by the following grammar.

$$S \rightarrow aA \mid bC \mid b$$
$$A \rightarrow aS \mid bB$$
$$B \rightarrow aC \mid bA \mid a$$
$$C \rightarrow aB \mid bS$$

Solution : Construct transition graph :

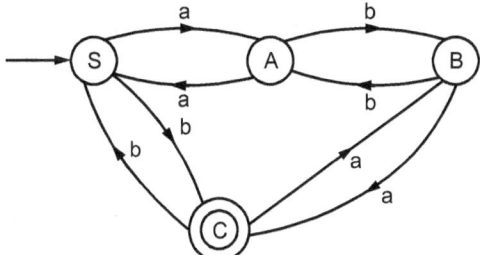

Fig. 3.21

The language accepted in the DFA is, which is containing even number of a's and odd number of b's. It is a right linear grammar. L = {w ∈ {a, b}* | w contains even number of a's and odd number of b's}.

Example 3.26 : Draw NFA accepting the language generated by grammar with productions :

$$S \rightarrow abA \,|\, bB \,|\, aba$$
$$A \rightarrow b \,|\, aB \,|\, bA$$
$$B \rightarrow aB \,|\, aA$$

Solution : (1) First draw the transition diagram for the first production rule as

$$S \rightarrow abA \,|\, bB \,|\, aba$$

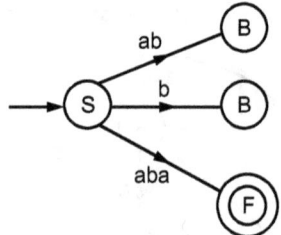

Fig. 3.22

(2) Draw the DFA for $A \rightarrow b \,|\, aB \,|\, bA$.

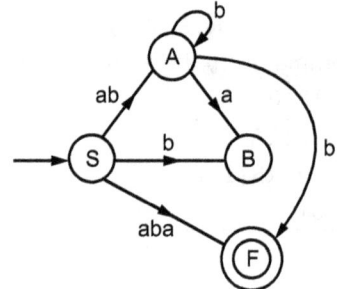

Fig. 3.22 (a)

(3) Draw the DFA for $B \rightarrow aB \,|\, bA \,|\, b$

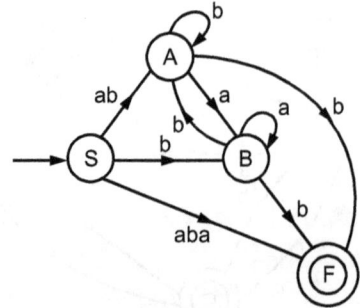

Fig. 3.22 (b)

3.5 AMBIGUOUS GRAMMAR

A grammar is said to be ambiguous if the language generated by the grammar contain some string that has two different parse tree (either leftmost or rightmost but not one leftmost and other rightmost.)

e.g. $E \rightarrow E + E \mid E * E \mid a \mid b$

For $a + b * a$

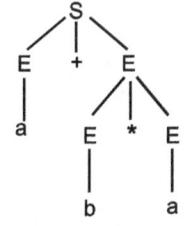 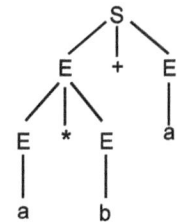

(a) Leftmost derivation   (b) Leftmost derivation

Fig. 3.23

3.5.1 Removing Ambiguity

(1) There is no general rule for that.
(2) Find out the production rules due to which ambiguity occurs.
(3) Rewrite that production rule such that ambiguity gets removed.

Example 3.27 : $E \rightarrow E + E \mid a \mid b$

Solution :

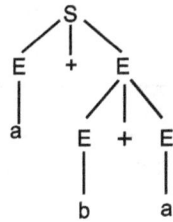 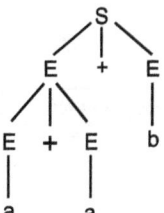

Fig. 3.24

Here for the (a + a + b), there are more than one leftmost parse trees. Hence given grammars is ambiguous.

Removing Ambiguity :

Ambiguity occurs due to E + E Hence
This rules is rewritten as

$$E + T \mid T$$

Hence final grammar is

$$E \rightarrow E + T \mid T$$
$$T \rightarrow a \mid b$$

Example 3.28 : E → E +E | E *E | (E) | I
$$I → a | b$$
(a) Show the grammar is ambiguous.
(b) Remove ambiguity.

Solution :

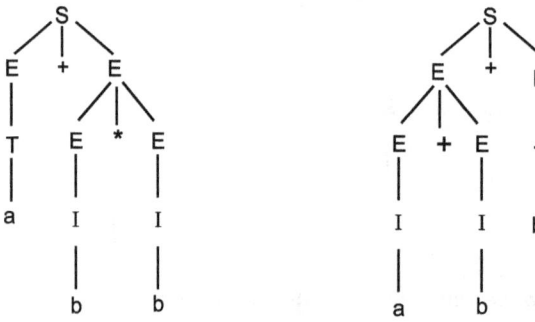

Fig. 3.25

Hence for the string (a + b * b), we get more than one leftmost parse trees.

Hence given grammar is ambiguous.

Removing Ambiguity :

Ambiguity is due to E + E and E * E produced

Hence it is rewritten as
E → E + T | T
T → T * F | F
F → (E) | a | b

3.6 SIMPLIFICATION OF CFG

For satisfying some restrictions on grammar, we are required to convert it in its equivalent form.

CFG can be simplified by using :
1. Eliminating useless symbols.
2. Eliminating ∈ production.
3. Eliminating unit production.

3.6.1 Eliminate the Useless Symbols from the Grammar

In grammar there are two types of symbols which are useless.
1. Non-generating symbol.
2. Non-reachable symbol.

(1) Non-Generating Symbol : If every variable present in grammar generates the terminal symbol then we call that variable as generating variable and other we call that variable as non-generating variable.

Example :
$$S \to AB \mid a \mid b$$
$$A \to a$$
$$B \to bB$$

The production $B \to bB$ does not generate any terminal symbol, so B is non-generating symbol.

Rules for finding the non-generating symbols :

1. Every symbol in T is generating.
2. If there is a production $A \to \alpha$ and every symbol in α is generating then A is generating where $\alpha \in (V + T)^*$.

A symbol not in set of generating symbols is said to be non-generating symbol.

Example 3.29 :
$$P = \begin{cases} S \to aAa \\ A \to Sb \mid bCC \\ C \to abb \\ E \to aC \end{cases}$$

Solution :

1. Number of terminals in P = {a, b} → Generating symbol group
2. Find out which production rule generates these symbols.
   (C → abb using this production generate a, b then add C in the step 1 group).
   $$\{C, a, b\}$$
3. Again repeat step 2.
   $$A \to bCC$$
   $$E \to a\in \quad \text{add A, E into group}$$
   {A, E, C, a, b}
4. S → aAa   Add S in group.
   {A, E, C, S, a, b}   All these symbols are generating

Example 3.30 :
$$P = \begin{cases} S \to aAa \\ A \to Sb \mid bCC \mid DaA \\ C \to abb \mid DD \\ E \to aC \\ D \to aDA \end{cases}$$

Solution :   Terminal symbols → {a, b}
$$\downarrow \quad C \to abb$$

Unit III | 3.27

{a, b, C}
↓   A → bCC, E → aC
{a, b, C, E, A}
↓   S → aAa
{a, b, C, E, A, S}

D is not present in the set. So D is the non-generating symbol.

(2) Non-Reachable Symbol :

- A symbol X is reachable if it can be reached from start symbol S.
- Finding non-reachable symbols : Non-reachable symbols can be located with the help of a dependency graph. A variable X is said to be dependent on S if there is a production

$$S \to \alpha_1 \times \alpha_2$$

The dependency graph is given below.

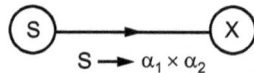

Fig. 3.26

(a) First draw dependency graph for all productions.

(b) If there is no path from start symbol to variable X then we call X is non-reachable symbol.

Examples :

1. P = {S → aS | AB, A → bA, B → AA}

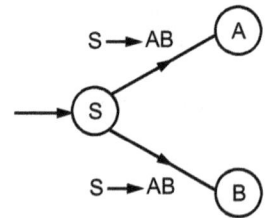

Fig. 3.27 : Dependency graph

2. P = {S → aAa, A → bBB, C → aB, B → ab}

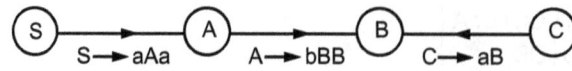

Fig. 3.27 (a) : Dependency graph

Variable C which is non-reachable from start state S, then we call C as non-reachable symbol.

3. P = {S → aBa | BC, A → aC | BCC, C → a, B → bCC, D → E, E → d}

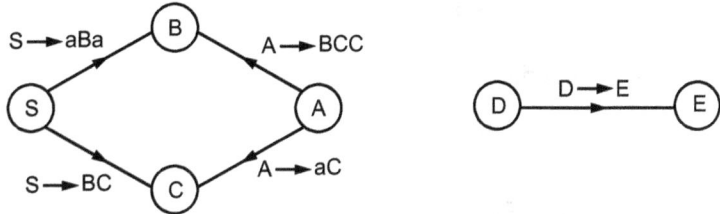

Fig. 3.27 (b)

A, D not reached from start state. A, D are non-reachable.

$$S \to B \quad\quad A \to aA \,|\, a$$
$$S \to AA \quad\quad B \to bB \,|\, b$$
$$S \to A$$

Finally, we are getting $S \to ABA \,|\, AB \,|\, BA \,|\, B \,|\, A \,|\, AA$
$$A \to aA \,|\, a$$
$$B \to bB \,|\, b$$

4. $S \to AB$
    $A \to aAA \,|\, \epsilon$
    $B \to bBB \,|\, \epsilon$

(a) $\left. \begin{array}{l} A \to \epsilon \\ B \to \epsilon \end{array} \right\}$ Null production

(b) $S \to AB \,|\, A \,|\, B$
    $A \to aAA \,|\, aA \,|\, AA \,|\, a$
    $B \to bBB \,|\, bB \,|\, b$

3.6.2 Elimination of ∈-production

A production of the form P → ∈ is called null production because P generate the ∈ symbol. How to eliminate ∈-production, we will see by one example.

$$S \to aS$$
$$S \to \epsilon$$

1. S → ∈, this is a null production.
2. So eliminate ∈ production.

$$S \to aS$$
Replace $\quad S \to \epsilon$
$$S \to aS \,|\, a$$

Eliminate, $\quad S \to \epsilon$ production

3. Final productions are $S \to aS \,|\, a$

$$S \to ABA$$

FORMAL LANGUAGE & AUTOMATA THEORY (TE COMP. SEM-V NMU)   GRAMMARS

$$A \to \epsilon \,|\, aA$$
$$B \to \epsilon \,|\, bB$$

$\left.\begin{array}{l} A \to \epsilon \\ A \to \epsilon \end{array}\right\}$ these are the nullable production.

$$S \to ABA$$
$$S \to BA$$
$$S \to AB$$

Example 3.31 : Eliminate all ϵ productions from the grammar without changing the language generated by the grammar.

Solution : Step - 1 :

Find out all nullable variables.

(a) Find out all the productions of the form

$$A \to \epsilon$$

(b) Find out all the productions whose right hand side is made up of combination of N.T. which are came in step a.

e.g. If $A \to \epsilon, B \to \epsilon$

and $C \to AB$

Then A , B and C all are nullable variables.

In our example

$$A \to \epsilon, B \to \epsilon$$

Hence A and B are nullable.

Step - 2 :

(a) Write down all the productions which contain A or B or both on RHS of the production. In our example

$$S \to ABAC$$
$$A \to aA$$
$$B \to bB$$

(b) Replace all the occurrences of A first, then all the occurrences of B, and then both A and B.

e.g.

(i) S → ABAC. Now it becomes

$$S \to BAC\,|\, ABC \,|\, AAC \,|\, AC \,|\, BC \,|\, C$$

Hence, $S \to ABAC\,|\, BAC \,|\, ABC \,|\, AA \,|\, AC \,|\, BC \,|\, C$

(ii) A → aA

Hence, $A \to aA \,|\, Aa$

(iii) B → bB

Hence, $B \to bB \,|\, b$

Step - 3 : Write down all newly formed productions as well as production which are not changed.

e.g.
$S \rightarrow ABAC \mid BAC \mid ABC \mid AAC \mid AC \mid BC \mid C$
$A \rightarrow aA \mid a$
$B \rightarrow bB \mid b$
$C \rightarrow c$

Example 3.32 :
$S \rightarrow AaA$
$A \rightarrow Sb \mid bCC \mid \epsilon$
$C \rightarrow cc \mid abb$

Solution :

(i) $A \rightarrow \epsilon$

Hence nullable variable is A.

(ii) $S \rightarrow AaA \mid aA \mid Aa \mid a$

Hence Grammar without ϵ–productions is
$S \rightarrow AaA \mid aA \mid Aa \mid a$
$A \rightarrow Sb \mid bCC$
$C \rightarrow cc \mid abb$

Example 3.33 :
$S \rightarrow aA$
$A \rightarrow b \mid \epsilon$

Solution :

(i) $A \rightarrow \epsilon$

Hence A is nullable variable.

(ii) $S \rightarrow aA \mid a$

Hence, final grammar is
$S \rightarrow aA \mid a$
$A \rightarrow b$

3.6.3 Elimination of Unit Production

$A \rightarrow B$, the production is the unit production and A and B both are variables.

How to find the unit production? The procedure of finding unit production is as follows.

The technique is based on expansion of unit production until it disappears, this technique is not applicable, when the cycle of unit production occurs.

For example : $A_1 \rightarrow A_2, A_2 \rightarrow A_3, A_2 \rightarrow A_1$

Example 3.34 : Remove unit production from the following grammar.
$P \Rightarrow S \rightarrow ASB \mid \epsilon$
$A \rightarrow aAS \mid a$
$B \rightarrow SbS \mid A \mid bb$

Solution : In given grammar,

$$B \to A \text{ is a unit production}$$

$B \to A$ this unit production is removed by expanding A.

So $A \to aAS \mid a$ is also generated by B. We are getting final production after elimination of unit production as follows.

$$S \to ASB \mid \epsilon$$
$$A \to aAS \mid a$$
$$B \to SbS \mid bb \mid aAS \mid a$$

Example 3.35 : Eliminate unit productions from

$$P = \begin{cases} S \to ABA \mid BA \mid AA \mid AB \\ A \to aA \mid a \\ B \to bB \mid b \\ S \to A \mid B \end{cases}$$

Solution : In above grammar

$$S \to A$$
$$S \to B, \text{ these two are unit productions.}$$

So expand A and B for removing unit productions from the grammar.

$$S \to ABA \mid BA \mid AA \mid AB \mid aA \mid a \mid bB \mid b$$
$$A \to aA \mid a$$
$$B \to bB \mid b$$

Example 3.36 :
$$S \to AB$$
$$A \to a$$
$$B \to C \mid b$$
$$C \to D$$
$$D \to E$$
$$E \to a$$

Solution : (i) Find out all the production of type

$$\text{N.T} \to \text{N.T}$$

In above example,
$$B \to C$$
$$C \to D$$
$$D \to E$$

(ii) Find out any production for which

N.T.→ T and do the replacement as follows.

In above example, $\qquad E \to a$

∴ $\qquad\qquad\qquad D \to a \qquad [\because D \to a \text{ and } E \to a]$

FORMAL LANGUAGE & AUTOMATA THEORY (TE COMP. SEM-V NMU)　　　　　GRAMMARS

$$C \to a \quad [\because D \to a \text{ and } C \to D]$$
$$B \to a \quad [\because C \to a \text{ and } B \to C]$$

Hence all the unit productions of above example get replaced by newly formed productions as

$$C \to D \text{ is } C \to a$$
$$B \to C \text{ is } B \to a$$
$$D \to E \text{ is } D \to a$$

Therefore after eliminating unit productions grammar is

$$S \to AB$$
$$A \to a$$
$$B \to a \mid b$$
$$C \to a$$
$$D \to a$$
$$E \to a$$

Example 3.37 : Eliminate unit productions

$$S \to ABA \mid BA \mid AA \mid AB \mid A \mid B$$
$$A \to aA \mid a$$
$$B \to bB \mid b$$

Solution: In this example, unit productions are

$$S \to A$$
$$S \to B$$
$$S \to A \quad \text{is replaced as } S \to aA \mid a \mid bB \mid b$$

Hence after removing unit productions a grammar is

$$S \to ABA \mid BA \mid AA \mid AB \mid aA \mid a \mid bB \mid b$$
$$A \to aA \mid a$$
$$B \to bB \mid b$$

Example 3.38 : Simplify the following grammar

$$S \to aC \mid SB$$
$$A \to bSCa$$
$$B \to aSB \mid bBC$$
$$C \to aBC \mid ad$$

Solution : (1) Find useless symbol from the given grammar.

(a) Find non-generating symbols from the grammar

$$\boxed{a, d} \longrightarrow \boxed{a, c, d} \longrightarrow \boxed{a, c, d, S} \longrightarrow \boxed{a, c, A, d, S}$$
$$\quad\quad C \to ad \quad\quad\quad S \to aC \quad\quad\quad A \to bSCa$$

Non-generating symbol is {B}.

Unit III | 3.33

Thus, production after elimination of non-generating symbol.

$$P = \begin{cases} S \to aC \\ A \to bSCa \\ C \to ad \end{cases}$$

(b) Find non-reachable symbols from the grammar :

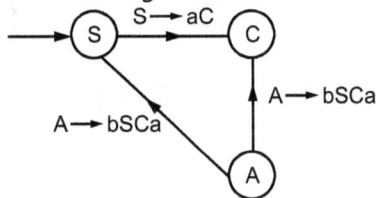

Fig. 3.28

A is non-reachable symbol, eliminate productions rule related to A.

$$P = \begin{cases} S \to aC \\ C \to ad \end{cases}$$

(2) ϵ production is not present in the grammar.

(3) Unit production is not present in the grammar.

Simplified grammar P = S → aC

C → ad

Example 3.39 : Simplify the following grammar :

S → ASB | ϵ

A → aAS | a

B → SbS | A | bb

Solution : 1. Find useless symbols from the grammar :

(a) Find non-generating symbols, (b)

| a, b | → | A, B | → | A, S, B |

A→0, B→bb S→ASB

All are generating symbols.

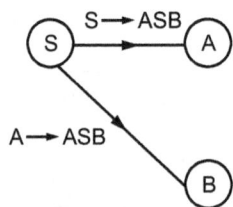

Fig. 3.29

All are reachable symbols.

2. Find ϵ production and eliminate ϵ production :

S → ϵ is a null production

S → ASB | AB

A → aAS | aA | a

B → Sb | SbS | bS | b | A | bb

3. Find unit production from the grammar and eliminate it.

  B → A is a unit production.

Expand variable A and assign production of A to B.

$$P = \begin{cases} S \to ASB \mid AB \\ A \to aAS \mid aA \mid a \\ B \to Sb \mid bS \mid SbS \mid b \mid aAS \mid aA \mid a \mid bb \end{cases}$$

This is simplified CFG.

3.7 NORMAL FORMS OF CFG

Normalization means representing the available information in the specified form without changing the contents.

Normalizing grammar means representing each production rule in the specified form without changing the language represented by the grammar.

There are two normalized forms.

3.7.1 Chomsky Normal Form (CNF)

A CFG without ∈-production is said to be in CNF if every production rule should be of the form

  N.T → T   or
  N.T → (N.T.) (N.T.)

e.g.
  S → AB
  S → a

where S, A, B ∈ V and a ∈ T

3.7.2 Griebach Normal Form (GNF)

A CFG is said to be GNF, if every production is in the form

  N.T → T . (NT.)*

i.e. S → aα

where a ∈ T and α is string of zero or more N.T

Example 3.40 : Check whether following grammar is in CNF or not.

  S → aAb| bAa
  A → aBA | bB | a
  B → b

Solution : Step - 1 : Simplification of grammar

i.e. (1) Removing ∈ production

  (2) Removing unit production

  (3) Removing useless symbol.

  Step : Convert it into the CNF.

Step - 2 :
 (1) No ∈ production
 (2) No unit production
 (3) No useless symbol.
Hence given grammar is simplified grammar.

Step - 3 : Find out production which are already in CNF.
 A → a and B → b

For converting other productions into CNF, see the following method.

(1) S → aAb | bAa

By adding new productions as:
 T_1 → a and T_2 → b
 S → $T_1 AT_2$ | $T_2 AT_1$

By adding new productions as:
 T_3 → $T_1 A$ and T_4 → $T_2 A$
 S → $T_3 T_2$ | $T_4 T_1$

(2) A → aBA | bB | a
 A → $T_1 BA$ | $T_2 B$ | a

By adding new productions as :
 T_5 → $T_1 B$
 A → $T_5 A$ | $T_2 B$ | a

Hence final grammar in CNF is
 S → $T_3 T_2$ | $T_4 T_1$
 A → $T_5 A$ | $T_2 B$ | a
 B → b
 T_1 → a
 T_2 → b
 T_3 → $T_1 A$
 T_4 → $T_2 A$
 T_5 → $T_1 B$

Example 3.41 :
 S → PQP
 P → 0P | ∈
 Q → 1Q | ∈

Solution : Step - 1 :
 (a) Removing ∈ -productions

Find out nullable variables.

i.e. $P \to \epsilon$
$Q \to \epsilon$
and $S \to PQP$
Hence $S \to \epsilon$

So, nullable variables are S, P, Q.

Hence, grammar after eliminating ϵ–production is

$S \to PQP \mid QP \mid PP \mid PQ \mid P \mid Q$
$P \to 0P \mid 0$
$Q \to 1Q \mid 1$

(b) Removal of unit production

Here $S \to \epsilon$ and $S \to Q$ are unit production.

Hence to remove it replace P by its production, and Q by its production.

Hence, grammar becomes

$S \to PQP \mid QP \mid PP \mid PQ \mid OP \mid 0 \mid 1Q \mid 1$
$P \to 0P \mid 0$
$Q \to 1Q \mid 1$

(c) Finding out useless symbol.

$P \to 0$, $Q \to 0$ and $S \to PQ$

Hence no non–generating symbol.

Hence no non–reachable symbols.

Hence no useless symbol.

Hence, simplified grammar is

$S \to PQP \mid QP \mid PP \mid PQ \mid OP \mid 0 \mid 1Q \mid 1$
$P \to 0P \mid 0$
$Q \to 1Q \mid 1$

Step - 2 : Conversion to CNF

(i) $S \to PQP$ $S \to T_1 P$
     $T_1 \to PQ$
     $S \to QP \mid PP \mid PQ$ are already in CNF
     $S \to 0P$
     $S \to 0 \mid 1$ are already in CNF
$S \to 1Q$ $S \to T_3 Q$
     $T_3 \to 1$

Hence 1st production becomes

$S \to T_1 P \mid QP \mid PP \mid PQ \mid T_2 P \mid 0 \mid T_3 Q \mid 1$

$T_1 \to PQ$

$T_2 \to 0$

$T_2 \to 1$

(ii) $P \to 0P$ $P \to T_2P$ $[\because T_2 \to 0]$

(iii) $Q \to 1Q$

$Q \to T_3Q$ $[\because T_3 \to 1]$

Hence, $Q \to T_3Q \mid 1$

Hence final grammar in CNF is

$S \to T_1P \mid QP \mid PP \mid PQ \mid T_2P \mid 0 \mid T_3Q \mid 1$

$P \to T_2P \mid 0$

$Q \to T_3Q \mid 1$

$T_1 \to PQ$

$T_2 \to 0$

$T_3 \to 1$

Example 3.42 : Check whether the given grammar is in CNF

$S \to bA \mid aB$

$A \to bAA \mid aS \mid a$

$B \to aBB \mid bS \mid b$

Solution : Given grammar is not in CNF.

Conversion into CNF :

Step - 1 : Simplification of grammars

(a) Elimination of ϵ–production – Not Required

(b) Elimination of unit production – Not Required

(c) Elimination of useless symbol

- No Non–generating symbol
- No Non–reachable symbol

Hence given grammar is already simplified grammars.

Step - 2 : Conversion

(i) $S \to bA \Rightarrow S \to T_b A$ and $T_b \to b$

$S \to aB \Rightarrow S \to T_a B$ and $T_a \to a$

(ii) $A \to bAA \Rightarrow T_b AA \Rightarrow T_b T_1$ and $T_1 \to AA$

$A \to aS \Rightarrow T_a S$

$A \to a$

(iii) $B \to aBB \Rightarrow T_aBB \Rightarrow T_a T_2$ and $T_2 \to BB$

$B \to bS \Rightarrow T_bS$

$B \to b$

Hence final grammar in CNF is

$$S \to T_1A \mid T_1b$$
$$A \to T_1T_1 \mid a$$
$$B \to T_2T_4 \mid b$$
$$T_1 \to b$$
$$T_2 \to a$$
$$T_3 \to AA$$
$$T_4 \to BB$$

Example 3.43 :
$$S \to Aba \mid aab$$
$$B \to AC$$

Solution : No, $\in$–production and unit production. But B is non–reachable. Hence, after eliminating useless symbol, grammar is

$S \to Aba \mid aab$

Conversion

$S \to Aba \Rightarrow AT_b T_a \Rightarrow AT_1$ and $T_1 \to T_b T_a$

$S \to aab \Rightarrow T_a T_a T_b \Rightarrow T_1 T_2$ and $T_2 \to T_a T_b$

Hence grammar in CNF is

$$S \to AT_1 \mid T_1 T_4$$
$$T_3 \to T_2 T_a 1$$
$$T_4 \to T_1 T_2$$
$$T_a \to a$$
$$T_b \to b$$

Example 3.44 :

$S \to AACD$

$A \to aAb \mid \in$

$C \to aC \mid a$

$A \to aDa \mid bDb \mid \in$

Solution : Step - 1 :

(a) Removal of $\in$–productions

$A \to \in$

Hence grammar becomes

$$S \to AACD \mid ACD \mid CD$$
$$A \to aAb \mid ab$$

C → aC | a
A → aDa | bDb

(b) No unit productions
(c) C → a
    A → ab

But S and D are non generating.

Since, starting symbol is non-generating, it is invalid grammar.

Find CNF equivalent to the following grammars.

(i)   S → aAbB
     A → aA | a
     B → bB | b

(ii)   S → Aba
     A → aab
     B → Ac

(iii)   S → a | 0B
     A → AA | 0S | 0
     B → 0BB | | S | 1

Griebach Normal Form :

The production rule is of the form

$$N.T \rightarrow T \cdot (N.T.)^*$$

(1) In CNF, we never replace a terminal which is at first position and non-terminal, which is at other than first position.

(2) To get a terminal at first position, we can either replace a non-terminal with its production rule to get a terminal or to get a left recursion on it. So that, we can achieve a terminal at a first position.

(3) Write introducing new production rule for N.T., we should introduce a new production rule in GNF.

Example 3.45 : Convert the following grammar in GNF.

Solution :
$$P \rightarrow QR \mid pqR$$
$$Q \rightarrow p \mid qR$$
$$R \rightarrow QRP \mid PQR$$

Step - 1 : Simplification of grammars :

(a) Elimination of ε – production – NA

(b) Elimination of unit production – NA

(c) Elimination of useless symbol

Non-generating symbol

Old variable	New variable	Reason
φ	φ	—
—	{Q}	Q → p
{Q}	{Q}	—

Here starting symbol is useless

Example 3.46 :
$S \rightarrow AA \mid 0$
$A \rightarrow SS \mid 1$

Solution : Grammar is already in simplified format.

Hence, directly convert it into GNF.

Conversion

$S \rightarrow 0$, $A \rightarrow 1$ is already in GNF.

We have to convert the remaining productions into GNF.

(1) $S \rightarrow AA$

$\rightarrow SSA \mid 1A \mid 0$ [∵ $A \rightarrow SS \mid 1$]

Above type of production have left recession.

i.e. $S \rightarrow SSA$

For such type of production, we have to remove left recession first.

Removal of left recursion :

Rules

$A \rightarrow BA' \mid \beta$

$A' \rightarrow \alpha A' \mid \alpha$

Now,

(i) $S \rightarrow S\,SA \mid 1A \mid 0 \mid \epsilon$

     A   A α β_1 β_2 β_3

Now, using rule,

For $S \rightarrow S\,SA \mid 1A$

(a) $S \rightarrow 1A\,S' \mid 1A$ $S' \rightarrow SA' \mid SA$

For $S \rightarrow S\,SA \mid 0$

(b) $S \rightarrow 0S' \mid 0$ $S' \rightarrow SA' \mid SA$

Hence after eliminating recursion on S we get,

$S \rightarrow 1AS' \mid 1A \mid 0S' \mid 0$ GNF

$S \rightarrow SAS' \mid SA$

Replace S with its production

$S' \rightarrow 1AS'A\,S' \mid 1\,A\,S' \mid 0\,S'\,AS' \mid 0\,AS' \mid 1\,AS'\,A \mid 1AA \mid 0\,S'A \mid 0A$

Now S' is also in GNF.

(ii) A → SS

Replace S by its productions

A → 1AS'**S** | 1 A **S** | 0 S' **S** | 0 **S**

Hence final grammar in GNF is

S → 1AS' | 1 A | 0 S' | 0

A → 1AS'S | 1 A S | 0 S' S | 0 S | 0

S' → 1AS'A S' | 1 A S' | 0 S' AS' | 0 AS' | 1 AS' A | 1AA | 0 S'A | 0A

Example 3.47 :

E → E + T | T

T → T * F | F

F → (E) | a

Solution : Simplification of grammar

(a) Removal of ∈ – productions–NA

(b) Removal of unit productions

	E → T
	T → F
Now,	F → (E)	a
Hence,	T → (E)	a
Hence,	E → (E)	a	T * F
Hence grammar is	E → E + T	T * F	(E)	a
	T → T * F	(E)	a
	F → (E)	a

(c) No useless symbol.

Hence simplified GNF.	E → E + T	T * F	(E)	a
	T → T * F	(E)	a
	F → (E)	a

Conversion

F → a, T → a, F → a is in GNF

Now (i) Substitute new productions as

A → + , B → * , D → ⊃

Hence,	E → EAT	+ TBF	CED	a
	T → TBF	CED	a
	F → CED	a
Now,	E → CED	a
	T → CED	a
	F → CED	a

are already in GNF, remaining are $E \to EAT \mid TBF$

$T \to TBF$

(i) $T \to TBF \mid CED \mid a$

$A \quad A\ \alpha \quad \beta_1 \quad \beta_2$

Using rules $T \to (EDT' \mid CED \mid a\ T' \mid a$

$T' \to BF\ T' \mid BF$

$\to *F\ T' \mid * F$ $[B \to *]$

(ii) $E \to EAT \mid TBF \mid CED \mid a$

$\dfrac{E}{A} \to \dfrac{E\ AT}{A\ \alpha} \mid (EDT'BF \mid CED\ BF \mid a\ T'BF \mid a\ BF \mid CED \mid a$

$\quad\quad\quad \beta_1 \quad \beta_2 \quad \beta_3 \quad \beta_4 \quad \beta_5 \quad \beta_6$

By T get replaced by

$E' \to ATE' \mid AT$

$\to +TE' \mid +T$

Hence, final grammar in GNF is

$E \to (EDT'\ BF\ E' \mid CEDBFE' \mid aT'BFE' \mid a\ BFE' \mid$

$(EDT' \mid aE' \mid EDT'BF \mid CEDBF \mid aT'BFE' \mid$

$(ED \mid a \mid aBF$

$T \to (EDT' \mid CED \mid a\ T' \mid a$

$F \to (ED \mid a$

$E' \to +TE' \mid +T$

$T' \to * FT' \mid * F$

$A \to +$

$B \to *$

$D \to)$

Example 3.48 :

$S \to AB$

$A \to BS \mid b$

$B \to SA \mid a$

Solution : Given grammar is simplified grammar.

Consider,

(i) $A \to BS \mid b$

$A \to SAS \mid aS \mid b$ $[\because B \to SA \mid a]$

(ii) $S \to AB$

$S \to SASB \mid aSB \mid bB$

$A \quad A\ \alpha \quad \beta_1 \quad \beta_2$

Now using rules

$S \to aSBS' \mid aB\ S' \mid aSB \mid bB$ — GNF

$S' \to ASBS' \mid ASB$

(iii) Consider,

$A \to SAS \mid aS \mid b$

Replace S by its production.

$A \to aSBS'AS \mid aB\ S'\ AS \mid aSBAS \mid bBAS \mid aS \mid b$

It is in GNF.

Hence,

$S' \to aSBS'AS\ SBS' \mid aB\ S'\ AS\ SBS' \mid aSBAS\ SBS \mid$
$bBASSBS' \mid aSSBS' \mid bSBS' \mid aSBS'SB \mid$
$bBS'ASSB \mid aSBASSB \mid bBASSB \mid$
$aSSB \mid bSB$

(iv) Now,

$B \to SA \mid a$

$\to aSSBS' \mid bBS'A \mid aSBA \mid bBA \mid a$

By replacing S with its production.

Hence final grammar in GNF is

$S \to aSBS' \mid bB\ S' \mid aSB \mid bB$

$S' \to aSBS'AS\ SBS' \mid aB\ S'\ AS\ SBS' \mid aSBAS\ SBS' \mid$
$bBASSBS' \mid aSSBS' \mid bSBS' \mid aSBS'SB \mid$
$bBS'ASSB \mid aSBASSB \mid bBASSB \mid aSSB \mid bSB$

$A \to aSBS'AS \mid aB\ S'\ AS \mid aSBAS \mid bBAS \mid aS \mid b$

$B \to aSBS'A \mid bBS'A \mid aSBA \mid bBA \mid a$

3.8 CHOMSKY HIERARCHY

Chomsky classified grammar in 4 types as follows :
1. Type 0 : Unrestricted grammar.
2. Type 1 : Context sensitive grammar.
3. Type 2 : Context free grammar.
4. Type 3 : Regular grammar.

3.8.1 Type 0 or Unrestricted Grammar

In this type the productions can be written without any restriction as its name is unrestricted grammar.

Consider a production $\alpha \to \beta$

where, length (α) > length (β)

As it is an unrestricted grammar, we summarise as follows.

Every grammar is also a type 0 grammar.

3.8.2 Type 1 or Context Sensitive Grammar

The production in the form $\alpha \to \beta$, where the β is atleast as long as α. Such type of grammar is called a type 1 or context sensitive grammar.

A type 2 grammar is also a type 1 grammar.

3.8.3 Type 2 or Context Free Grammar

The production in the form $A \to \alpha$

where $A \in V$
and $\alpha \in (V \cup T)^*$
  V – Set on variable
  T – Set of terminals

Such type of grammar is called as a type 2 or context free grammar.

Type 2 generates a language, that language is called as a context free grammar.

A type 3 grammar is also a type 2 grammar.

3.8.4 Type 3 or Regular Grammar

The productions in the following form :

$A \to \epsilon$
$A \to aB$
$A \to Ba$
$A \to a$

where, $a \in \Sigma$ [$\because \Sigma$ – set of input symbols]
and $A, B \in V$ [$\because V$ – set of variables]

Type 3 generates a language, that language is called as a regular language.

3.9 PUMPING LEMMA FOR CFG

Let G be a context tree grammar, then m is a constant such that any string $W \in L(G)$ with $|W| \geq m$ can be written as w = uvxyz, conditional to

1. $|vxy| \leq m$, middle portion is less than m
2. $vy \neq \epsilon$ i.e. strings v and y will be pumped.
3. For all $i \geq 0$, $uv^i xy^i z$ is in L, that means the string of v and y can be pumped zero or more times.

Proof : Consider a grammer G

$$G = (V, T, P, S)$$

then φ (G) denotes largest number of symbols on the right-hand side of production in P.
In pumping lemma, constant m should satisfy the condition as

$$m \geq \phi(G)^{|V-T|}$$

Consider string W ∈ L (G) such that |W| ≥ n. Now construct parse tree T which generates W with smallest number of leaves.

The tree T will have a path length of at least |V − T| + 1. Here we have |V − T| + 2 nodes with the last node labeled with terminal and nonterminals.

In this way we will say that a string of the form $uv^i xy^i z$ where i ≥ 0.

Example 3.49 : Prove that L = $\{a^i b^i i^i \mid i \geq 1\}$ is not a CFL.

Solution :

(a) Consider a given language L is CFL.
(b) W = $a^m b^m c^m$ where the m is given as per pumping lemma.
(c) Now W is rewritten as uvxyz where |vxy| ≤ m and v · y ≠ ∈
(d) From pumping lemma, if uvxyz ∈ L then $uv^i xy^i z$ is in L (G) for each i = 0, 1, 2, ...

There are two cases :

Case I : vy contains all three symbols a, b, c. If vy contains all three symbols a, b and c then either v or y contains two symbols. Now broke the exacts location of a, b and c then either v or y contains two symbols. Now broke the exact location of a, b and c then either v or y contains two symbols.

Now broke the exact location of a, b and c $uv^2 xy^2 z$ and hence $uv^2 xy^2 z \notin$ L (G)

Case II : If vy does not contains three symbols a, b and c then $uv^2 xy^2 z$ will have unequal number of a's, b's and c's.

∴ $\quad uv^2 xy^2 z \notin$ L (G)

Hence proved by contradiction.

Example 3.50 : Prove that L = $\{a^i b^i c^j \mid j \geq i\}$ is not a CFL.

Solution :

(a) Consider a given language L is CFL.
(b) W = $a^m b^m c^m$ where the m is given as per pumping lemma.
(c) Now w is rewritten as uvxyz where |vxy| ≤ m and v · y ≠ ∈.
(d) From pumping lemma, if uvxyz ∈ L then $uv^i xy^i z$ is in L (G) for each i = 0, 1, 2, ...

There are two cases :

Case I : As it is from example 3.49.

Case II : If vy does not contain three symbols a, b and c then $uv^2 xy^2 z$ will have either :

(a) Unequal number of a and b
(b) Count of either a and b can be increased from the count of c.

Hence proved by contradiction.

Example 3.51 : Prove that the language
$$L = \{ww \mid w \text{ is in } (0 + 1)^*\} \text{ is not a CFL}$$

Solution :
(a) Assume $L = \{ww \mid w \text{ is in } (0 + 1)^*\}$ is a CFL.
(b) $w = 0^m 1^m 0^m 1^m$, where the m is given as per pumping lemma.
(c) w is rewritten as uvxyz, where $|vxy| \leq m$ and $vy \neq \epsilon$.
(d) From pumping lemma, if $uvxyz \in L$, them $uv^i xy^i z$ is in $L(G)$ for each $i = 0, 1, 2, \ldots$
(e) vxy must be in one of following form : 0^j, 1^j, 0^j, 1^k

Case I : vxy is of the form 0^j
Case II : vxy is of the form 1^j
Case III : vxy is of the form 0^j, ^{k} or $1^j 0^k$
Thus the string $uv^0 xy^0 z \notin L$
Hence proved by contradiction.

3.10 CLOSURE PROPERTIES OF CFL'S

A closure properties of CFL :
A context free language is closed under :
 1. Union
 2. Concatenation
 3. Kleene star
 4. Reversal

A context free language is not closed under :
 1. Intersection
 2. Complementation.

3.10.1 CFL is Closed Under Union

Statement : If L_1 and L_2 are CFL, then $L_1 \cup L_2$ is a CFL.
Proof : Let, L_1 is CFL which is generated by CFG
$$G_1 = (V_1, T_1, P_1, S_1)$$
Let, L_2 is CFL which is generated by CFG
$$G_2 = (V_2, T_2, P_2, S_2)$$
Now, $G = G_1 \cup G_2$ [∵ G final grammar generated from G_1 and G_2]
and S will be the start symbol of G.
∴ $S \rightarrow S_1$
    $S \rightarrow S_2$
∴ $G_1 = (G_1) \cup (G_2)$
    $G_1 = (V_1 \cup V_2 \cup \{S\}, \{T_1 \cup T_2\}, P_1 \cup P_2 \cup \{S \rightarrow S_1 | S_2\}, S)$
where $S \rightarrow S_1 | S_2$ generating string from S_1 or S_2 which are the start symbols of G_1 and G_2 respectively.
∴ $L(G) = L_1 \cup L_2$

3.10.2 CFL is Closed Under Concatenation

Statement : If L_1 and L_2 are CFL, then L_1L_2 is a CFL.
Proof : Let L_1 is CFL which is generated by CFG
$$G_1 = (V_1, T_1, P_1, S_1)$$
Let, L_2 is CFL which is generated by CFG
$$G_2 = (V_2, T_2, P_2, S_2)$$
Now, $\quad G = G_1 G_2$
and S will be the start symbol of G
$\therefore \quad S \to S_1 S_2$
$\therefore$ Final grammar G is as follows
$$G = (V_1 \cup V_2 \cup \{S\}, T_1 \cup T_2, P_1 \cup P_2 \cup \{S \to S_1 S_2\}, S)$$

3.10.3 CFL is Closed Under Kleene Star

Statement : If L is a CFL, then L* is a CFL
Proof : Let L_1 be a CFL with $G_1 = (V_1, T_1, P_1, S_1)$
Now we will generate $\quad L = L_1^*$
For this, we add S as a start symbol of G in L. Also we have to add new productions
$$S \to SS_1$$
$$S \to \epsilon$$
These productions generate a string w^* for L.
$\therefore$ Final G is $\quad G = (V_1, T_1, P_1 \cup \{S \to SS_1 | \epsilon\}, S)$

3.10.4 CFL is Closed Under Reversal

Statement : If L is a CFL, then L^* is a CFL.
Proof : Consider L = L(G) for CFG, G = (V, T, P, S)
$\therefore \quad G^R$ is given by $\quad G^R = (V, T, P^R, S)$
As P is a production rule, therefore reversing the right hand side of the production, we will get P^R.

3.10.5 CFL is not Closed Under Intersection

Statement : CFL's are not closed under intersection.
Proof : Consider two CFLs L_1 and L_2
$$L_1 = \{0^n 1^n 2^m | n, m \geq 0\}$$
$$L_2 = \{0^m 1^n 2^n | n, m \geq 0\}$$
(a) Productions set for L_1 as
$$S \to AB$$
$$A \to 0A1 | \epsilon$$
$$B \to 2B | \epsilon$$
(b) Productions set for L_2 as
$$S \to AB$$
$$A \to 0A | \epsilon$$
$$B \to 1B2 | \epsilon$$

Productions (a) show the equal number of a's and b's.
Productions (b) show the equal number of b's and c's.
   i.e. $w_1 \in L_1$ and $w_2 \in L_2$
∴ $w \in L_1 \cap L_2$ contains equal number of a's and b's, and b's and c's.
∴ $L_1 \cap L_2 = \{a^n b^n c^n \mid n \geq 0\}$ but this cannot be generated by CFG.

3.10.6 CFL is not Closed Under Complementation

Statement : CFL is not closed under complementation.

Proof : Consider CFL is closed under complementation.

i.e. If L_1 is context free then L_m' is also context free and if L_2 is context free then L_2' is also context free.

We can write $(L_1 \cap L_2)$ as $(L_1' \cup L_2')'$, which should be a context free.

But $(L_1 \cap L_2)$ is not fixed to be a context free, that means whatever our consideration that the CFL is closed under complementation is wrong.

Hence, by contradiction it is proved that CFL is not closed under complementation.

3.11 DECISION ALGORITHMS FOR CFL

A CFL may be represented using a CFG or PDA, these are several algorithms available to test given CFG, G = = (V, T, P, S) and string x, whether x is in L(G)

(1) Testing emptiness

Given any CFL L, there is a CFG G to generate it, we can determine using the context of elimination of useless symbols, where start symbol is useless if so, then L(G) = ∅, otherwise not.

(2) Testing membership

Given a CFL L and a string x, the membership problem is to determine whether $x \in L$?
Given a PDA P for L.

We assume that5 CFG G = (V, T, P, S) is given such that L = L(G)

QUESTIONS

1. Compare the FA and Grammar.
2. Explain the context free Grammar.
3. Define Recursive production ?
4. What are the concatenation Rules for Grammar ?
5. Discuss the conversion of DFA to RLG (Right linear Regular Grammar)
6. Explain the conversion steps of RLG to DFA.
7. Explain the conversion steps of DFA to LLG (Linear Left Grammar).
8. Define Ambiguous Grammar ? How to Remove Ambiguity ?

9. Explain the simplication of CFG.
10. Explain the Normal form of CFG.
11. Brief discuss about Chomsky Hiearchy.
12. Explain the closure properties of CFLs.
13. Explain the Decision Algorithm for CFLs.
14. Is the following CFG ambiguous?
    G = ({S,A} , {a,b} , {P, S})
    where P consists of
    $$S \to aAS|a$$
    $$A \to SbA|SS|ba$$
15. Construct the grammar G to represent
    L = {wcw^T| w∈ {a,b}*}
16. Convert the following grammar to CNF
    S → Aba, S → aab, B → Ac
17. Convert the following grammar to GNF
    (a) S → Bs, S → Aa, A → bc, B → Ac.
    (b) S → AA|0, A → SS|1
18. Show that the language
    (i) $L_1 = \{a^i b^i c^j | i, j > , 1\}$ and
    (ii) $L_2 = \{a^i b^i c^j | i, j >, 1\}$ are content free language
19. Find CFF generating each of these languages
    (i) $L_1 = \{a^i b^j c^k | i = j + k\}$
    (ii) $L_2 = \{a^i b^j c^k | j = i + k\}$
    (iii) $L_3 = \{a^i b^j c^k | i = j \text{ or } j = k\}$
20. Using pumping lemma for CFL prove that the language $L = \{a^i b^j c^k\}\ i < j < k$ is not CFL.
21. Convert the following grammar to CNF
    S → AACD
    A → aAb|∈
    C → ac|a
    A → aDa|bDb|∈.
22. In each ease, show that the grammar is ambiguous and find the equivalent unambiguous grammar.
    (a) S → SS|a|b
    (b) S → ABA, A → aAb|∈, B → bB|∈
    (c) S → asb|aasb|∈

Unit - IV

PUSH DOWN STACK MEMORY MACHIENS AND PRODUCTION SYSTEMS

4.1 INTRODUCTION

As we have seen regular expression represented by finite automata. We can construct CFG for regular expression as well as for non-regular languages like $0^n\ 1^n$ i.e. for every regular expression, we can draw the FA, whereas FA cannot be drawn for any non-regular language. In the same way to construct or design any content free language, FA is not sufficient, so we introduce push down machine/automata (PDA), as it has a stack which is used to store the input.

4.2 PUSH DOWN STACK MEMORY MACHINES

The push down machine consists of input tape, stack and finite control as shown in Fig. 4.1.

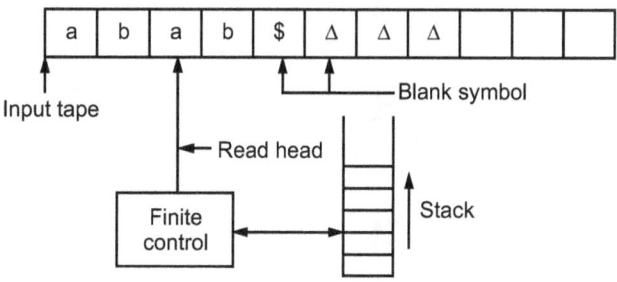

Fig. 4.1 : Push down Stack Memory Machine

Input Tape : Consists of input symbols with blank symbol at the end of input symbol of a string.

Read head : Which gives the movement of the control on input symbols.

Finite Control : Which points the current symbol which is to be read.

Blank Symbol : $, or Δ which indicates end of input.

Stack : We can push and remove (POP) the items from one end only.

4.2.1 Definition of PDM (PDA)

A PDM is a 7 - tuple

$$M = (Q, \Sigma, \Gamma, q_0, Z_0, F, \delta)$$

where,
- Q – is a finite set of states
- Σ – is a finite set of input symbols
- Γ – is a finite set of stack symbols
- q_0 – is a initial state, $q_0 \subseteq Q$
- Z_0 – is a initial stack symbol, $Z_0 \subseteq \Gamma$
- F – is a finite set of final states, $F \subseteq Q$
- δ – is a transition function as given below

$$Q \times \Sigma \times \Gamma \text{ to } Q \times \Gamma^*$$

4.2.2 Graphical Representation of PDA

Following symbols are used while representing the PDA.

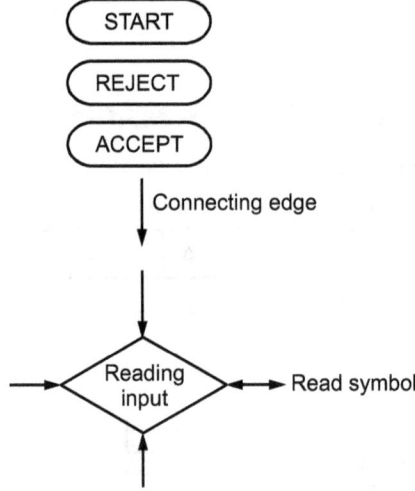

Fig. 4.2 : Symbols used in PDA

Example 4.1 :

Simulate or construct PDA for language $L = \{a^n b^n | \Sigma = \{a, b\}\}$ where $n \geq 1$. Also construct FA.

Solution :

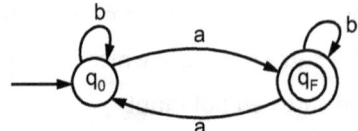

Fig. 4.3 : FA for $a^n b^n$

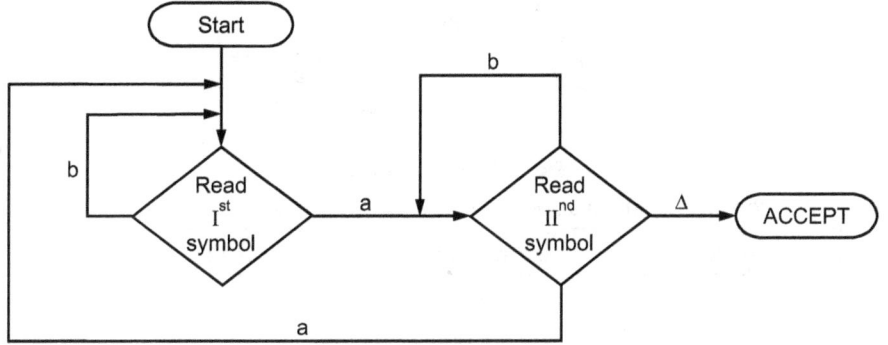

Fig. 4.4 : PDA for $a^n b^n$

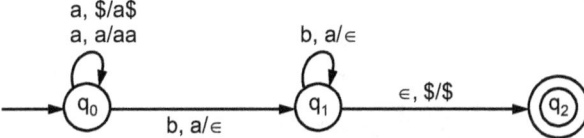

Fig. 4.5 : PDA for $a^n b^n$, $n \geq 1$

We can represent a transition graph in other way also, as follows :

$$\delta(p, x, y) \rightarrow (q_1, Z)$$

Following is a transition graph for Fig. 4.5.

$$\delta(q_0, a, \$) \rightarrow (q_0, a\$)$$
$$\delta(q_0, a, a) \rightarrow (q_0, aa)$$
$$\delta(q_0, b, a) \rightarrow (q_1, \epsilon)$$
$$\delta(q_1, b, a) \rightarrow (q_1, \epsilon)$$
$$\delta(q_1, \epsilon, \$) \rightarrow (q_2, \epsilon)$$
↑ end of string

Example 4.2 :

Design a PDA to accept the language

$$L = \{wcw^R : w \in \{a, b\}^*\}$$

Solution : Let, $M = \{Q, \Sigma, \Gamma, q_0, Z_0, F, \delta\}$

where,
$Q = \{q_0, q_1\}$
$\Sigma = \{a, b, c\}$
$\Gamma = \{a, b\}$
$F = \{q_1\}$

and δ having the following transitions

$$\delta(q_0, a, \epsilon) \rightarrow (q_0, a)$$
$$\delta(q_0, b, \epsilon) \rightarrow (q_0, b)$$
$$\delta(q_0, c, \epsilon) \rightarrow (q_1, \epsilon)$$
$$\delta(q_1, a, a) \rightarrow (q_1, \epsilon)$$
$$\delta(q_1, b, b) \rightarrow (q_1, \epsilon)$$

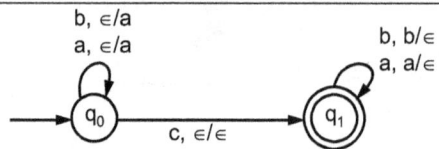

Fig. 4.6 : PDA for wcw^R

For example, consider a string abbcbba ∈ L.

State	Unread Input	Stack
q_0	abbcbba	ϵ
q_0	bbcbba	a
q_0	bcbba	ba
q_0	cbba	bba
q_1	bba	bba
q_1	ba	ba
q_1	a	a
q_1	ϵ	ϵ

Example 4.3 :

Design a PDA to accept the language

$$L = \{ww^R : w \in (a, b)^*\}$$

Solution : Let, $M = \{Q, \Sigma, \Gamma, q_0, Z_0, F, \delta\}$

where,
$Q = \{q_0, q_1\}$
$\Sigma = \{a, b\}$
$F = \{q_1\}$

δ is a transition function,

$\delta(q_0, a, \epsilon) \rightarrow (q_0, a)$
$\delta(q_0, b, \epsilon) \rightarrow (q_0, b)$
$\delta(q_0, \epsilon, \epsilon) \rightarrow (q_1, \epsilon)$
$\delta(q_1, a, a) \rightarrow (q_1, \epsilon)$
$\delta(q_1, b, b) \rightarrow (q_1, \epsilon)$

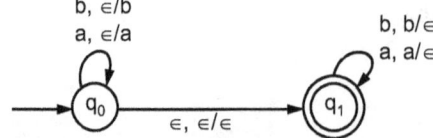

Fig. 4.7 : PDA for ww^R

For example, consider a string abbbba ∈ L.

State	Unread Input	Stack
q_0	abbbba	∈
q_0	bbbba	a
q_0	bbba	ba
q_0	bba	bba
q_1	ba	ba
q_1	a	a
q_1	∈	∈

Example 4.4 :

Design a PDA accepts the language

$L = \{w \in \{a, b\}^* : w \text{ has the same number of a's and b's}\}$

Solution : Let, $M = \{Q, \Sigma, \Gamma, q_0, Z_0, F, \delta\}$

where, $Q = \{q_0, q_1, q_2\}$

$\Sigma = \{a, b\}$

$\Gamma = \{a, b, c\}$

$F = \{q_2\}$

δ is as shown below.

$\delta(q_0, \epsilon, \epsilon) \rightarrow (q_1, c)$
$\delta(q_1, a, c) \rightarrow (q_1, ac)$
$\delta(q_1, a, a) \rightarrow (q_1, aa)$
$\delta(q_1, a, b) \rightarrow (q_1, \epsilon)$
$\delta(q_1, b, c) \rightarrow (q_1, bc)$
$\delta(q_1, b, b) \rightarrow (q_1, bb)$
$\delta(q_1, b, a) \rightarrow (q_1, \epsilon)$
$\delta(q_1, \epsilon, c) \rightarrow (q_2, \epsilon)$

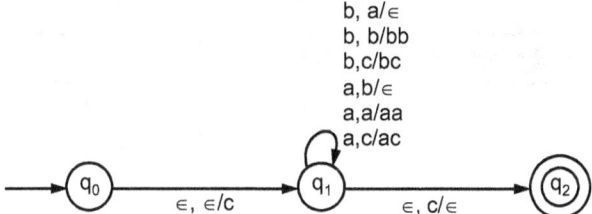

Fig. 4.8 : PDA for w which has same number of a's and b's

For example, consider a string abbbabaa

State	Unread Input	Stack
q_0	abbbabaa	ϵ
q_1	abbbabaa	c
q_1	bbbabaa	ac
q_1	bbabaa	c
q_1	babaa	bc
q_1	abaa	bbc
q_1	baa	bc
q_1	aa	bbc
q_1	a	bc
q_1	ϵ	c
q_2	ϵ	ϵ

Example 4.5 :

Consider a PDA $M = \{Q, \Sigma, \Gamma, \delta, q_0, Z_0, F\}$

where,
$$Q = \{q_0, q_1\}$$
$$F = \{q_1\}$$
$$\Sigma = \{a, b\}$$
$$\Gamma = \{a\}$$

δ is as follows :
$$\delta(q_0, a, \epsilon) \rightarrow (q_0, a)$$
$$\delta(q_0, b, \epsilon) \rightarrow (q_0, a)$$
$$\delta(q_0, a, \epsilon) \rightarrow (q_1, \epsilon)$$
$$\delta(q_1, a, a) \rightarrow (q_1, \epsilon)$$
$$\delta(q_1, b, a) \rightarrow (q_1, \epsilon)$$

Solution :

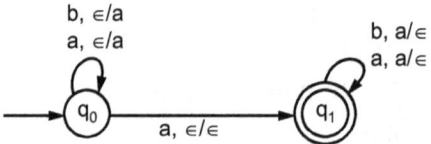

Fig. 4.9 : PDA

4.3 INSTATANEOUS DESCRIPTION

As we know that in FA, we can show the stepwise acceptance of final state, here we use same representation for acceptance, for the same, we use instantaneous description of PDA.

An instantaneous description (ID) of a PDA is a triplet (q, w, s).

Where,
q : is a current state
w : is unread input string
s : is stack contents

"⊢" symbol is used to indicate a move of PDA.

For example: $\delta(q_0, w, Z_0) = \delta(q_1, wZ_0)$

- q_0 → Current state
- w → Input string
- Z_0 → Stack top
- q_1 → Change state from q_0 to q_1
- wZ_0 → Push string on stack

Example 4.6:

Given ID for Fig. 4.5 [$a^n b^n$, $n \geq 1$]

$(q_0, aaabbb, Z_0)$ ⊢ $(q_0, aabbb, aZ_0)$
⊢ $(q_0, abbb, aaZ_0)$
⊢ $(q_0, bbb, aaaZ_0)$
⊢ (q_1, bb, aaZ_0)
⊢ (q_1, b, aZ_0)
⊢ (q_1, ϵ, Z_0)
⊢ (q_2, ϵ) Accept state

Example 4.7:

Given PDA,

$M = \{Q, \Sigma, \Gamma, \delta, q_0, F, Z_0\}$
$Q = \{q_0, q_1, q_2\}$
$\Sigma = \{a, b, c\}$
$\Gamma = \{a, b, Z_0\}$
$F = \{q_2\}$
$Z_0 =$ Stack top symbol
$q_0 =$ Initial state

δ mapping function as follows:

$\delta(q_0, a, Z_0) = \delta(q_0, aZ_0)$
$\delta(q_0, b, Z_0) = \delta(q_0, bZ_0)$
$\delta(q_0, a, a) = \delta(q_0, aa)$
$\delta(q_0, b, b) = \delta(q_0, bb)$
$\delta(q_0, b, a) = \delta(q_0, ba)$
$\delta(q_0, a, b) = \delta(q_0, ab)$
$\delta(q_0, c, Z_0) = \delta(q_1, Z_0)$
$\delta(q_0, c, a) = \delta(q_1, a)$
$\delta(q_0, c, b) = \delta(q_1, b)$
$\delta(q_1, a, a) = \delta(q_1, \epsilon)$
$\delta(q_1, b, b) = \delta(q_1, \epsilon)$
$\delta(q_1, \epsilon, Z_0) = \delta(q_2, Z_0)$

Give ID for bbacabb.

Solution : Construct PDA from given δ mapping function.

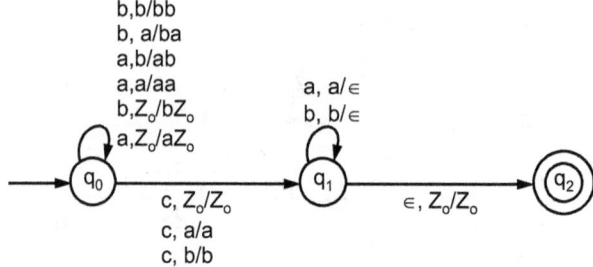

Fig. 4.10 : L = wcw^R | w ∈ (a + b)*

Now we will see ID for given string.

$(q_0, bbacabb, Z_0) \vdash (q_0, bacabb, bZ_0)$
$\vdash (q_0, acabb, bbZ_0)$
$\vdash (q_0, cabb, abbZ_0)$
$\vdash (q_1, abb, abbZ_0)$
$\vdash (q_1, bb, bbZ_0)$
$\vdash (q_1, b, bZ_0)$
$\vdash (q_1, \epsilon, Z_0)$
$\vdash (q_2, Z_0)$ Accept state

Example 4.8 :

Design a PDA for the language L = {$a^m b^m c^n$ | m, n ≥ 1}

Solution : Let,
where,
$M = \{Q, \Sigma, \Gamma, \delta, q_0, F, Z_0\}$
$Q = \{q_0, q_1, q_2\}$
$\Sigma = \{a, b, c\}$
$\Gamma = \{a, b, c, Z_0\}$
$F = \{q_2\}$

δ mapping function is as follows :

$\delta(q_0, a, Z_0) = \delta(q_0, aZ_0)$
$\delta(q_0, a, a) = \delta(q_0, aa)$
$\delta(q_0, b, a) = \delta(q_1, \epsilon)$
$\delta(q_1, b, a) = \delta(q_1, \epsilon)$
$\delta(q_1, c, Z_0) = \delta(q_1, Z_0)$
$\delta(q_1, \epsilon, Z_0) = \delta(q_2, Z_0)$

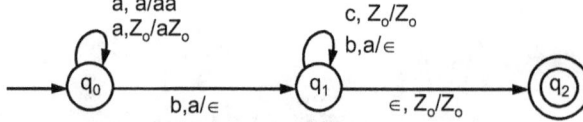

Fig. 4.11 : PDA for $a^m b^m c^n$

Now we will see ID for a given PDA. Consider a string aabbccc

∴ $\delta(q_0, aabbccc, Z_0) \vdash \delta(q_0, abbccc, aZ_0)$
$\vdash \delta(q_0, bbccc, aaZ_0)$
$\vdash \delta(q_1, bccc, aZ_0)$
$\vdash \delta(q_1, ccc, Z_0)$
$\vdash \delta(q_1, cc, Z_0)$
$\vdash \delta(q_1, c, Z_0)$
$\vdash \delta(q_1, \epsilon, Z_0)$
$\vdash \delta(q_2, Z_0)$ Accept state

Example 4.9 :

Design a PDA for the language, $L = \{a^n b^{2n} | n \geq 1\}$

Solution : Here string contains n number of a's followed by 2n number of b's.

Let, $M = \{Q, \Sigma, \delta, q_0, \Gamma, F, Z_0\}$
where, $Q = (q_0, q_1, q_2)$
$\Sigma = \{a, b\}$
$\Gamma = \{a, Z_0\}$
$F = \{q_2\}$
$Z_0 = $ Stack top symbol
$q_0 = $ Initial state

δ is as follows :

$\delta(q_0, a, Z_0) = (q_0, aaZ_0)$ ∵ For single a we are pushing 2a's
$\delta(q_0, a, a) = (q_0, aaa)$
$\delta(q_0, b, a) = (q_1, \epsilon)$ ∵ Changes q_0 to q_1 and popping corresponding a
$\delta(q_1, b, a) = (q_1, \epsilon)$

Now after reading all b's here, we can pop all corresponding a's. Finally ϵ is an input symbol.

∴ $\delta(q_1, \epsilon, Z_0) \rightarrow (q_2, \epsilon)$

Now we will see ID for a given PDA. Consider a string aabbbb

$\delta(q_0, aabbbb, Z_0) \vdash (q_0, abbbb, aaZ_0)$
$\vdash (q_0, bbbb, aaaaZ_0)$
$\vdash (q_1, bbb, aaaZ_0)$
$\vdash (q_1, bb, aaZ_0)$
$\vdash (q_1, b, aZ_0)$
$\vdash (q_1, \epsilon, Z_0)$
$\vdash (q_2, Z_0)$ or (q_2, ϵ) Accept state

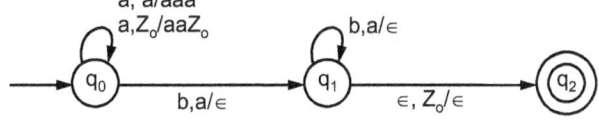

Fig. 4.12 : PDA for $a^n b^{2n} | n \geq 1$

Example 4.10 :

Construct a PDA that accepts a string of well formed parenthesis as (,), [,], { , }.

Solution : Well formed parenthesis are nothing but left parenthesis come first and then corresponding right parenthesis comes. For example, if [, (or { then],) or } is called well formed parenthesis.

Now we can construct PDA for the same.

$$\delta(q_0, (, Z_0) \to (q_1, (Z_0)$$
$$\delta(q_0, [, Z_0) \to (q_1, [Z_0)$$
$$\delta(q_0, \{, Z_0) \to (q_1, \{Z_0)$$

If there are more parenthesis on left side, then we just push it on to the stack.

$$\delta(q_1, (, () = (q_1, (()$$
$$\delta(q_1, [, [) = (q_1, [[)$$
$$\delta(q_1, \{, \{) = (q_1, \{\{)$$
$$\delta(q_1, (, [) = \{q_1, ([)$$
$$\delta(q_1, (, \{) = (q_1, (\{)$$
$$\delta(q_1, [, () = (q_1, [()$$
$$\delta(q_1, \{, () = (q_1, \{()$$
$$\delta(q_1, \{ [) = (q_1, \{[)$$
$$\delta(q_1, [, \{) = (q_1, [\{)$$

If we read closing parenthesis on right side then we start to pop the stack contents.

$$\delta(q_1,), () \to (q_1, \epsilon)$$
$$\delta(q_1,], [) \to (q_1, \epsilon)$$
$$\delta(q_1, \}, \{) \to (q_1, \epsilon)$$

After reading complete string, we will get ϵ, i.e. final state.

$$\delta(q_1, \epsilon, Z_0) \to (q_0, Z_0)$$

$\therefore$ PDA M = ($\{q_0, q_1\}$, $\{\{, (, [,],), \}\}$, $\{[, (, \{, Z_0\}$, δ, q_0, Z_0, $\{q_0\}$)

Now we will see ID for a given PDA. Consider a string (({ } [ ])

$$\delta(q_0, (\{\}[]), Z_0) \vdash (q_1, \{\}[]), (Z_0)$$
$$\vdash (q_1, \}[]), \{(Z_0)$$
$$\vdash (q_1, []), (Z_0)$$
$$\vdash (q_1,]), [(Z_0)$$
$$\vdash (q_1,), (Z_0)$$
$$\vdash (q_1, \epsilon, Z_0)$$
$$(q_0, Z_0) \quad \text{Final/Accept state}$$

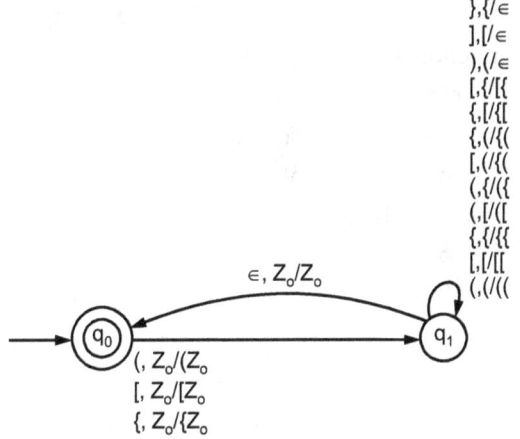

Fig. 4.13 : PDA for well formed parenthesis

4.4 ACCEPTANCE BY PDA (THE LANGUAGE OF PDA)

Following are the two approaches to accept the language of PDA.

1. **Acceptance by Empty Stack :**

   Let after reading the input string from initial state, for that PDA, the stack is empty.

   Let the PDA, $M = \{Q, \Sigma, \Gamma, \delta, q_0, F, Z_0\}$

   then the language accepted by empty stack is

   $$E(M) = \{w \mid (q_0, w, Z_0) \vdash^* (q_1, \epsilon, \epsilon)\}$$

   $\vdash^*$ shows multiple transition functions.

2. **Acceptance by Final State :**

   The PDA accept the input string, after getting final input symbol of acceptance string then it reach to the final state.

   Let the PDA, $M = \{Q, \Sigma, \Gamma, \delta, q_0, F, Z_0\}$

   then the language accepted by final state is

   $$F(M) = \{w \mid (q_0, w, Z_0) \vdash^* (q_1, \epsilon, X)\}$$

   i.e. after accepting the complete string it reach to the final state q_1.

Example 4.11 :

Design a PDA for the language, $L = \{0^n 1^m 0^n \mid m, n \geq 1\}$ by empty stack.

Solution : Here string contains n number of 0's followed by m number of 1's followed by n number of 0's.

(I) Push all 0's onto stack.

(II) Then read 1 only.

(III) Then read 0 and each reading, pop 0 from stack.

Let, $\quad M = (\{q_0, q_1\}, \{0, 1\}, \{q_0, \delta, \{q_1\}, Z_0\}$
where δ is mapping function which is as follows

$$\delta(q_0, 0, Z_0) = \delta(q_0, 0Z_0)$$
$$\delta(q_0, 0, 0) = \delta(q_0, 00)$$
$$\delta(q_1, 1, 0) = \delta(q_1, 0)$$
$$\delta(q_1, 1, 0) = \delta(q_1, 0)$$
$$\delta(q_1, 0, 0) = \delta(q_1, \epsilon)$$
$$\delta(q_1, \epsilon, Z_0) = \delta(q_2, Z_0) \quad \text{Accept state}$$

Now we will see the ID for a given PDA.

$$\delta(q_0, 0011100, Z_0) \vdash \delta(q_0, 011100, 0Z_0)$$
$$\vdash \delta(q_0, 11100, 00Z_0)$$
$$\vdash \delta(q_0, 1100, 00Z_0)$$
$$\vdash \delta(q_1, 100, 00Z_0)$$
$$\vdash \delta(q_1, 00, 00Z_0)$$
$$\vdash \delta(q_1, 0, 0Z_0)$$
$$\vdash \delta(q_1, \epsilon, Z_0)$$
$$\vdash \delta(q_2, Z_0)$$

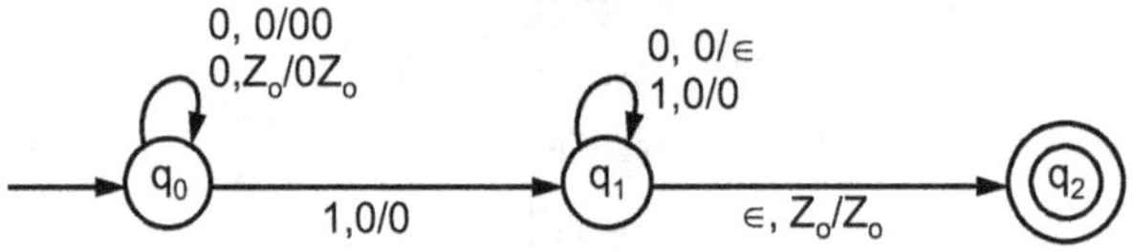

Fig. 4.14 : PDA for $0^n 1^m 0^n | m, n \geq 1$

4.5 DETERMINISTIC PUSH DOWN AUTOMATA (DPDA)

A deterministic push down automata (DPDA) is a push down automata in which one and only one transition is applicable at any time.

i.e. if $\quad \delta(p, x, y) \rightarrow (q, z)$
$\quad\quad\quad\quad \delta(p, x, y) \rightarrow (r, w)$
then $\quad$ q must be equal to r and
$\quad\quad\quad$ z must be equal to w.

Definition of DPDA :

PDAM is deterministic if it satisfies both the following conditions :
1. The set $\delta(q, a, X)$ has at most one element for any q in Q, or input symbol a in Σ or $a = \epsilon$ and $X \in \Gamma$.
2. For any $q \in Q$ and $X \in \Gamma$, if $\delta(q, \epsilon, X) \neq \phi$, then $\delta(q, a, X) = \phi$ for every $a \in \Sigma$.

Example 4.12 : Construct a DPDA to accept strings with more a's than b's.

i.e. $L = \{x \in \{a, b\}^* \mid n_a(x) > n_b(x)\}$

Solution : Here
- $n_a(x)$ – Total number of a's in input string
- $n_b(x)$ – Total number of b's in input string

Logic
- If we read a or b simply push it on stack
- If stack top is a and we read a, then push it on stack
- If stack top is b and we read b, then push it on stack
- If we read a stack top is b then pop and vice versa

Finally, we read ϵ.

$$\delta(q_0, a, Z_0) \rightarrow (q_0, aZ_0)$$
$$\delta(q_0, b, Z_0) \rightarrow (q_0, bZ_0)$$
$$\delta(q_0, a, a) \rightarrow (q_0, aa)$$
$$\delta(q_0, b, b) \rightarrow (q_0, bb)$$
$$\delta(q_0, a, b) \rightarrow (q_0, \epsilon)$$
$$\delta(q_0, b, a) \rightarrow (q_0, \epsilon)$$
$$\delta(q_0, \epsilon, a) \rightarrow (q_1, a)$$

where, $M = (\{q_0, q_1\}, \{a, b\}, \{a, b, Z_0\}, \delta, q_0, Z_0, \{q_1\})$

Now we will see ID for a given PDA, consider the input string abbabaa

$$(q_0, abbabaa, Z_0) \vdash (q_0, bbabaa, aZ_0)$$
$$\vdash (q_0, babaa, Z_0)$$
$$\vdash (q_0, abaa, bZ_0)$$
$$\vdash (q_0, baa, Z_0)$$
$$\vdash (q_0, aa, bZ_0)$$
$$\vdash (q_0, a, Z_0)$$
$$\vdash (q_0, \epsilon, aZ_0)$$
$$\vdash (q_1, a) \quad \text{Accept state}$$

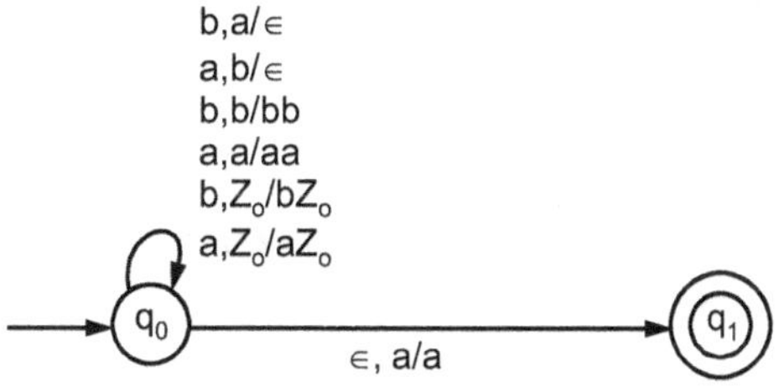

b,a/ϵ
a,b/ϵ
b,b/bb
a,a/aa
b,Z_0/bZ_0
a,Z_0/aZ_0

q_0 ϵ, a/a q_1

Fig. 4.15 : PDA for $x \in \{a, b\}^* \mid n_a(x) > n_b(x)$

Example 4.13 : Construct PDA for following language, $L = \{a^m b^n \mid n < m\}$
  (i) PDA accepting L by empty stack
  (ii) PDA accepting L by final state.

Solution : (i) By empty stack :

Push m number of a's onto the stack,
$$\delta(q_0, a, Z_0) = (q_1, aZ_0)$$
$$\delta(q_0, a, a) = (q_0, aa)$$

a should be popped for every b as input
$$\delta(q_0, b, a) = (q_1, \epsilon)$$
$$\delta(q_1, b, a) = (q_1, \epsilon)$$

As $n < m$ i.e. pop the number of a's in $(m - n)$ way.
$$\delta(q_1, \epsilon, a) = (q_1, \epsilon)$$

Finally, the symbol Z_0 should be popped out to make the stack empty.
$$\delta(q_1, \epsilon, Z_0) = (q_1, \epsilon)$$

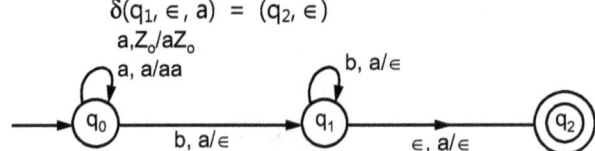

Fig. 4.16 (a) : PDA accepting by empty stack

(ii) By final state : Modify the last two equations from above transitions as follows and just add the following equation
$$\delta(q_1, \epsilon, a) = (q_2, \epsilon)$$

Fig. 4.16 (b) : PDA accepting by final state

Example 4.14 :

Design a PDA for accepting a language, $L = \{a^n b^n c^m d^m \mid n, m \geq 1\}$

Solution : Number of a's should be pushed on stack. a should be popped for every input symbol b. Number of c's should be pushed on stack, c should be popped for every input symbol d.

∴   PDA, $M = (\{q_0, q_1, q_2, q_3\} \{a, b, c, d\}, \{a, c, Z_0\}, \delta, q_0, Z_0, \phi\}$

where δ is a transition graph as follows :
$$\delta(q_0, a, Z_0) = (q_0, aZ_0)$$
$$\delta(q_0, a, a) = (q_0, aa)$$

$\delta(q_0, b, a) = (q_1, \epsilon)$
$\delta(q_1, b, a) = (q_1, \epsilon)$
$\delta(q_1, c, Z_0) = (q_2, cZ_0)$
$\delta(q_2, c, c) = (q_2, cc)$
$\delta(q_2, d, c) = (q_3, \epsilon)$
$\delta(q_3, d, c) = (q_3, \epsilon)$
$\delta(q_3, \epsilon, Z_0) = (q_3, \epsilon)$

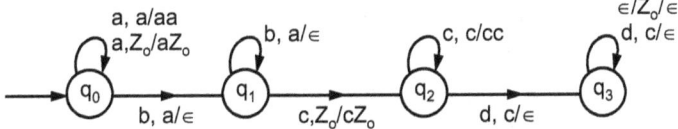

Fig. 4.17 : PDA for $a^n b^n c^m d^m | n, m \geq 1$

4.6 NON-DETERMINISTIC PDA (NPDA)

NPDA is similar like NFA as in NPDA multiple moves under a situation.

A NPDA is 7 tuples, $M = \{Q, \Sigma, \Gamma, \delta, q_0, F, Z_0\}$
where,
- Q — finite set of states
- Σ — finite set of input symbols
- Γ — stack alphabet
- δ — transition function
- $q_0 \in Q$ — initial state
- $Z_0 \in \Gamma$ — stack top symbol
- F — set of final state $F \subseteq Q$

4.6.1 Difference between DPDA and NPDA

DPDA	NPDA
1. Deterministic PDA.	1. Non-deterministic PDA.
2. Only one move in every situation.	2. Multiple moves under a situation.
3. DPDA is less powerful than NPDA.	3. NPDA is more powerful than DPDA.
4. Every context free language cannot be recognized by a DPDA.	4. Every context free language can be recognized by a NPDA.
5. A palindrome cannot be accepted by DPDA.	5. A palindrome can be accepted by NPDA.

Example 4.15 :
Design a PDA for detection of odd palindrome over {a, b}.

Solution : An odd palindrome is of two forms :
   (a) waw^R e.g. ababa, aaaaa
   (b) wbw^R e.g. abbba, aabaa

Now firstly, n characters (a or b) are pushed onto the stack.
- Match the n characters from first to last of input string.
- As n is non-deterministic, it should be having two cases.

(a) It is not the middle character
$$\delta(q_0, a, \epsilon) \rightarrow (q_0, a)$$
$$\delta(q_0, b, \epsilon) \rightarrow (q_0, b)$$

(b) It is a middle character
$$\delta(q_0, a, \epsilon) \rightarrow (q_1, \epsilon)$$
$$\delta(q_0, b, \epsilon) \rightarrow (q_1, \epsilon)$$

Now we have some more transitions
$$\delta(q_1, a, a) \rightarrow \{(q_1, \epsilon)\}$$
$$\delta(q_1, b, b) \rightarrow \{(q_1, \epsilon)\}$$
$$\delta(q_1, \epsilon, Z_0) \rightarrow \{(q_1, \epsilon)\} \quad \text{Accept by an empty stack}$$

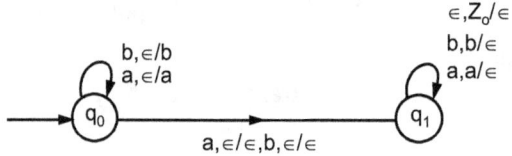

Fig. 4.18 : PDA of odd palindrome

Example 4.16 :
Design a PDA for even palindrome over {a, b}

Solution :
- Firstly, push n characters (a or b) onto stack.
- Match the n characters from first to last of input string.
- As n is non-deterministic, there are following two cases, we have to follow (whose previous character is same)

(a) It is first character of the second half, pop the current stack.
$$\delta(q_0, a, a) \rightarrow (q_1, \epsilon)$$
$$\delta(q_0, b, b) \rightarrow (q_1, \epsilon)$$

(b) It belongs to first half; push the current stack

$$\delta(q_0, a, \epsilon) \rightarrow (q_0, a)$$
$$\delta(q_0, b, \epsilon) \rightarrow (q_0, b)$$

As n is non-deterministic, whose previous character is not the same then it should be pushed on stack.

$$\delta(q_0, a, b) = (q_0, ab)$$
$$\delta(q_0, b, a) = (q_0, ba)$$

Now we will write the transitions for PDA.

$$\delta(q_0, a, Z_0) = \{(q_0, aZ_0)\}$$
$$\delta(q_0, b, Z_0) = \{(q_0, bZ_0)\}$$
$$\delta(q_0, a, a) = \{(q_0, aa), (q_1, \epsilon)\}$$
$$\delta(q_0, a, b) = \{(q_0, ab)\}$$
$$\delta(q_0, b, a) = \{(q_0, ba)\}$$
$$\delta(q_0, b, b) \rightarrow \{(q_0, bb), (q_1, \epsilon)\}$$
$$\delta(q_1, a, a) \rightarrow \{(q_1, \epsilon)\}$$
$$\delta(q_1, b, b) \rightarrow \{(q_1, \epsilon)\}$$
$$\delta(q_1, \epsilon, Z_0) \rightarrow \{(q_1, \epsilon)\}$$

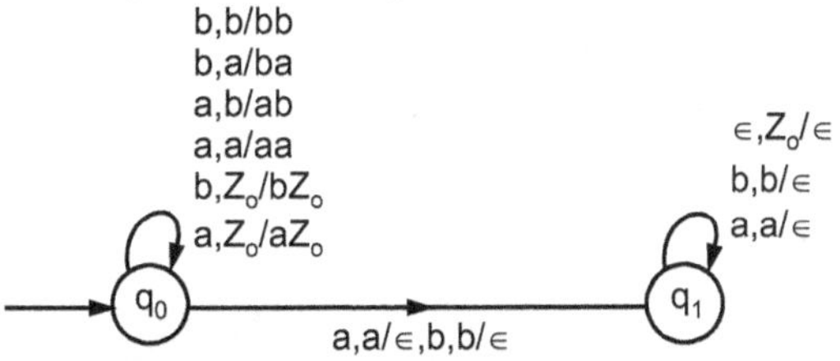

Fig. 4.19 : PDA for even palindrome

4.7 EQUIVALENCE OF PDA AND CFG

4.7.1 Construction of PDA from CFG

We can construct PDA from a given CFG G,

where, $\quad = (V, T, P, S)$

The PDA accepting L(G) is as follows

$$M = (\{q\}, T, V \cup T, \delta, q, S, \phi)$$

where δ is defined by,

(1) For each variable $A \in V$.

$$\delta(q, \epsilon, A) \rightarrow \{(q, \alpha) \mid A \rightarrow \alpha \text{ is production in G}\}$$

(2) For each terminal $a \in T$,

$$\delta(q, a, a) \rightarrow \{(q, \epsilon)\}$$

Example 4.17 :

Convert the grammar given below to PDA by empty stack.

$$S \to 0S1 \mid A$$
$$A \to 1A0 \mid S \mid \epsilon$$

Solution : (1) For each variable $A \in V$,

$$\delta(q, \epsilon, A) \to \{(q, \alpha) \mid A \to \alpha \text{ is in G}]$$
$$\delta(q, \epsilon, S) \to \{(q, 0S1), (q, A)\}$$
$$\delta(q, \epsilon, A) \to \{(q, 1A0), (q, S), (q, \epsilon)\}$$

(2) For each terminal $a \in T$,

$$\delta(q, a, a) \to (q, \epsilon)$$
$$\therefore \delta(q, 0, 0) \to \{(q, \epsilon)\}$$
$$\delta(q, 1, 1) \to \{(q, \epsilon)\}$$

Finally, PDA is as follows :

$$M = (\{q\}, \{0, 1\}, \{S, A, 0, 1\}, \delta, q, S, \phi\}$$

where δ is
$$\delta(q, \epsilon, S) = \{(q, 0S1), (q, A)\}$$
$$\delta(q, \epsilon, A) = \{(q, 1A0), (q, S), (q, \epsilon)\}$$
$$\delta(q, 0, 0) = \{(q, \epsilon)\}$$
$$\delta(q, 1, 1) = \{(q, \epsilon)\}$$

Example 4.18 :

Construct a PDA equivalent to the following CFG

$$S \to 0BB$$
$$B \to 0S \mid 1S \mid 0$$

Test if 010^4 is in the language.

Solution : (1) For each variable $A \in V$,

$$\delta(q, \epsilon, S) \to \{(q, 0BB)\} \qquad \ldots (1)$$
$$\delta(q, \epsilon, B) \to \{(q, 0S), (q, 1S), (q, 0)\} \qquad \ldots (2)$$

(2) For each terminal $a \in T$,

$$\delta(q, 0, 0) \to \{(q, \epsilon)\} \qquad \ldots (3)$$
$$\delta(q, 1, 1) \to \{(q, \epsilon)\} \qquad \ldots (4)$$

Equivalent PDA, M is given as follows

$$M = (\{q\}, \{0, 1\}, \{0, 1, S, B\}, \delta, q, S, \phi\}$$

Now check for 010^4

$$\delta(q, 010000, S) \to (q, 010000, 0BB) \qquad \text{by (1)}$$
$$\to (q, 10000, BB) \qquad \text{by (3)}$$
$$\to (q, 10000, 1SB) \qquad \text{by (2)}$$

→ (q, 0000, SB)	by (4)
→ (q, 0000, 0BBB)	by (1)
→ (q, 000, BBB)	by (3)
→ (q, 000, 0BB)	by (2)
→ (q, 00, BB)	by (3)
→ (q, 00, 0B)	by (2)
→ (q, 0, B)	by (3)
→ (q, 0, 0)	by (2)
→ (q, ∈, ∈)	by (3)

↑ accepted by empty stack

Example 4.19 :
Construct PDA for

$$S \to 0AB$$
$$A \to 1A \mid 1$$
$$B \to 0B \mid 1A \mid 0$$

Also show that whether it is a DPDA or NPDA.

Solution : (1) For each variable A ∈ V,

$$\delta(q, \epsilon, S) \to (q, 0AB)$$
$$\delta(q, \epsilon, A) \to \{(q, 1A), (q, 1)\}$$
$$\delta(q, \epsilon, B) \to \{(q, 0B), (q, 1A), (q, 0)\}$$

(2) For each terminal a ∈ T,

$$\delta(q, 0, 0) = \{(q, \epsilon)\}$$
$$\delta(q, 1, 1) = \{(q, \epsilon)\}$$

where, PDA $M = (\{q\} \{0, 1\}, \{0, 1, S, A, B\}, \delta, q, S, \phi)$

∴ Given PDA is an NPDA.

Example 4.20 :
Design a PDA for following grammar

$$S \to S + S \mid S * S \mid 4 \mid 2$$

Also show the acceptance of the following string 2 + 2 * 4.

Solution : (1) For each variable A ∈ V

$$\delta(q, \epsilon, S) \to \{(q, S + S), (q, S * S), (q, 4), (q, 2)\} \quad \ldots (1)$$

(2) For each terminal a ∈ T,

$$\delta(q, +, +) = \{(q, \epsilon)\} \quad \ldots (2)$$
$$\delta(q, *, *) = \{(q, \epsilon)\} \quad \ldots (3)$$
$$\delta(q, 2, 2) = \{(q, \epsilon)\} \quad \ldots (4)$$

$$\delta(q, 4, 4) = \{(q, \epsilon)\} \quad \ldots (5)$$

where, PDA $M = (\{q\}, \{+, *, 4, 2\}, \{+, *, 4, 2, S\}, \delta, q, S, \phi)$

Now check for $2 + 2 * 4$.

$$\begin{aligned}
\delta(q, 2 + 2 * 4, S) &\to (q, 2 + 2 * 4, S + S) & \text{by (1)} \\
&\to (q, 2 + 2 * 4, 2 + S) & \text{by (1)} \\
&\to (q, +2 * 4, +S) & \text{by (4)} \\
&\to (q, 2 * 4, S) & \text{by (2)} \\
&\to (q, 2 * 4 S * S) & \text{by (1)} \\
&\to (q, 2 * 4, 2 * S) & \text{by (1)} \\
&\to (q, *4, *S) & \text{by (4)} \\
&\to (q, 4, S) & \text{by (3)} \\
&\to (q, 4, 4) & \text{by (1)} \\
&\to (q, \epsilon, \epsilon) & \text{by (5)}
\end{aligned}$$

Example 4.21 :

Construct NPDA from given grammar

$$S \to aABB \mid aAA$$
$$A \to aBB \mid a$$
$$B \to bBB \mid A$$

Solution : (1) For each variable $A \in V$,

$$\delta(q, \epsilon, S) \to \{(q, aABB), (q, aAA)\}$$
$$\delta(q, \epsilon, A) \to \{(q, aBB), (q, a)\}$$
$$\delta(q, \epsilon, B) \to \{(a, bBB), (q, A)\}$$

(2) For each terminal $a \in T$,

$$\delta(q, a, a) \to \{(q, \epsilon)\}$$
$$\delta(q, b, b) \to \{q, \epsilon)\}$$

where, PDA $M = (\{q\}, \{a, b\}, \{a, b, S, A, B\}, \delta, q, S, \phi)$

4.7.2 Construction of CFG from PDA

We can construct an equivalent CFG from a PDA. The variable of the CFG is constructed as follows $[p \times q]$,

where, $p, q \in Q$ and $X \in T$

$\therefore \quad$ PDA $M = (Q, \Sigma, \Gamma, \delta, q_0, Z, \phi)$

Steps to convert PDA to CFG (productions)

1. For start state | symbol add production as follows

$$S \to [q_0, Z, q_n] \text{ where } Z \text{ is stack, top symbol}$$

2. For each transition of the form
$$\delta(q_i, a, Z) \to (q_j, Y)$$
where, $Z, Y \in (\Gamma \cup \epsilon)$
$a \in (\Sigma \cup \epsilon)$
$\therefore \quad [q_i, Z, q] \to a[q_j\ Y\ a]$

3. For each transition of the form
$$\delta(q_i, a, Z) \to (q_j, Y_1 Y_2)$$
$\therefore$ For each $P_1, P_2 \in Q$ productions are
$$[q_i, Z, P_1] \to a[q_j, Y_1, P_2][P_2, Y_2, P_1]$$

Example 4.22 : Give a CFG generating the language accepted by the following PDA
$$M = (\{q_0, q_1\}, \{0, 1\}, \{Z_0, x\}, \delta, q_0, Z_0, \phi)$$
where δ is as follows
$\delta(q_0, 1, Z_0) = \{(q_0, xZ_0)\}$
$\delta(q_0, 1, x) = \{(q_0, xx)\}$
$\delta(q_1, 0, x) = \{(q_1, x)\}$
$\delta(q_0, \epsilon, Z_0) = \{(q_1, \epsilon)\}$
$\delta(q_1, 1, x) = \{(q_1, \epsilon)\}$
$\delta(q_1, 0, Z_0) = \{(q_1, Z_0)\}$

Solution : (1) Add production for start state
$$S \to [q_0\ Z_0\ q_0]$$
$$S \to [q_0\ Z_0\ q_1]$$

(2) Add productions for $\delta[q_0, 1, Z_0] = \{(q_0, xZ_0)\}$
$[q_0\ Z_0\ q_0] \to 1\ [q_0\ x\ q_0]\ [q_0\ Z_0\ q_0]$
$[q_0\ Z_0\ q_0] \to 1\ [q_0\ x\ q_1]\ [q_1\ Z_0\ q_0]$
$[q_0\ Z_0\ q_1] \to 1\ [q_0\ x\ q_0]\ [q_0\ Z_0\ q_1]$
$[q_0\ Z_0\ q_1] \to 1\ [q_0\ x\ q_1]\ [q_1\ Z_0\ q_1]$

(3) Add productions for $\delta(q_0, 0, x) \to \{(q_1, x)\}$
$[q_0\ x\ q_0] \to 0\ [q_1\ x\ q_0]$
$[q_0\ x\ q_1] \to 0\ [q_1\ x\ q_1]$

(4) Add productions for $\delta(q_0, \epsilon, Z_0) = \{(q_1, \epsilon)\}$
$[q_0\ Z_0\ q_1] \to \epsilon$

(5) Add productions for $\delta(q_1, 1, x) \to \{(q_1, \epsilon)\}$
$[q_1\ x\ q_1] \to 1$

(6) Add productions for $\delta(q_1, 0, Z_0) \to \{(q_0, Z_0)\}$
$[q_1\ Z_0\ q_0] \to 0\ [q_0\ Z_0\ q_0]$
$[q_1\ Z_0\ q_1] \to 0\ [q_0\ Z_0\ q_1]$

Now for conversion to CFG, we can rename the variables as below.

$[q_0 \ Z_0 \ q_0]$ – A $\quad [q_0 \ x \ q_0]$ – E
$[q_0 \ Z_0 \ q_1]$ – B $\quad [q_0 \ x \ q_0]$ – F
$[q_1 \ Z_0 \ q_0]$ – C $\quad [q_1 \ x \ q_0]$ – G
$[q_1 \ Z_0 \ q_1]$ – D $\quad [q_1 \ x \ q_1]$ – H

$S \to A \mid B$
$A \to 1EA \mid 1FC$
$B \to 1EB \mid 1FD$
$C \to 0A$
$D \to 0B$
$E \to 1EE \mid 1FG$
$F \to 1EF \mid 1FH$
$E \to 0G$
$F \to 0H$
$A \to \epsilon$
$H \to 1$

This is a CFG for a given PDA but it consists of unit, ϵ production, and non-generating symbols.

So we remove all these from given grammar.

(1) Remove ϵ - production, nullable set = {S, A}

$S \to A \mid B$
$A \to 1EA \mid 1FC \mid 1E$
$B \to 1EB \mid 1FD$
$C \to 0A \mid 0$
$D \to 0B$
$E \to 1EE \mid 1FG \mid 0G$
$F \to 1EH \mid 1FH \mid 0H$
$H \to 0$

(2) Remove non-generating symbols.

B, D, E, G are non-generating symbols.

∴
$S \to A$
$A \to 1FC$
$C \to 0A \mid 0$
$F \to 1FH \mid 0H$
$H \to 0$

(3) Remove unit production $S \to A$. Final set of productions are

$$S \to 1FC$$
$$C \to 0A \mid 0$$
$$F \to 1FH \mid 0H$$
$$H \to 0$$

$\therefore \quad L = \{1^n 01^n 0 \ldots 1^n 0 \mid n > 1\} \cup \epsilon$

Example 4.23 :

Obtain CFG for following PDA

$(\{q_0, q_1\}, \{0, 1\}, \{0, 1, Z_0\}, \delta, q_0, Z_0, \phi)$

where δ is
$\delta(q_0, \epsilon, Z_0) = \{(q_1, \epsilon)\}$
$\delta(q_0, 0, Z_0) = \{(q_0, 0Z_0)\}$
$\delta(q_0, 0, 0) = \{(q_0, 00)\}$
$\delta(q_0, 1, 0) = \{(q_0, 10)\}$
$\delta(q_0, 1, 1) = \{(q_0, 11)\}$
$\delta(q_0, 0, 1) = \{(q_1, \epsilon)\}$
$\delta(q_1, 0, 1) = \{(q_1, \epsilon)\}$
$\delta(q_1, 0, 0) = \{(q_1, \epsilon)\}$
$\delta(q_1, \epsilon, Z_0) = \{(q_1, \epsilon)\}$

Solution : (1) Productions for start state

$$S \to [q_0 \, Z_0 \, q_0]$$
$$S \to [q_0 \, Z_0 \, q_1]$$

(2) For $\delta(q_0, \epsilon, Z_0) = (q_1, \epsilon)$

$$[q_0 \, Z_0 \, q_1] \to \epsilon$$

(3) For $\delta(q_0, 0, Z_0) = (q_0, 0Z_0)$

$$[q_0 \, Z_0 \, q_0] \to 0[q_0 \, 0 \, q_0][q_0 \, Z_0 \, q_0]$$
$$[q_0 \, Z_0 \, q_0] \to 0[q_0 \, 0 \, q_1][q_1 \, Z_0 \, q_0]$$
$$[q_0 \, Z_0 \, q_1] \to 0[q_0 \, 0 \, q_0][q_0 \, Z_0 \, q_1]$$
$$[q_0 \, Z_0 \, q_1] \to 0[q_0 \, 0 \, q_1][q_1 \, Z_0 \, q_1]$$

(4) For $\delta(q_0, 0, 0) = (q_0, 00)$

$$[q_0 \, 0 \, q_0] \to 0[q_0 \, 0 \, q_0][q_0 \, 0 \, q_0]$$
$$[q_0 \, 0 \, q_0] \to 0[q_0 \, 0 \, q_1][q_1 \, 0 \, q_0]$$
$$[q_0 \, 0 \, q_1] \to 0[q_0 \, 0 \, q_0][q_0 \, 0 \, q_1]$$
$$[q_0 \, 0 \, q_1] \to 0[q_0 \, 0 \, q_1][q_1 \, 0 \, q_1]$$

(5) For $\delta(q_0, 1, 0) = (q_0, 10)$

$$[q_0 \, 0 \, q_0] \to 1[q_0 \, 1 \, q_0][q_0 \, 0 \, q_0]$$

$[q_0\ 0\ q_0] \rightarrow 1[q_0\ 1\ q_1]\ [q_1\ 0\ q_0]$
$[q_0\ 0\ q_1] \rightarrow 1[q_0\ 1\ q_0]\ [q_0\ 0\ q_1]$
$[q_0\ 0\ q_1] \rightarrow 1[q_0\ 1\ q_1]\ [q_1\ 0\ q_1]$

(6) For $\delta(q_0, 1, 1) = (q_0, 11)$

$[q_0\ 1\ q_0] \rightarrow 1[q_0\ 1\ q_0]\ [q_0\ 1\ q_0]$
$[q_0\ 1\ q_0] \rightarrow 1[q_0\ 1\ q_1]\ [q_1\ 1\ q_0]$
$[q_0\ 1\ q_1] \rightarrow 1[q_0\ 1\ q_0]\ [q_0\ 1\ q_1]$
$[q_0\ 1\ q_1] \rightarrow 1[q_0\ 1\ q_1]\ [q_1\ 1\ q_1]$

(7) For $\delta(q_0, 0, 1) = (q_1, \epsilon)$

$[q_0\ 1\ q_1] \rightarrow 0$

(8) For $\delta(q_1, 0, 1) = (q_1, \epsilon)$

$[q_1\ 1\ q_1] \rightarrow 0$

(9) For $\delta(q_1, 0, 0) = (q_1, \epsilon)$

$[q_1\ 0\ q_1] \rightarrow 0$

(10) For $\delta(q_1, \epsilon, Z_0) = (q_1, \epsilon)$

$[q_1\ Z_0\ q_1] \rightarrow \epsilon$

Now for conversion to CFG, we can rename the variables as below.

$[q_0\ Z_0\ q_0]$ – A $[q_1\ 0\ q_0]$ – G
$[q_0\ Z_0\ q_1]$ – B $[q_1\ 0\ q_1]$ – H
$[q_1\ Z_0\ q_0]$ – C $[q_0\ 1\ q_0]$ – I
$[q_1\ Z_0\ q_1]$ – D $[q_0\ 1\ q_1]$ – J
$[q_0\ 0\ q_0]$ – E $[q_1\ 1\ q_0]$ – K
$[q_0\ 0\ q_1]$ – F $[q_1\ 1\ q_1]$ – L

S → A | B
B → ϵ
A → 0EA | 0FC
B → 0EB | 0FD
E → 0EE | 0FG
F → 0EF | 0FH
E → 1IE | 1JG
F → 1IF | 1JH
I → 1II | 1JK
J → 1IJ | 1JL
J → 0
L → 0

$$H \to 0$$
$$D \to \epsilon$$

Now remove ϵ, unit and null productions.

(1) Remove ϵ productions, Nullable set = {D, B, S}

$\therefore$
$$S \to A \mid B$$
$$A \to 0EA \mid 0FC$$
$$B \to 0EB \mid 0FD \mid 0E \mid 0F$$
$$E \to 0EE \mid 0FG \mid 1IE \mid 1JG$$
$$F \to 0EF \mid 0FH \mid 1IF \mid 1JH$$
$$H \to 0$$
$$I \to 1II \mid 1JK$$
$$J \to 1IJ \mid 1JL \mid 0$$
$$L \to 0$$

(2) Removing non-generating symbols
{A, C, D, E, G, I}

$\therefore$
$$S \to B$$
$$B \to 0F$$
$$F \to 0FH \mid 1JH$$
$$H \to 0$$
$$J \to 1JL \mid 0$$
$$L \to 0$$

(3) Remove unit productions $S \to B$

$\therefore$
$$S \to 0F$$
$$F \to 0FH \mid 1JH$$
$$H \to 0$$
$$J \to 1JL \mid 0$$
$$L \to 0$$

$\therefore$ $L = \{0^n 1^m 0^{n+m} \mid n, m \geq 1\} \cup \epsilon$.

Example 4.24 :

Obtain CFG for the following PDA

$$P = (\{q_0, q\}, \{0, 1\}, \{A, Z\}, \delta, q_0, Z, \phi)$$

where δ transitions are

$$\delta(q_0, 0, Z) = (q_0, AZ)$$
$$\delta(q_0, 0, A) = (q_0, AA)$$
$$\delta(q_0, 1, A) = (q_1, \epsilon)$$

$\delta(q_1, 1, A) = (q_1, \epsilon)$
$\delta(q_1, \epsilon, A) = (q_1, \epsilon)$
$\delta(q_1, \epsilon, Z) = (q_1, \epsilon)$

Solution : (1) For $\delta(q_0, 0, Z) = (q_0, AZ)$

$[q_0 Z q_0] \rightarrow 0[q_0 A q_0] [q_0 Z q_0]$
$[q_0 Z q_0] \rightarrow 0[q_0 A q_1] [q_1 Z q_0]$
$[q_0 Z q_1] \rightarrow 0[q_0 A q_0] [q_0 Z q_1]$
$[q_0 Z q_1] \rightarrow 0[q_0 A q_1] [q_1 Z q_1]$

(2) For $\delta(q_0, 0, A) \rightarrow (q_0, AA)$

$[q_0 A q_0] \rightarrow 0[q_0 A q_0] [q_0 A q_0]$
$[q_0 A q_0] \rightarrow 0[q_0 A q_1] [q_1 A q_0]$
$[q_0 A q_1] \rightarrow 0[q_0 A q_0] [q_0 A q_1]$
$[q_0 A q_1] \rightarrow 0[q_0 A q_1] [q_0 A q_1]$

(3) For $\delta(q_0, 1, A) = (q_1, \epsilon)$

$[q_0 A q_1] \rightarrow 1$

(4) For $\delta(q_1, 1, A) = (q_1, \epsilon)$

$[q_1 A q_1] \rightarrow 1$

(5) For $\delta(q_1, \epsilon, A) = (q_1, \epsilon)$

$[q_1 A q_1] \rightarrow \epsilon$

(6) For $\delta(q_1, \epsilon, Z) = (q_1, \epsilon)$

$[q_1 Z q_1] \rightarrow \epsilon$

Productions are in CFG.

4.9 POST MACHINE

As we have seen push down automata overcomes the limitations of the finite automata as PDA having the stack to store data or input string. But PDA is also having some limitations as PDA cannot accept context sensitive languages.

To overcome the limitations of FA and PDA, Emil post introduced concept of post machine as this machine has a capability to accept any language.

Post machine is most powerful than FA and PDA that means PM accepts regular, non-regular, context free and non-context free language.

As PM consists of FA with queue which provides memory and increases the capability of PM. As it uses a queue, so we can add the input only to the rear of the queue, and deleted from front only.

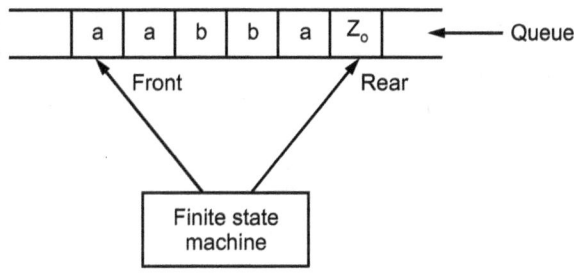

Fig. 4.20 : Post machine

Moves in Post Machine :

Move in post machine depends on :
1. State of the machine.
2. Symbol of the front of the queue.

Components of Post Machine's Move :

(a) Next state
(b) Information of the current symbol whether it is removed or not from front of queue.
(c) Details of adding new symbol to the rear of the queue with null symbol.

Definition of Post Machine :

A post machine is defined as 7 tuple.

$$M = (Q, \Sigma, \Gamma, \delta, q_0, Z_0, F)$$

where,
- Q – Set of states
- Σ – Input alphabet
- Γ – Queue symbol with $\Sigma \subseteq \Gamma$
- δ – Transition function
- q_0 – Initial state, $q_0 \subseteq Q$
- Z_0 – Rear end symbol, $Z_0 \notin \Sigma$
- F – Set of final states $F \subseteq Q$

Here transition function consists :

(a) Current state.
(b) Front symbol of the queue.

Post machines having the following four types of transitions.

1. $\delta(q_1, a) \rightarrow (q_2, b)$
        ↑   ↑
      Delete Insert

2. $\delta(q_1, a) \to (q_2, \epsilon)$

   ↑   ↑

   Delete   No insert

3. $\delta(q_1, \epsilon) \to (q_2, a)$

   ↑   ↑

   No delete   Insert

4. $\delta(q_1, \epsilon) \to (q_2, \epsilon)$

   ↑   ↑

   No delete   No insert

IMP transition (a, ϵ) means (delete a, insert ϵ).

Example 4.25 :

Draw a post machine that accepts even and odd palindrome.

Solution :

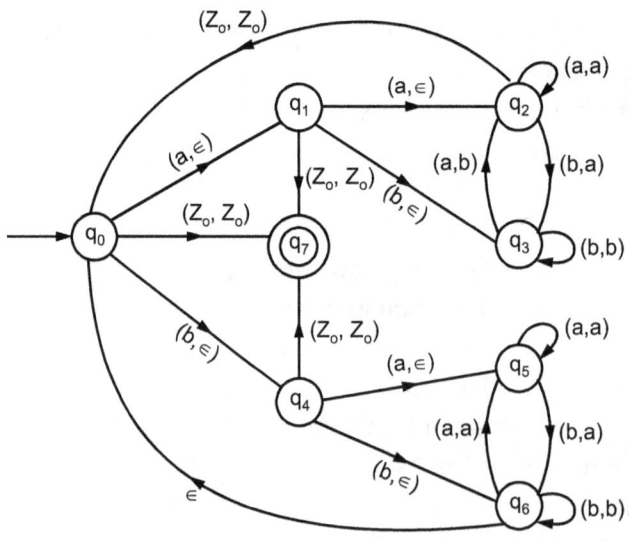

Fig. 4.21 : PM for palindrome

Post machine,   M = ({$q_0, q_1, q_2, q_3, q_4, q_5, q_6, q_7$}, {a, b}, {a, b, Z_0}, δ, q_0, Z_0, {q_7})

Logic : Considering the deletion at front and addition at rear for every input symbol, changing the states as per the requirement.

Transition Table

	a	b	Z_0	
→ q_0	(q_1, ϵ)	q_4, ϵ	q_7, Z_0	← Front symbol delete
q_1	(q_2, ϵ)	q_3, ϵ	–	
q_2	(q_2, a)	(q_3, a)	q_0, Z_0	← Insert symbol
q_3	q_2, b	q_3, b	–	
q_4	q_5, ϵ	q_6, ϵ	q_7, Z_0	
q_5	q_5, a	q_6, a	–	
q_6	q_5, a	q_6, b	q_0, Z_0	
q_7	q_7	q_7	q_7	← Final state

Example 4.26 :
Design PM for
$$L = \{a^n b^n c^n \mid n \geq 0\}$$

Solution :

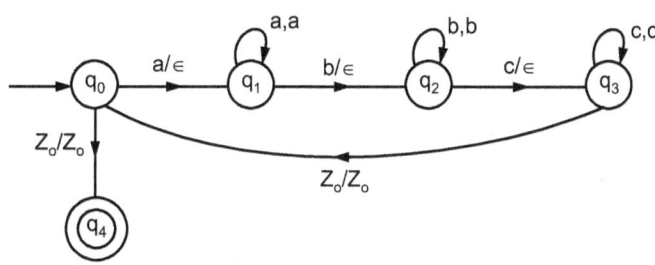

Fig. 4.22 : PM for $\{a^n b^n c^n \mid n \geq 0\}$

Post machine, $M = (\{q_0, q_1, q_2, q_3, q_4\}, \{a, b, c\}, (a, b, c, Z_0), \delta, q_0, Z_0, \{q_4\})$

Logic : Here leftmost symbol is deleted.
i.e. firstly, delete leftmost a
       delete leftmost b
       delete leftmost c

Repeat this process till the end of the string.

Transition Table

	a	b	Z_0	C
→ q_0	q_1, ϵ	–	q_4, Z_0	–
q_1	q_1, a	q_2, ϵ	–	–
q_2	–	q_2, b	–	q_3, ϵ
q_3	–	–	q_0, Z_0	q_3, C
q_3	q_4	q_4	q_4	q_4

Example 4.27 :

Design a post machine for the following language, L = $\{a^n b^n | n \geq 0\}$

Solution :

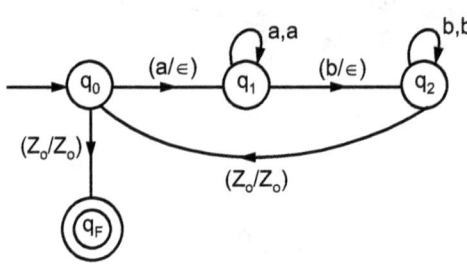

Fig. 4.23 : PM for $\{a^n b^n | n \geq 0\}$

Post machine, M = $(\{q_0, q_1, q_2, q_3\}, \{a, b\}, \{a, b, Z_0\}, \delta, q_0, Z_0, \{q_3\})$

Execution of PM for aaaabbbb

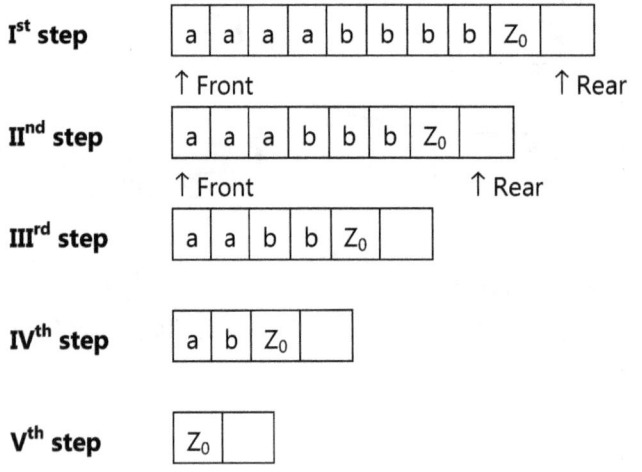

Final state

Transition Table

	a	b	Z_0
q_0	q_1, ϵ	–	q_3, Z_0
q_1	q_1, a	q_2, ϵ	–
q_2	–	q_2, b	q_0, Z_0
q_F	q_F	q_F	q_F

4.10 POWER OF PDA

- A PDA is less powerful than a post machine. A string of $a^n b^n c^n$ can be handled by a post machine but it can not be handled by a PDA.
- An NPDA is more powerful than a DPDA. A string of the form WWR can be handled by an NPDA but it cannot be handled by an NPDA but it can not be handled by a NPDA.
- DPDA is more powerful than FA. A string of the form $a^n b^n$ can be handled by a DPDA but it cannot be handled by FA.

4.11 MARKOV ALGORITHMS

A Markov algorithm is a string rewriting system that uses grammar-like rules to operate on stringsof symbols. Markov algorithms have been shown to be Turing-complete, which means that they are suitable as a general model of computationand can represent any mathematical expressionfrom its simple notation. Markov algorithms are named after the mathematician Andrey Markov, Jr.

There are three types of Markov Algorithms
1. Markov Chain Algorithm
2. Markov Theory Algorithm
3. Markov Process Algorithm

4.11.1 Markov Chain Algorithm

A Markov chain (discrete-time Markov chain or DTMC), named after Andrey Markov,is a mathematical system that undergoes transitions from one state to another on a state space. It is a random process usually characterized as memoryless: the next state depends only on the current state and not on the sequence of events that preceded it. This specific kind of "memorylessness" is called the Markov property. Markov chains have many applications as statistical models of real-world processes.

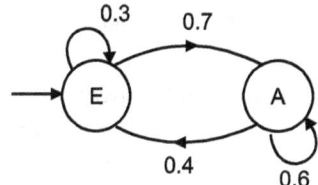

Fig. 4.24 : A simple two state markov chain

Formal Definition

A Markov chain is a sequence of random variables $X_1, X_2, X_3, \ldots$ with the Markov property, namely that, given the present state, the future and past states are independent. Formally, $Pr = (X_{n+1} = x \mid X_1 = x_1, X_2 = x_2 \ldots, X_n = x_n) = Pr(X_{n+1} = x \mid X_n = x_n)$, if both conditional probabilities are well defined, i.e. if $Pr(X_1 = x_1 = \ldots, X_n = x_n) > 0$.

The possible values of Xi form a countable setS called the state space of the chain.

Markov chains are often described by a sequence of directed graphs, where the edges of graph n are labeled by the probabilities of going from one state at time n to the other states at time n+1, $Pr(X_{n+1} = x \mid X_n = x_n)$. The same information is represented by the transition matrix from time n to time n+1. However, Markov chains are frequently assumed to be time-homogeneous (see variations below), in which case the graph and matrix are independent of n and so are not presented as sequences.

These descriptions highlight the structure of the Markov chain that is independent of the initial distribution $Pr(X_1 = x_1)$. When time-homogenous, the chain can be interpreted as a state machine assigning a probability of hopping from each vertex or state to an adjacent one. The probability $Pr(X_n = x \mid X_1 = x_1)$ of the machine's state can be analyzed as the statistical behavior of the machine with an element x_1 the state space as input, or as the behavior of the machine with the initial distribution $Pr(X_1 = y) = [x_1 = y]$ of states as input, where [P] is the Iverson bracket. The stipulation that not all sequences of states must have nonzero probability of occurring allows the graph to have multiple connected components, suppressing edges encoding a 0 transition probability, as if a has a nonzero probability of going to b but a and x lie in different connected components, then $Pr(X_{n+1} = b \mid X_n = a)$ is defined, while $Pr(X_{n+1} = b \mid X_1 = x, \ldots, X_n = a)$ is not.

4.11.2 Properties of Markov Chain Algorithm

1. Reducibility

A state j is said to be accessible from a state i (written i → j) if a system started in state i has a non-zero probability of transitioning into state j at some point. Formally, state j is accessible from state i if there exists an integer nij ≥ 0 such that

$$Pr(X_{n_{ij}} = j \mid X_0 = i) = P_{ij}^{(n_{ij})} > 0$$

This integer is allowed to be different for each pair of states, hence the subscripts in nij. Allowing n to be zero means that every state is defined to be accessible from itself.

This integer is allowed to be different for each pair of states, hence the subscripts in nij. Allowing n to be zero means that every state is defined to be accessible from itself.

A state i is said to communicate with state j (written i ↔ j) if both i → j and j → i. A set of states C is a communicating class if every pair of states in C communicates with each other, and no state in C communicates with any state not in C. It can be shown that communication in this sense is an equivalence relationand thus that communicating classes are the equivalence classes of this relation. A communicating class is closed if the probability of leaving the class is zero, namely that if iis in C but j is not, then j is not accessible from i.

A state i is said to be essential or final if for all j such that i → j it is also true that j → i. A state iisinessential if it is not essential. A Markov chain is said to be irreducible if its state space is a single communicating class; in other words, if it is possible to get to any state from any state.

2. Periodicity

A state i has period k if any return to state i must occur in multiples of k time steps. Formally, the period of a state is defined as

$$k = \gcd\{n : \Pr(X_n = i \mid X_0 = i) > 0\}$$

(where "gcd" is the greatest common divisor). Note that even though a state has period k, it may not be possible to reach the state in k steps. For example, suppose it is possible to return to the state in {6, 8, 10, 12, ...} time steps; k would be 2, even though 2 does not appear in this list.

If k = 1, then the state is said to be aperiodic: returns to state i can occur at irregular times. In other words, a state i is aperiodic if there exists n such that for all n' ≥ n,

$$\Pr(X_{n'} = i \mid X_0 = i) > 0$$

Otherwise (k > 1), the state is said to be periodic with period k. A Markov chain is aperiodic if every state is aperiodic. An irreducible markov chain only needs one aperiodic state to imply all states are aperiodic.

Every state of a bipartite graph has an even period.

3. Recurrence

A state i is said to be transient if, given that we start in state i, there is a non-zero probability that we will never return to i. Formally, let the random variable T_i be the first return time to state i (the "hitting time"):

$$T_i = \inf\{n \geq 1 : X_n = i \mid X_0 = i\}$$

The number

$$f_{ii}^{(n)} = \Pr(T_i = n)$$

is the probability that we return to state i for the first time after n steps. Therefore, state i is transient if

$$\Pr(T_i < \infty) = \sum_{n=1}^{\infty} n \cdot f_{ii}^{(n)}$$

State i is recurrent (or persistent) if it is not transient. Recurrent states are guaranteed to have a finite hitting time.

Mean Recurrence Time

Even if the hitting time is finite with probability 1, it need not have a finite expectation. The mean recurrence time at state i is the expected return time M_i:

$$M_i = E[T_i] = \sum_{n=1}^{\infty} n \cdot f_{ii}^{(n)}$$

State i is positive recurrent (or non-null persistent) if M_i is finite; otherwise, state i is null recurrent (or null persistent).

Expected Number of Visits

It can be shown that a state i is recurrent if and only if the expected number of visits to this state is infinite, i.e.,

$$\sum_{n=1}^{\infty} p_{ii}^{(n)} = \infty$$

Absorbing States

A state i is called absorbing if it is impossible to leave this state. Therefore, the state i is absorbing if and only if

$p_{ii} = 1$ and $p_{ij} = 0$ for $i \neq j$

If every state can reach an absorbing state, then the Markov chain is an absorbing Markov chain.

4. Ergodicity

A state i is said to be ergodic if it is aperiodic and positive recurrent. In other words, a state i is ergodic if it is recurrent, has a period of 1 and it has finite mean recurrence time. If all states in an irreducible Markov chain are ergodic, then the chain is said to be ergodic.

It can be shown that a finite state irreducible Markov chain is ergodic if it has an aperiodic state. A model has the ergodic property if there's a finite number N such that any state can be reached from any other state in exactly N steps. In case of a fully connected transition matrix where all transitions have a non-zero probability, this condition is fulfilled with N=1. A model with more than one state and just one out-going transition per state cannot be ergodic.

4.11.3 Steady-State Analysis and Limiting Distributions

If the Markov chain is a time-homogeneous Markov chain, so that the process is described by a single, time-independent matrix p_{ij}, then the vector π is called a stationary distribution (or invariant measure) if $\forall j \in S_{it}$ it satisfies

$$0 \leq \pi_j \leq 1$$

$$\sum_{j \in s} \pi_j = 1$$

$$\pi_j = \sum_{j \in s} \pi_i p_{ij}$$

An irreducible chain has a stationary distribution if and only if all of its states are positive recurrent. In that case, π is unique and is related to the expected return time:

$$\pi_j = \frac{C}{M_j}$$

where C is the normalizing constant. Further, if the positive recurrent chain is both irreducible and aperiodic, it is said to have a limiting distribution; for any i and j,

$$\lim_{n \to \infty} p_{ij}^{(n)} = \frac{C}{M_j}$$

Note that there is no assumption on the starting distribution; the chain converges to the stationary distribution regardless of where it begins. Such π is called the equilibrium distribution of the chain.

If a chain has more than one closed communicating class, its stationary distributions will not be unique (consider any closed communicating class C in the chain; each one will have its own unique stationary distribution π_i. Extending these distributions to the overall chain, setting all values to zero outside the communication class, yields that the set of invariant measures of the original chain is the set of all convex combinations of the π_i's). However, if a state j is aperiodic, then

$$\lim_{n \to \infty} p_{jj}^{(n)} = \frac{C}{M_j}$$

and for any other state i, let fij be the probability that the chain ever visits state j if it starts at i,

$$\lim_{n \to \infty} p_{ij}^{(n)} = C \frac{f_{xj}}{M_j}$$

If a state i is periodic with period k > 1 then the limit

$$\lim_{n \to \infty} p_{ij}^{(n)}$$

does not exist, although the limit

$$\lim_{n \to \infty} p_{ii}^{(kn+r)}$$

does exist for every integer r.

Steady-State Analysis and the Time-Inhomogeneous Markov chain

A Markov chain need not necessarily be time-homogeneous to have an equilibrium distribution. If there is a probability distribution over states π such that

$$\pi_j = \sum_{j \in s} \pi_i \Pr(X_{n+1} = j \mid X_n = i)$$

for every state j and every time n then π is an equilibrium distribution of the Markov chain. Such can occur in Markov chain Monte Carlo (MCMC) methods in situations where a number of different transition matrices are used, because each is efficient for a particular kind of mixing, but each matrix respects a shared equilibrium distribution.

A Markov Algorithm over an alphabet A is a finite ordered sequence of productions x→y, where x, y ∈ A*. Some productions may be "Halt" productions. e.g.

abc→ b

ba→ x (halt)

Execution Proceeds as Follows :
1. Let the input string be w
2. The productions are scanned in sequence, looking for a production x → y where x is a substring of w
3. The left-most x in w is replaced by y
4. If the production is a halt production, we halt
5. If no matching production is found, the process halts
6. If a replacement was made, we repeat from step 2.

Note that a production ∧→ a inserts a at the start of the string.

- What does this Markov algorithm do?

    aba → b
    ba → b
    b → a
    aabaaa
    abaa
    ba
    b
    a

Example 4.28 : The following example shows the basic operation of a Markov algorithm.

Rules
1. "A" -> "apple"
2. "B" -> "bag"
3. "S" -> "shop"
4. "T" -> "the"
5. "the shop" -> "my brother"
6. "a never used" ->."terminating rule"

Symbol String
"I bought a B of As from T S."

Execution
If the algorithm is applied to the above example, the Symbol string will change in the following manner.
1. "I bought a B of apples from T S."
2. "I bought a bag of apples from T S."
3. "I bought a bag of apples from T shop."
4. "I bought a bag of apples from the shop."

5. "I bought a bag of apples from my brother."

The algorithm will then terminate.

Example 4.29 : (Binary to Unary)

These rules give a more interesting example. They rewrite binary numbers to their unary counterparts. For example: 101 will be rewritten to a string of 5 consecutive bars.

Rules

1. "|0" -> "0||"
2. "1" -> "0|"
3. "0" -> ""

Symbol String

"101"

Execution

If the algorithm is applied to the above example, it will terminate after the following steps.

1. "0|01"
2. "00||1"
3. "00||0|"
4. "00|0|||"
5. "000|||||"
6. "00|||||"
7. "0|||||"
8. "|||||"

QUESTIONS

1. Define Push Down Machine, what are the different types of PDM ? What are the applications of PDM ?
2. Let G be the grammar given by

   S → aABB | aAA, A → aBB | a, B → bBB | A construct NPDA that accepts the language generated by this grammar.
3. Construct Push Down Automata for each of the following language.

   (i) The set of polindrames over alphabet {a, b}

   (ii) The set of all string over alphabet {a, b} with exactly twice many a's as b's.

   (iii) $\{a^i b^j c^k \mid i \neq j \text{ or } j \neq k\}$
4. Let L = $\{a^n b^n c^m d^m \mid n, m \geq 1\}$ find a PDA that accepts L.

5. Let L = {$a^i b^j c^k$ | i, j, k ≥ 0 and i + j = k}
   (a) Find a PDA that recognizes L by final state.
   (b) Find a PDA that recognizes L by empty stack.
6. Design a PDA and then corresponding CFG for : the language that accepts the simple palindrome.
   $$L = \{xcx^r \mid x \in (A, B)^*\}$$
7. Consider the PDA with the following moves :
   $$\delta(q_0, a, z_0) = \{(q_0, az_0)\}$$
   $$\delta(q_0, a, a) = \{(q_0, aa)\}$$
   $$\delta(q_0, b, a) = \{(q_1, \epsilon)\}$$
   $$\delta(q_1, b, a) = \{(q_1, \epsilon)\}$$
   $$\delta(q_1, \epsilon, z_0) = \{(q_1, \epsilon)\}$$
   obtain CFG equivalent to PDA.
8. Give the CFG generating the language accepted by the following PDA :
   m = ({q_0, q_1}, {0, 1}, {x, z_0}, δ, q_0, z_0, φ}
   when δ is given below
   $$\delta(q_0, 1, z_0) = \{(q_0, xz_0\}$$
   $$\delta(q_0, 1, x) = \{(q_0, xx)\}$$
   $$\delta(q_0, 0, x) = \{(q_1, x)\}$$
   $$\delta(q_0, \epsilon, z_0) = \{(q_0, \epsilon)\}$$
   $$\delta(q_0, 1, x) = \{(q_1, \epsilon)\}$$
   $$\delta(q_1, 0, z_0) = \{(q_0, z_0)\}$$
9. Describe the language L (m) in English for push down automation.
   M = (K, Σ, Γ, Δ, S, F)
   where k = (S, F)
   F = (F)
   Σ = (a, b)
   Γ = (a)
   Δ = {(S, a, ∈), (S, a)), ((S, b, ∈), (S, a)), ((S, a, ∈), (F, ∈)), ((F, a, a), (F, ∈),
   ((F, b, a), (F, ∈))}
10. Write the definitation of DPDA and NPDA ? Differentiate between NPDA and DPDA.

Unit - V

TURING MACHINE

5.1 INTRODUCTION

Uptil now we have studied finite state machine, push down machine and post machine. All of these machines do not have control over the input and they can not modify their own inputs. As turing machine is a writing machine, so it can modify its own inputs. Turing machine is most powerful than all other machines.

Features :

(1) Unlimited memory capacity. (2) External memory is available.

(3) Easy movement on left or right side on tape.

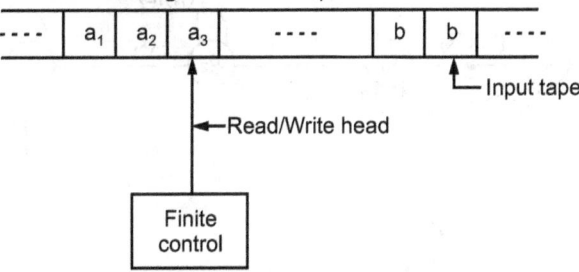

Fig. 5.1 : Turing machine

Here, Input tape provides inputs to a TM.

Read/write head provides the movement.

Finite control controls the input by read/write head.

5.1.1 Definition of Turing Machine

The TM is a 7 tuple.

$$M = (Q, \Sigma, \Gamma, \delta, q_0, \Delta \text{ or } B, F)$$

where,
- Q – Finite set of states
- Σ – Finite set of input symbols
- Γ – Finite set of external symbols
- Δ or B – Blank symbol Δ or $B \in \Gamma$.
- δ – Transition function
- q_0 – Initial state
- F – Final state

5.1.2 Instantaneous Description

Turing Machine, $M = (Q, \Sigma, \Gamma, \delta, q_0, B, F)$ having ID of a TM can be given as follows

$(q_0, a) = (q_1, A, R)$

- q_0 → Current state
- a → Input symbol
- q_1 → Next state
- A → Replacing current input symbol i.e. a
- R → Direction

5.1.3 Movement of Read/Write Head

L → Move to left side
R → Move to right side
N → No movement

Example 5.1 : Design a TM which accepts the strings of the form 0011.

Solution :

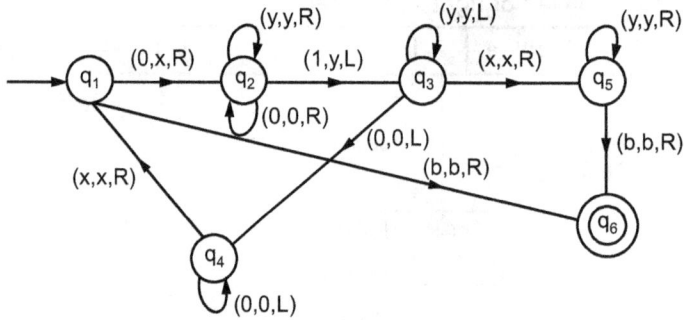

Fig. 5.2 : TM for 0011

Now we will see the acceptance of 0011

$$b\ 0011\ b \xrightarrow{(0,x,R)} bx\ 011\ b \xrightarrow{(0,0,R)} bx\ 011\ b$$
$$q_1 \qquad\qquad q_2 \qquad\qquad q_2$$

$$\xrightarrow{(1,y,L)} bx\ 0y1\ b \xrightarrow{(0,0,L)} bx\ 0y1\ b \xrightarrow{(x,x,R)} bx\ 0y1b$$
$$q_3 \qquad\qquad q_4 \qquad\qquad q_1$$

$$\xrightarrow{(0,x,R)} bxxy1\ b \xrightarrow{(y,y,R)} bxx\ y1\ b \xrightarrow{(1,y,L)} bxx\ yyb$$
$$q_2 \qquad\qquad q_2 \qquad\qquad q_3$$

$$\xrightarrow{(y,y,L)} bxx\ yy\ b \xrightarrow{(x,x,R)} bxx\ yy\ b \xrightarrow{(y,y,R)} bxx\ yy\ b$$
$$q_3 \qquad\qquad q_5 \qquad\qquad q_5$$

$$\xrightarrow{(y,y,R)} bxx\ yy\ b \xrightarrow{(b,b,R)} bxx\ yy\ bb$$
$$q_5 \qquad\qquad q_6$$

Example 5.2 : Design a TM which accepts all strings of the form $a^n b^n$ for $n \geq 1$ and rejects all other strings.

Solution :

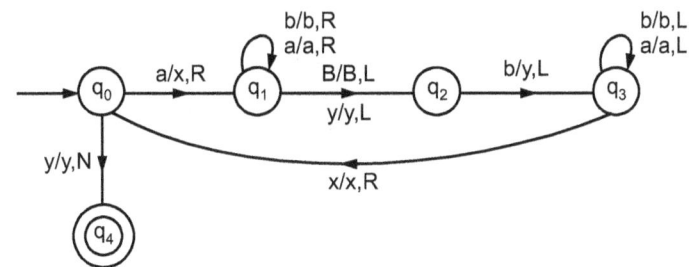

Fig. 5.3 : TM for $a^n b^n$, $n \geq 1$

Transition Table

	a	b	x	y	B
→ q_0	(q_1, x, R)	–	–	(q_4, y, N)	–
q_1	(q_1, a, R)	(q_1, b, R)	–	(q_2, y, L)	(q_2, B, L)
q_2	–	(q_3, y, L)	–	–	–
q_3	(q_3, a, L)	(q_3, b, L)	(q_0, x, R)	–	–
(q_4)	q_4	q_4	q_4	q_4	q_4

Here we can perform n number of cycles for acceptance.

Each cycle consists of three steps :

(a) Leftmost a is changed to x.

(b) Rightmost b is changed to y.

(c) Head returns to first a.

Now we define the TM.

$$M = (Q, \Sigma, \Gamma, \delta, q_0, B, F)$$

where,
$Q = \{q_0, q_1, q_2, q_3, q_4\}$

$\Sigma = \{a, b\}$

$\Gamma = \{a, b, B\}$

q_0 = Initial state

B = Blank symbol

F = Final state $\{q_4\}$

Example 5.3 : Design a TM to check whether a string over {a, b} contains equal number of a's and b's.

Solution :

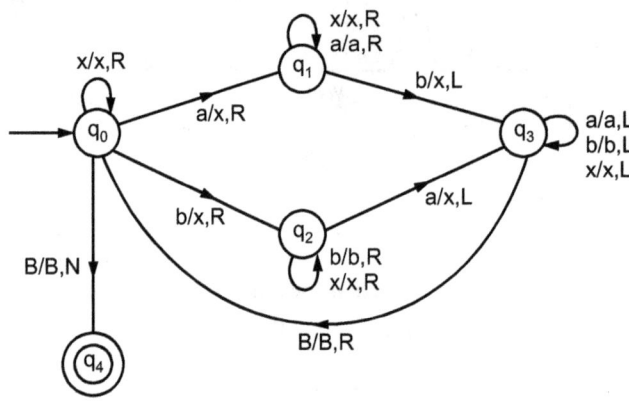

Fig. 5.4 : TM for x(a) − x(b)

Transition Table

	a	b	X	B
→ q_0	(q_1, X, R)	(q_2, X, R)	(q_0, X, R)	(q_4, B, N)
q_1	(q_1, a, R)	(q_3, X, L)	(q_1, X, R)	–
q_2	(q_3, X, L)	(q_2, b, R)	(q_2, X, R)	–
q_3	(q_3, a, L)	(q_3, b, L)	(q_3, X, L)	(q_0, B, R)
((q_4))	q_4	q_4	q_4	q_4

∴ Turing Machine, M = {Q, Σ, Γ, δ, q_0, B, F)
where,
Q = {q_0, q_1, q_2, q_3, q_4}
Σ = {a, b}
Γ = {a, b, X, B}
q_0 = Initial state
B = Blank symbol
F = {q_4}

Consider input string abba

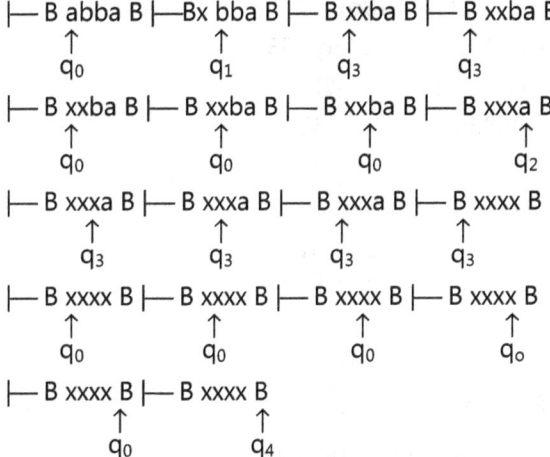

⊢ B abba B ⊢ Bx bba B ⊢ B xxba B ⊢ B xxba B
    ↑   ↑   ↑   ↑
  q_0 q_1 q_3 q_3

⊢ B xxba B ⊢ B xxba B ⊢ B xxba B ⊢ B xxxa B
  ↑   ↑   ↑   ↑
 q_0 q_0 q_0 q_2

⊢ B xxxa B ⊢ B xxxa B ⊢ B xxxa B ⊢ B xxxx B
  ↑   ↑   ↑   ↑
 q_3 q_3 q_3 q_3

⊢ B xxxx B ⊢ B xxxx B ⊢ B xxxx B ⊢ B xxxx B
  ↑   ↑   ↑   ↑
 q_0 q_0 q_0 q_0

⊢ B xxxx B ⊢ B xxxx B
  ↑   ↑
 q_0 q_4

Example 5.4 : Design a TM for a language, L = $\{1^n\ 2^n\ 3^n\ |\ n \geq 1\}$

Solution :

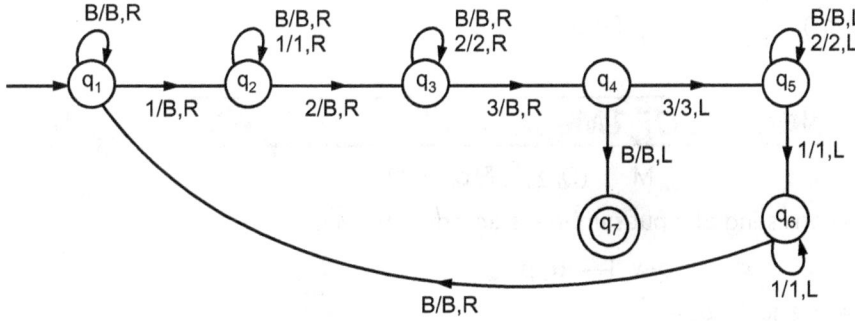

Fig. 5.5 : TM for $1^n\ 2^n\ 3^n\ |\ n \geq 1$

Logic :

- On q_1, R/W head replaces leftmost 1 by b with right move and enters to q_2.
- On scanning the leftmost 2, the R/W head replaces leftmost 2, by b with right move and enters to q_3.
- On scanning the leftmost 3, the R/W head replaces 3 by b, and moves to the right and enters q_4.
- After scanning rightmost 3, R/W head moves to the left until it finds leftmost 1.
- Repeat above all steps till final output.

Consider string 112233

q_1 112233 ⊢ Bq_2 12233 ⊢ B1$q_2$2233 ⊢ B1B$q_3$233
⊢ B1B2$q_3$33 ⊢ B1B2B$q_4$3 ⊢ B1B2q_5B3 ⊢ B1B$q_5$2B3
⊢ B1q_5B2B3 ⊢ B$q_5$1B2B3 ⊢ q_6B1B2B3 ⊢ B$q_1$1B2B3
⊢ BB$q_2$2B3 ⊢ BBB$q_2$2B3 ⊢ BBBBq_3B3 ⊢ BBBBB$q_3$3
⊢ BBBBBBq_4B ⊢ BBBBBq_7BB

Transition Table

	1	2	3	b
→ q_1	(q_2, B, R)	–	–	(q_1, B, R)
q_2	(q_2, 1, R)	(q_3, B, R)	–	(q_2, B, R)
q_3	–	(q_3, 2, R)	(q_4, B, R)	(q_3, B, R)
q_4	–	–	(q_5, 3, L)	(q_7, B, L)
q_5	(q_6, 1, L)	(q_5, 2, L)	–	(q_5, B, L)
q_6	(q_6, 1, L)	–	–	(q_1, B, R)
ⓠ₇		Final state		

5.2 LANGUAGE OF TM

Consider TM, $M = (Q, \Sigma, \Gamma, \delta, q_0, B, F)$

A string w consisting of input symbols is accepted by M if

$$q_0 w \vdash^* \alpha_1 p \alpha_2$$

where $P \in F$ and $\alpha_1 \alpha_2 \in \Gamma^*$

If machine M halts in non-accepting state then M does not accept w.

Example 5.5 : Construct TM to accept the set L of all strings over {0, 1} ending with 010.

Solution :

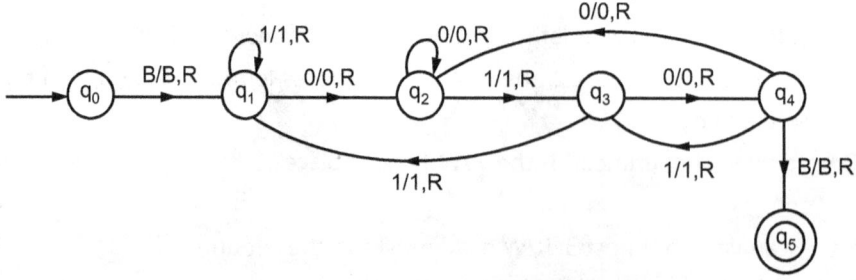

Fig. 5.6 : TM for end with 010

Transition Table

	0	1	B
→ q_0	–	–	(q_1, B, R)
q_1	$(q_2, 0, R)$	$(q_1, 1, R)$	–
q_2	$(q_2, 0, R)$	$(q_3, 1, R)$	–
q_3	$(q_4, 0, R)$	$(q_1, 1, R)$	–
q_4	$(q_2, 0, R)$	$(q_3, 1, R)$	(q_5, B, R)
ⓠ$_5$	Final State		

Example 5.6 : Construct a TM that accepts L = $\{0^{2n} \mid n \geq 0\}$.

Solution : Logic :

1. It writes B on leftmost 0 of the input string w.
2. It reads symbols of w from left to right and replaces the alternate 0's with x's.
3. If tape contains a single 0 in above step, then M accepts w.
4. If the tape contains more than one 0 and the number of 0's is odd in step 2, M rejects w.
5. M returns head to the left end of the tape.
6. M goes to step 2.

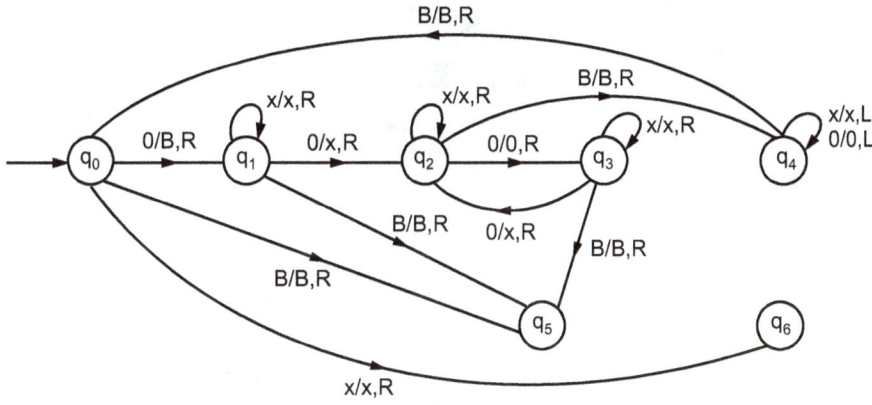

Fig. 5.7

Transition Table

	0	B	x
→ q_0	(q_1, B, R)	(q_5, B, R)	(q_6, x, R)
q_1	(q_2, x, R)	(q_5, B, R)	(q_1, x, R)
q_2	$(q_3, 0, R)$	(q_4, b, R)	(q_2, x, R)
q_3	(q_2, x, R)	(q_5, B, R)	(q_3, x, R)
q_4	$(q_4, 0, L)$	(q_1, b, R)	(q_4, x, L)
((q_5))	–	–	–
q_6	–	–	–

Turing Machine, $M = (Q, \Sigma, \Gamma, \delta, q_0, B, F)$

where,
$Q = \{q_0, q_1, q_2, q_3, q_4, q_5, q_6\}$
$\Sigma = \{0\}$
$\Gamma = \{0, x, B\}$
$F = \{q_5\}$

Consider a string 0000

$q_00000 \vdash Bq_1000 \vdash Bxq_200 \vdash Bxq_30 \vdash Bx0xq_2 \vdash Bx0q_4xB \vdash Bxq_40xB$
$\vdash Bq_4x0xB \vdash q_4Bx0xB \vdash Bq_1x0xB \vdash Bxq_10xB \vdash Bxxq_2xB \vdash Bxxxq_2B$
$\vdash Bxxq_4xB \vdash Bxq_4xxB \vdash Bq_4xxxB \vdash q_4BxxxB \vdash Bq_1xxxB \vdash Bxq_1xxB$
$\vdash Bxxq_1xB \vdash Bxxxq_1B \vdash BxxxBq_5$

Example 5.7 : Design a TM that replaces every occurrence of abb by baa.
Solution :

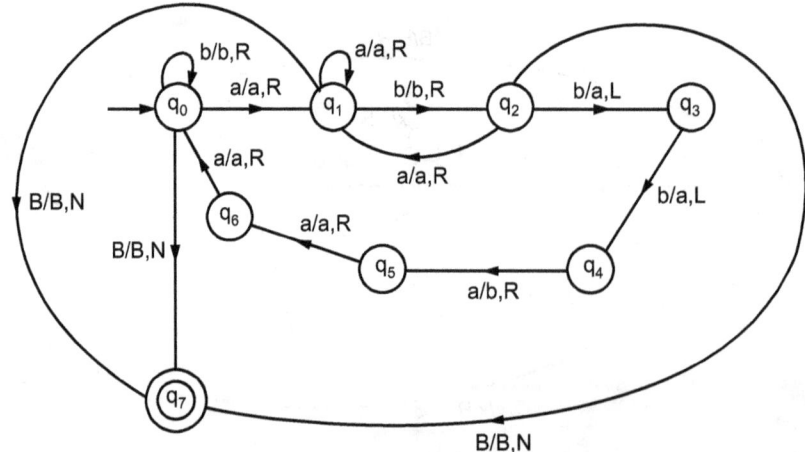

Fig. 5.8 : TM

$M = \{Q, \Sigma, \Gamma, \delta, q_0, B, F\}$

$Q = \{q_0, q_1, q_2, q_3, q_4, q_5, q_6, q_7\}$

$\Sigma = \{a, b\}$

$\Gamma = \{a, b, B\}$

$F = \{q_7\}$

Transition Table

	a	b	B
→ q_0	q_1, a, R	q_0, b, R	q_7, B, N
q_1	q_1, a, R	q_2, b, R	q_7, B, N
q_2	q_1, a, R	q_3, a, L	q_7, B, N
q_3	–	q_4, a, L	–
q_4	q_5, b, R	–	–
q_5	q_6, a, R	–	–
q_6	q_6, a, R	–	–
(q_7)	–	–	–

Example 5.8 : Design a TM to replace string 110 by 101.

Solution :

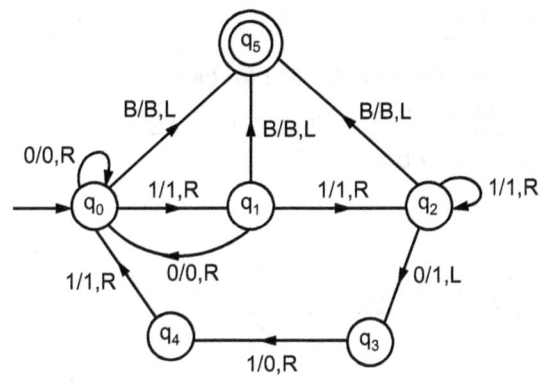

Fig. 5.9

Turing Machine, where,

$M = (Q, \Sigma, \delta, \Gamma, q_0, B, F)$

$Q = \{q_0, q_1, q_2, q_3, q_4, q_5\}$

$\Sigma = \{0, 1\}$

$\Gamma = \{0, 1, B\}$

$F = \{q_5\}$

Transition Table

	0	1	B
→ q_0	(q_0, 0, R)	(q_1, 1, R)	(q_5, B, L)
q_1	(q_0, 0, R)	(q_2, 1, R)	(q_5, B, L)
q_2	(q_3, 1, L)	(q_2, 1, R)	(q_5, B, L)
q_3	–	(q_4, 0, R)	–
q_4	–	(q_0, 1, R)	–
ⓠ$_5$	Final State		

Example 5.9 : Design a TM with no more than three states that accept the language (a(a + b)*).

Solution : First draw DFA for (a(a + b)*)

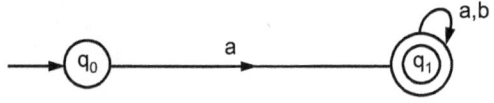

Fig. 5.10 (a)

Now construct TM from the DFA.

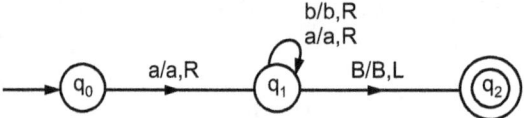

Fig. 5.10 (b) : TM for (a(a + b)*)

Turing Machine, $M = (\{q_0, q_1, q_2\} \{a, b\} \{a, b, B\}, \delta, q_0, B, \{q_2\})$

Example 5.10 : Design a TM for $a^n b^n c^n | n \geq 1$.

Solution :

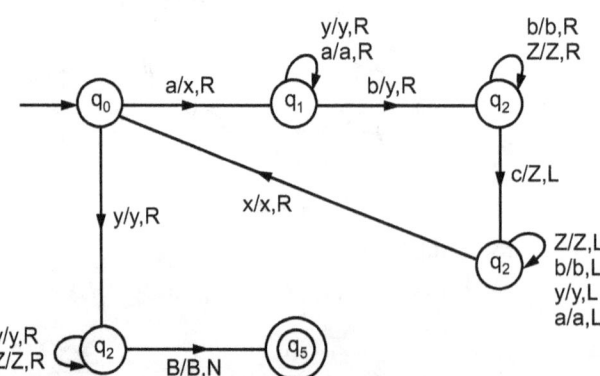

Fig. 5.11 : TM for $a^n b^n c^n | n \geq 1$

Transition Table

	a	b	c	x	y	z	B
→ q_0	(q_1, x, R)	–	–	–	(q_4, Y, R)	–	–
q_1	(q_1, a, R)	(q_2, Y, R)	–	–	(q_1, Y, R)	–	–
q_2	–	(q_2, b, R)	(q_3, Z, R)	–	–	(q_2, Z, R)	–
q_3	(q_3, a, L)	(q_3, b, L)	–	(q_0, x, R)	(q_3, Y, L)	(q_3, Z, L)	–
q_4	–	–	–	–	(q_4, Y, R)	(q_4, Z, R)	(q_5, B, N)
ⓠ$_5$	–	Final state					

Turing Machine gives $M = (Q, \Sigma, \Gamma, \delta, q_0, B, F)$
where,
$Q = \{q_0, q_1, q_2, q_3, q_4, q_5\}$
$\Sigma = \{a, b, c\}$
$\Gamma = \{a, b, c, x, y, z, B\}$
q_0 = initial state
$F = \{q_5\}$
B = blank symbol

Example 5.11 : Design a TM to find the 1's complement of a given binary input.

Solution :

Fig. 5.12 : TM for 1's complement

Transition Table

	0	1	B
q_0	$(q_0, 1, R)$	$(q_0, 0, R)$	(q_1, B, L)
ⓠ$_1$	Final state		

∴ Turing Machine, $M = (\{q_0, q_1\}, \{0, 1\}, \{0, 1, B\}, \delta, q_0, B, \{q_1\})$

Example 5.12 : Design a TM to find 2's complement of a binary machine.

Solution : 2's complement of any number can be found by moving from right end to left side till the first '1' without any change and then take complement of each bit.

For example : 2's complement of a binary number 11001010100

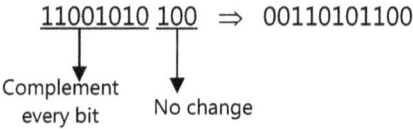

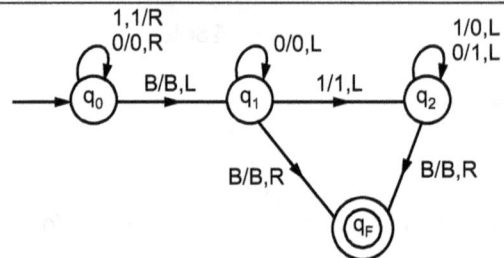

Fig. 5.13 : TM for 2's complement

Transition Table

	0	1	B
→ q_0	$(q_0, 0, R)$	$(q_0, 1, R)$	(q_1, B, L)
q_1	$(q_1, 0, L)$	$(q_2, 1, L)$	(q_3, B, R)
q_2	$(q_2, 1, L)$	$(q_2, 0, L)$	(q_3, B, R)
q_F		Final state	

Turing Machine, where,

$M = \{Q, \Sigma, \delta, \Gamma, q_0, B, F\}$

$Q = \{q_0, q_1, q_2, q_F\}$

$\Sigma = \{0, 1\}$

$\Gamma = \{0, 1, B\}$

q_0 = initial state

$F = \{q_F\}$

We will see acceptance of 0101101000

B0101101000 ⊢ B010110100B ⊢ B0101101000B ⊢ B0101101000
 ↑   ↑   ↑   ↑
 q_0 q_0 q_0 q_0

⊢ B0101101000B ⊢ B0101101000B ⊢ B0101101000 ⊢ B0101101000B
 ↑   ↑   ↑   ↑
 q_0 q_0 q_0 q_0

⊢ B0101101000B ⊢ B0101101000B ⊢ B0101101000B ⊢ B0101101000B
 ↑   ↑   ↑   ↑
 q_0 q_0 q_0 q_0

⊢ B0101101000B ⊢ B0101101000B ⊢ B0101101000B ⊢ B0101101000B
 ↑   ↑   ↑   ↑
 q_0 q_0 q_0 q_0

B0101101000B ⊢ B0101011000B ⊢ B0100011000B ⊢ B0110011000B
↑   ↑   ↑   ↑
q_0 q_0 q_0 q_0

⊢ B0010011000B ⊢ B1010011000B ⊢ B1010011000B
 ↑   ↑   ↑
 q_0 q_0 q_0

Example 5.13 : Construct a TM for checking well formedness of parenthesis.

Solution :

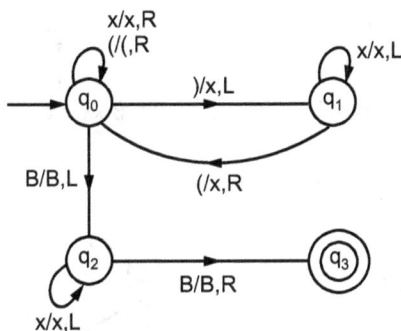

Fig. 5.14 : TM for parenthesis

Transition Table

	(	)	x	B
→ q_0	$(q_0, (, R)$	(q_1, x, L)	(q_0, x, R)	(q_2, B, L)
q_1	(q_0, x, R)	–	(q_1, x, L)	–
q_2	–	–	(q_2, x, L)	(q_3, B, R)
q_3	Final state			

∴ Turing Machine, $M = \{Q, \Sigma, \Gamma, \delta, q_0, B, F\}$
where,
$Q = \{q_0, q_1, q_2, q_3\}$
$\Sigma = P\{(,)\}$
$\Gamma = \{(,), x, B\}$
q_0 = initial state
B = blank symbol
$F = \{q_3\}$

We will have execution of (( ) ( ))

B (( ) ( )) B ⊢ B (( ) ( )) B ⊢ B (( ) ( )) B ⊢ B ((x ( )) B ⊢ B (xx ( )) B
↑   ↑   ↑   ↑   ↑
q_0 q_0 q_0 q_1 q_0

⊢ B (xx ( )) B ⊢ B (xx ( )) B ⊢ B (xx (x) B ⊢ B (xxxx) B ⊢ B (xxxx) B
↑   ↑   ↑   ↑   ↑
q_0 q_0 q_1 q_0 q_0

⊢ B (xxxxx B) ⊢ B (xxxxx B ⊢ B (xxxxx B ⊢ B (xxxxx B ⊢ B (xxxxx B
↑   ↑   ↑   ↑   ↑
q_1 q_1 q_1 q_1 q_1

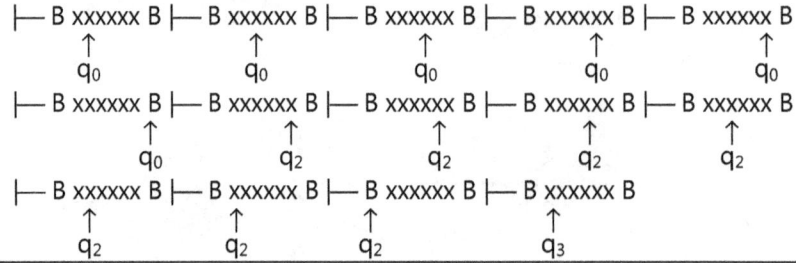

Example 5.14 : Design a TM for palindrome over {a, b}.

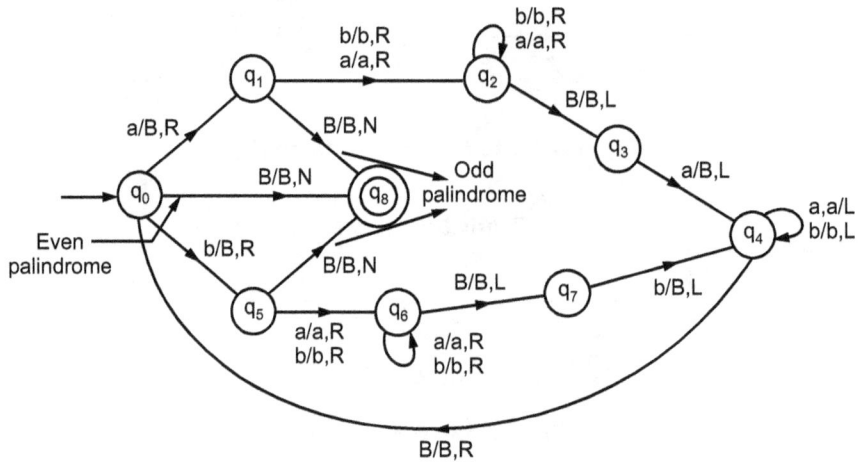

Fig. 5.15 : TM for palindrome

Turing Machine, $M = (\{q_0, q_1, q_2, q_3, q_4, q_5, q_6, q_7, q_8\}, \{a, b\}, \{a, b, B\}, \delta, q_0, B, \{q_8\})$

Consider string abbabba

$BabbabbaB \vdash BBbbabbaB \vdash BBbbabbaB \vdash BbbabbaB \vdash BbbabbaB$
$\quad\uparrow\qquad\qquad\uparrow\qquad\qquad\uparrow\qquad\qquad\uparrow\qquad\qquad\uparrow$
$\quad q_0\qquad\qquad q_1\qquad\qquad q_2\qquad\qquad q_2\qquad\qquad q_2$

$\vdash BbbabbaB \vdash BbbabbaB \vdash BbbabbaB \vdash BbbabbaB \vdash BBabbaBB$
$\quad\uparrow\qquad\qquad\uparrow\qquad\qquad\uparrow\qquad\qquad\uparrow\qquad\qquad\uparrow$
$\quad q_2\qquad\qquad q_2\qquad\qquad q_2\qquad\qquad q_3\qquad\qquad q_4$

$\vdash BbbabbB \vdash BbbabbB \vdash BbbabbB \vdash BbbabbB \vdash BbbabbB \vdash BbbabbB$
$\quad\uparrow\qquad\qquad\uparrow\qquad\qquad\uparrow\qquad\qquad\uparrow\qquad\qquad\uparrow\qquad\qquad\uparrow$
$\quad q_4\qquad\qquad q_4\qquad\qquad q_4\qquad\qquad q_4\qquad\qquad q_4\qquad\qquad q_0$

$\vdash BBbabbB \vdash BbabbB \vdash BbabbB \vdash BbabbB \vdash BbabbB \vdash BbabbB$
$\quad\uparrow\qquad\qquad\uparrow\qquad\qquad\uparrow\qquad\qquad\uparrow\qquad\qquad\uparrow\qquad\qquad\uparrow$
$\quad q_5\qquad\qquad q_6\qquad\qquad q_6\qquad\qquad q_6\qquad\qquad q_6\qquad\qquad q_7$

$\vdash BbabBB \vdash BbabB \vdash BbabB \vdash BbabB \vdash BbabB \vdash BBabB \vdash BabB$
$\quad\uparrow\qquad\qquad\uparrow\qquad\qquad\uparrow\qquad\qquad\uparrow\qquad\qquad\uparrow\qquad\qquad\uparrow\qquad\qquad\uparrow$
$\quad q_7\qquad\qquad q_7\qquad\qquad q_7\qquad\qquad q_7\qquad\qquad q_0\qquad\qquad q_5\qquad\qquad q_6$

$\vdash BabB \vdash BabB \vdash BaBB \vdash BaB \vdash BaB \vdash BBB \vdash BBB$
$\quad\uparrow\qquad\qquad\uparrow\qquad\qquad\uparrow\qquad\qquad\uparrow\qquad\qquad\uparrow\qquad\qquad\uparrow\qquad\qquad\uparrow$
$\quad q_6\qquad\qquad q_7\qquad\qquad q_4\qquad\qquad q_4\qquad\qquad q_0\qquad\qquad q_0\qquad\qquad q_0$

Example 5.15 : Design TM to compare two numbers, which will produce the output L if first number is less than the second number, output A if first is greater than the second number and D otherwise.

Solution :

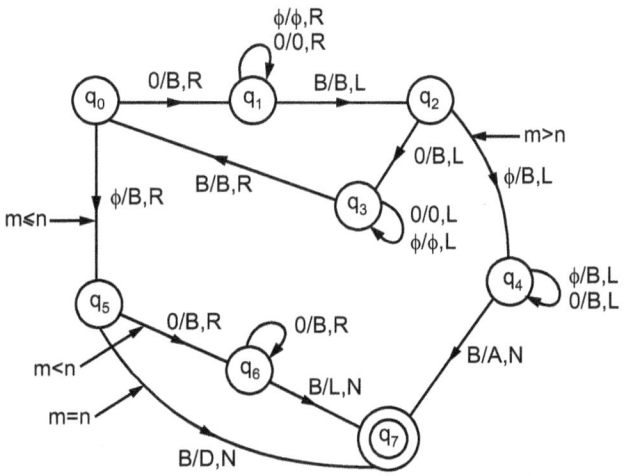

Fig. 5.16 : TM

Example 5.16 : Design a TM to compute remainder and quotient when a unary number is divided by another unary number.

Solution :

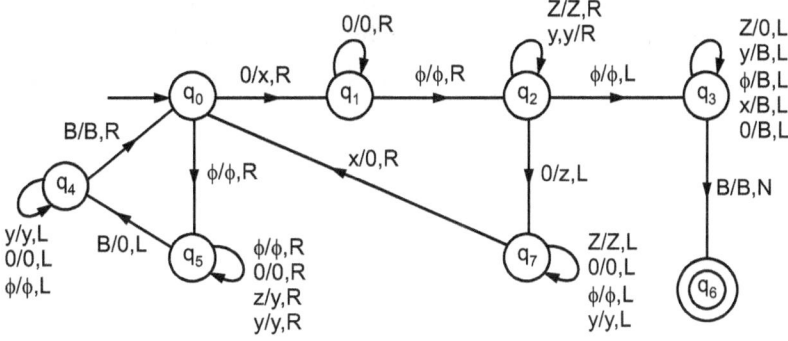

Fig. 5.17 : TM

Example 5.17 : Design a TM to add two unary numbers.

Solution :

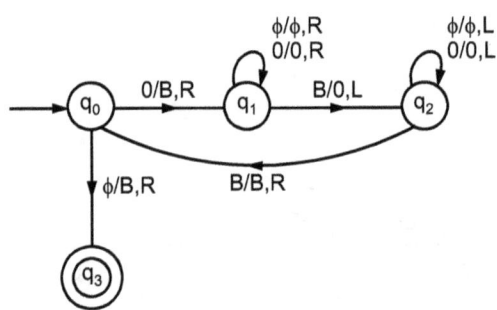

Fig. 5.18 : TM

Transition Table

	0	ϕ	B
→ q_0	(q_1, B, R)	(q_3, B, R)	–
q_1	(q_1, 0, R)	(q_1, ϕ, R)	(q_2, 0, L)
q_2	(q_2, 0, L)	(q_2, ϕ, L)	(q_0, B, R)
ⓠ$_3$	Final state		

Turing Machine $M = (\{q_0, q_1, q_2, q_3\} \{0, \phi\}, \{0, \phi, B\}, \delta, q_0, B, \{q_3\})$

5.3 THE HALTING PROBLEM

Halting problem of a TM is unsolvable.

"Consider a TM, M with input w, when the input w is given then machine M will halt."

As halting problem of TM is unsolvable, this can be proved by contradiction.

Consider the halting problem of TM is solvable and a machine $M_1(h_i)$ which takes two inputs.

(a) String of M

(b) An input w for machine M.

M_1 gives an output "halt" if M_1 determines that M stops on input w; otherwise M_1 gives output as "loop".

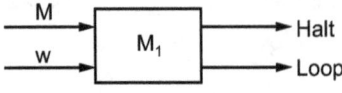

Fig. 5.19

Now consider M_1 as M_2 and M on both inputs and M_2 determines M will halt when M as its input. For this input string contain 0 and 1.

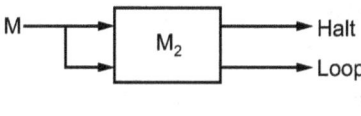

Fig. 5.20

Let us construct new TM M_3 which takes M_2 as input and works as follows :

(a) If output of M_2 is "loop" then M_3 halts.

(b) If output of M_2 is "halt" then M_3 will be in loop.

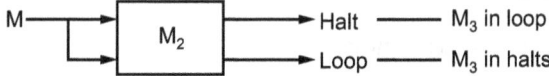

Fig. 5.21

Finally given M_3 is input to M_3 itself.

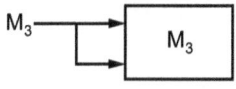

Fig. 5.22

Here we say that, M_3 halts on M_3 when input is M_3, then M_3 is in loop. M_3 loops forever when M_3 is input, then M_3 halts.

In either cases result is wrong. Hence we say that, M_3 does not exist, as M_3 does not exist that means M_2 and M_1 also do not exist as they are depend on each other.

5.4 COMPARISON OF DFA, PDA AND TM

Following is the comparison of DFA, PDA and TM :

1. DFA accepts regular language only, also NFA accepts regular language.
    ∴   DFA = NFA
2. PDA having two types : DPDA and NPDA. PDA has a memory so PDA accepts large class of languages than FA.
   PDA has more power than FA.
   NPDA accepts the language of CFG.
        Power (DPDA) < Power (NPDA)
3. Two stack/n-stack PDA's are more powerful.

4. Turing machines can be programmed. Hence TM accepts very large class of language.

TM accepts the type 0 class of languages.

$$TM > PDA > FM (FA)$$

Turing machine accepts all languages like regular non-regular, context free and context sensitive language.

5.5 APPLICATIONS OF DFA, PDA AND TM

5.5.1 Applications of DFA

1. It is used in computer algorithms.
2. It is used in design of digital circuit.
3. String matching.
4. Lexical analysis (compiler)
5. Information exchange.

5.5.2 Applications of PDA

1. PDA is used for CFL.
2. PDA is used for parsing.
3. As PDA is abstract machine; used for giving proofs of lemma on CFL.

5.5.3 Applications of TM

1. Turing machine is used as a recognizer which recognizes different languages easily.
2. Turing machine is used as a decider.
3. Turing machine is used as an enumerator that means TM with an output printer to print strings.
4. Turing machine is used as a function computer, which uses the function to define the working.

5.6 TUNING MACHINE LIMITATIONS

5.6.1 Computational Complexity Theory :

A limitation of Turing machines is that they do not model the strengths of a particular arrangement well. For instance, modern stored-program computers are actually instances of a more specific form of abstract machine known as the random access stored program machine or RASP machine model. Like the Universal Turing machine the RASP stores its "program" in "memory" external to its finite-state machine's "instructions". Unlike the universal Turing machine, the RASP has an infinite number of distinguishable, numbered but unbounded "registers"—memory "cells" that can contain any integer. The RASP's finite-state machine is equipped with the capability for indirect addressing (e.g. the contents of one register can be used as an address to specify another register); thus the RASP's "program" can address any register in the register-sequence. The upshot of this distinction is that there are computational optimizations that can be performed based on the memory indices, which are not possible in a general Turing machine; thus when Turing machines are used as the basis for bounding running times, a 'false lower bound' can be proven on certain algorithms' running times (due to the false simplifying assumption of a Turing machine). An example of this is binary search, an algorithm that can be shown to perform more quickly when using the RASP model of computation rather than the Turing machine model.

5.6.2 Concurrency :

Another limitation of Turing machines is that they do not model concurrency well. For example, there is a bound on the size of integer that can be computed by an always-halting nondeterministic Turing machine starting on a blank tape. By contrast, there are always-halting concurrent systems with no inputs that can compute an integer of unbounded size. (A process can be created with local storage that is initialized with a count of 0 that concurrently sends itself both a stop and a go message. When it receives a go message, it increments its count by 1 and sends itself a go message. When it receives a stop message, it stops with an unbounded number in its local storage.)

5.7 VARIANTS OF TURING MACHINES

There are number of other types of Turing machines in addition to the one we have seen such as Turing machines with multiple tapes, ones having one tape but with multiple heads, ones with two dimensional tapes, non-deterministic Turing machines etc. It turns out that computationally all these Turing machines are equally powerful. That is, what one type can compute any other can also compute. However, the efficiency of computation, that is, how fast they can compute, may vary.

5.7.1 Multi-Tape TM

Multi-Tape Turing Machine

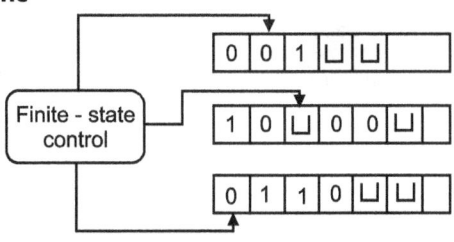

Fig. 5.25

- Input on Tape 1
- Initially all heads scanning cell 1, and tapes 2 to k blank
- In one step: Read symbols under each of the k-heads, and depending on the current control state, write new symbols on the tapes, move the each tape head (possibly in different directions), and change state.
- Formal Definition

A k-tape Turing Machine is $M = (Q, \Sigma, \Gamma, \delta, q_0, q_{acc}, q_{rej})$ where

- Q is a finite set of control states
- Σ is a finite set of input symbols
- $\Gamma \supseteq \Sigma$ is a finite set of tape symbols. Also, a blank symbol $\sqcup \in \Gamma \setminus \Sigma$
- $q_0 \in Q$ is the initial state
- $q_{acc} \in Q$ is the accept state
- $q_{rej} \in Q$ is the reject state, where $q_{rej} \neq q_{acc}$
- $\delta : (Q \setminus \{q_{acc}, q_{rej}\}) \times \Gamma^k \to Q \times (\Gamma \times (L, R))^k$ is the transition function.

Computation, Acceptance and Language

- A configuration of a multi-tape TM must describe the state, contents of all k-tapes, and positions of all k-heads. Thus, $C \in Q \times (\Gamma^* \{*\} \Gamma\Gamma^*)^k$, where * denotes the head position.
- Accepting configuration is one where the state is qacc, and starting configuration on input w is $(q_0, *\omega, *\sqcup, \ldots *\sqcup)$
- Formal definition of a single step is skipped.
- ω is accepted by M, if from the starting configuration with w as input, M reaches an accepting configuration.
- $L(M) = \{\omega \mid \omega \text{ accepted by M}\}$

Expressive Power of multi-tape TM

Theorem 1 : For any k-tape Turing Machine M, there is a single tape TM single(M) such that L(single(M)) = L(M).

Challenges

- How do we store k-tapes in one?
- How do we simulate the movement of k independent heads?

Storing Multiple Tapes

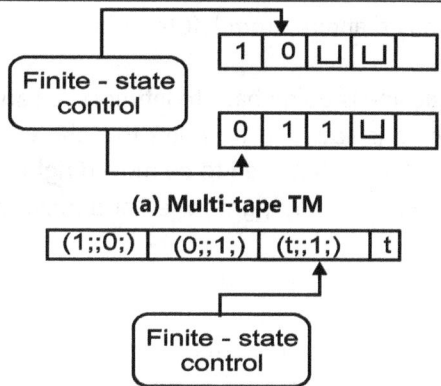

(a) Multi-tape TM

Fig. 5.26 : (b) 1-tape equivalent single (M)

Store in cell i contents of cell i of all tapes. "Mark" head position of tape with .

Simulating One Step

Challenge 1: Head of 1-Tape TM is pointing to one cell. How do we nd out all the k symbols that are being read by the k heads, which maybe in different cells?

- Read the tape from left to right, storing the contents of the cells being scanned in the state, as we encounter them.

Challenge 2: After this scan, 1-tape TM knows the next step of k-tape TM. How do we change the contents and move the heads?

- Once again, scan the tape, change all relevant contents, "move" heads (i.e., move s), and change state.

Overall Construction

First we outline the high-level algorithm for the 1-tape TM. On input w

1. First the machine will rewrite input w to be in "new" format.
2. To simulate one step
- Read from left-to-right remembering symbols read on each tape, and move all the way back to leftmost position.
- Read from left-to-right, changing symbols, and moving those heads that need to be moved right.
- Scan back from right-to-left moving the heads that need to be moved left.

Formally, let $M = (Q, \Sigma, \Gamma, \delta, q_0, q_{acc}, q_{rej}))$. To define the machine single(M) it is useful to identify modes that single(M) could be in while simulating M. The modes are

$$mode = \{init, back\text{-}init, read, back\text{-}read, x\text{-}right, x\text{-}left\}$$

where

- init means that the machine is rewriting input in new format
- back-init means the machine is just going back all the way to the leftmost cell after "initial-lizing" the tape

- read means the machine is scanning from left to right to read all symbols being read by k-tape machine
- back-read means the machine is going back to leftmost cell after the "read" phase
- x-right means the machine is scanning from left to right and is going to make all tape changes and move those heads that need to be moved right
- x-left means the machine is scanning right to left and moving all heads that need to be moved left

Now single(M) = $(Q', \Sigma', \Gamma', \delta', q'_0, q'_{acc}, q'_{rej})$ where

- Recall, based on the high-level description, single(M) needs to remember a few things in its state. It needs to keep track of the current "mode"; Ms state; during the read phase the symbols being scanned by each head of M; at the end of the read phase, the new symbols to be written and direction to move the heads. Thus,

$$Q' = \{q'_0, q'_{acc}, q'_{rej}\} \cup (\text{modes} \times Q \times \{\Gamma \times L, R, *\})^k)$$

where q'_0, q'_{acc}, q'_{rej} are new initial, accept and reject states, respectively. "*" is new special symbol that we will use to when placing new head positions, and can be ignored for now. Intuitively, when the mode is "read" the directions don't mean anything, and symbols in will be the symbols that M is scanning. During the "x" phases the directions are the directions each head needs to be moved, and the symbols are the new symbols to be written.

- $\Sigma' = \Sigma$; the input alphabet does not change
- On the tape, we write the contents of one cell of each of the k-tapes and whether the head scans that position or not. Thus, $\Gamma' = \{\triangleright, \sqcup\} \cup (\Gamma \times \{\cdot, *\})^k$, where $\triangleright$ B will be a new left-end-marker, as it will be useful for single(M) to know when it has finished scanning all the way to the left. $\sqcup$ as always is the blank symbol of the machine.

- The initial state, accept state and reject states are the new states q'_0, q'_{acc}, q'_{rej}.

We will now formally de ne the transition function . We will describe for various cases below; for a case not covered below, we will assume our usual convention that the machine single(M) goes to the reject state q'_{rej} and moves the head left.

Initial State: In the rst step, single(M) will move to the "initialization phase", which will write a (new) left endmarker, and rewrite the tape in the correct format for the future. Thus, from initial state q'_0 you go to a state whose "mode" is init. Since we are going to insert a new left end-marker, we need to "shift" all symbols of the input one-space to right, which can be accomplished by remembering the next symbol to be written in the state. So $\delta'(q'_0, a) = \{\{init, q_0, a, *, 0, L, 0, \ldots, 0, L\}, \triangleright\}$ the symbols 0 and L don't mean anything (and so can be changed to whatever you please), and the remembers that when we write the next symbol all heads must be in that position.

Initialization : In the initialization phase, we just read a symbol and write it in the "new format", which means writing blank symbols for all the other tape cells, and moving right. When we scan the entire input to go back left, i.e., change mode to back-init. There are two caveats to this. First we are shifting symbols of the input one position to the right because of the left endmarker ▷,; so we actually write what we remembered in our state, and remember what we read in the state. Also, in the rst position, we need to "place" all the heads; this is remembered because of . So we haven

$\delta'(\{init, q_0, a, *, 0, L, ..., 0, L\}, b) = \{(init, q_0, b, L, 0, L, L, ..., 0, L\}, (a, *, \sqcup, *, ..., \sqcup, *), R)$

$\delta'(\{init, q_0, a, L, 0, L, ..., 0, L\}, b) = \{(init, q_0, b, L, 0, L, L, ..., 0, L\}, (a, \cdot, \sqcup, *, ..., \sqcup, \cdot), R)$

$\delta'(\{init, q_0, a, L, 0,, L, ..., 0, L\}, \sqcup) = \{(back\text{-}init, q_0, 0, L, ..., 0, L\}, (a, \cdot, \sqcup, ..., \sqcup, \cdot), L)$

5.7.2 NONDETERMINISTIC TURING MACHINE

Deterministic TM: At each step, there is one possible next state, symbols to be written and direction to move the head, or the TM may halt.

Nondeterministic TM: At each step, there are nitely many possibilities. So formally, $M = (Q, \Sigma', \Gamma, \delta', q'_0, q'_{acc}, q'_{rej})$ where

- $Q, \Sigma, \Gamma, q_0, q_{acc}, q_{rej})$ are as before for 1-tape machine
- $\delta : (Q \setminus \{q_{acc}, q_{rej}\}) \times \Gamma \to P(Q \times \Gamma \times (L, R))$

Computation, Acceptance and Language

- A con guration of a nondeterministic TM is exactly the same as that of a 1-tape TM. So are notions of starting configuration and accepting configuration.
- A single step ⊢ is de ned similarly. $X_1 X_2 ... X_{i-1} q X_i X_n \vdash X_1 X_2 ... p X_{i-1} Y ... X_n$, if $(p, Y, L) \in (q, X_i)$; case for right moves is analogous.
- w is accepted by M, if from the starting con guration with w as input, M reaches an accepting configuration, for some sequence of choices at each step.
- $L(M) = \{w \mid w \text{ accepted by } M\}$

Expressive Power of Nondeterministic TM

Theorem 2 : For any nondeterministic Turing Machine M, there is a (deterministic) TM det(M) such that $L(det(M)) = L(M)$.

Proof Idea

det(M) will simulate M on the input.

- **Idea 1:** det(M) tries to keep track of all possible \con gurations" that M could possibly be after each step. Works for DFA simulation of NFA but not convenient here.
- **Idea 2:** det(M) will simulate M on each possible sequence of computation steps that M may try in each step.

Nondeterministic Computation

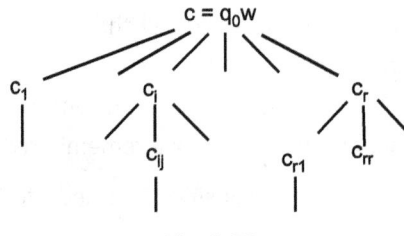

Fig. 5.27

- If $r = \max_{q;X} |(q; X)|$ then the runs of M can be organized as an r-branching tree.
- $c_{i_1 i_2 \ldots i_n}$ is the configuration of M after n-steps, where choice i_1 is taken in step 1, i_2 in step 2, and so on.
- Input w is accepted i 9 accepting con guration in tree.

Deterministic Simulation

Proof Idea

The machine det(M) will search for an accepting con guration in computation tree
- The configuration at any vertex can be obtained by simulating M on the appropriate sequence of nondeterministic choices
- det(M) will perform a BFS on the tree. Why not a DFS?

Observe that det(M) may not terminate if w is not accepted.

Proof Details

det(M) will use 3 tapes to simulate M (note, multitape TMs are equivalent to 1-tape TMs)
- Tape 1, called input tape, will always hold input w
- Tape 2, called simulation tape, will be used as M's tape when simulating M on a sequence of nondeterministic choices
- Tape 3, called choice tape, will store the current sequence of nondeterministic choices

Execution of det(M)

1. Initially: Input tape contains w, simulation tape and choice tape are blank
2. Copy contents of input tape onto simulation tape
3. Simulate M using simulation tape as its (only) tape
(a) At the next step of M, if state is q, simulation tape head reads X, and choice tape head reads i, then simulate the ith possibility in (q; X); if i is not a valid choice, then goto step 4
(b) After changing state, simulation tape contents, and head position on simulation tape, move choice tape's head to the right. If Tape 3 is now scanning t, then goto step 4
(c) If M accepts then accept and halt, else goto step 3(1) to simulate the next step of M.
4. Write the lexicographically next choice sequence on choice tape, erase everything on simula-tion tape and goto step 2.

Deterministic Simulation

In a nutshell

- det(M) simulates M over and over again, for different sequences, and for different number of steps.
- If M accepts w then there is a sequence of choices that will lead to acceptance. det(M) will eventually have this sequence on choice tape, and then its simulation M will accept.
- If M does not accept w then no sequence of choices leads to acceptance. det(M) will therefore never halt!

5.7.3 Turing Machines with Two Dimensional Tapes

This is a kind of Turing machine that have one finite control, one read-write head and one two dimensional tape. The tape has the top end and the left end but extends indefinitely to the right and down. It is divided into rows of small squares. For any Turing machine of this type there is a Turing machine with a one dimensional tape that is equally powerful, that is, the former can be simulated by the latter. To simulate a two dimensional tape with a one dimensional tape, first we map the squares of the two dimensional tape to those of the one dimensional tape diagonally as shown in the following tables:

(a) Two Dimensional Tape

<="" td="">

	v	v	v	V	v	v	v	......
H	1	2	6	7	15	16		......
H	3	5	8	14	17	26		......
H	4	9	13	18	25			....
H	10	12	19	24				....
H	11	20	23					....
H	21	22						....

....

Here the numbers indicate the correspondence of squares in the two tapes: **square i** of the two dimensional tape is mapped to **square i** of the one dimensional tape. **h** and **v** are symbols which are not in the tape alphabet and they are used to mark the left and the top end of the tape, respectively.

(b) One Dimensional Tape

v 1 v 2 3 h 4 5 6 v 7 8 9 10 h 11 ...... The head of a two dimensional tape moves one square up, down, left or right.

Let us simulate this head move with a one dimensional tape.

Let **i** be the head position of the two dimensional tape. If the head moves down from i, then move the head of the one dimensional tape to right until it hits **h** or **v** counting the number of squares it has visited after **i**. Let k be the number of squares visited by the head of the one dimensional tape. If **h** was hit first, then from h move the head of the one dimensional tape further right to the k-th square from **h**. That is the square corresponding to the square below **i** in the two dimensional tape. If **v** was hit first, then $(k+1)^{th}$ square to the right from **v** is the new head position.

For example, suppose that the head position is at 8 for the two dimensional tape in the above table, that is **i** = **8**. If the head moves down to position 13, then for the one dimensional tape, the head moves from position 8 to right. Then it meets h first, which is the third square from 8. Thus from h, move 3 positions to the right. That is the head position of the one dimensional tape corresponding to 13 on the two dimensional tape.

If **i** = **5** and the head moves down on the other hand, then on the one dimensional tape the head moves to the right and it hits v first, which is the second square from **i** = **5**. Thus this time the third square is the head position of the one dimensional tape corresponding to 9 on the two dimensional tape.

Similarly formulas can be found for the head position on the one dimensional tape corresponding to move up, right or left on the two dimensional tape. Details are omitted. Thus some Turing machines with a one dimensional tape can simulate every move of a Turing machine with one two dimensional tape. Hence they are at least as powerful as Turing machines with a two dimensional tape. Since Turing machines with a two dimensional tape obviously can simulate Turing machines with a one dimensional tape, it can be said that they are equally powerful.

5.7.4 Turing Machines with Multiple Heads

This is a kind of Turing machines that have one finite control and one tape but more than one read-write heads. In each state only one of the heads is allowed to read and write. It is denoted by a 5-tuple $< Q, \Sigma, \Gamma, q_0, \delta >$. The transition function is a partial function

$$\delta : Q \times \{H_1, H_2, ..., H_n\} \times (\Gamma \cup \{\Delta\}) \rightarrow (Q \cup \{h\}) \times (\Gamma \cup \{\Delta\} \times \{R, L, S\}$$

where $H_1, H_2 ... , H_n$ denote the tape heads.

It can be easily seen that this type of Turing machines are as powerful as one tape Turing machines.

5.7.5 Turing Machines with Infinite Tape

This is a kind of Turing machine that have one finite control and one tape which extends infinitely in both directions.

It turns out that this type of Turing machines are only as powerful as one tape Turing machines whose tape has a left end.

5.7.6 Random Access Machine

This is an idealized model of modern computers. Have a nite number of "registers", an infinite number of available memory locations, and store a sequence of instructions or "program" in memory.

- Initially, the program instructions are stored in a contiguous block of memory locations start-ing at location 1. All registers and memory locations, other than those storing the program, are set to 0.

Instruction Set

- add X, Y: Add the contents of registers X and Y and store the result in X.
- loadc X, I: Place the constant I in register X.
- load X, M: Load the contents of memory location M into register X.
- loadI X, M: Load the contents of the location \pointed to" by the contents of M into register X.
- store X, M: store the contents of register X in memory location M. jmp M: The next instruction to be executed is in location M.
- jmz X, M: If register X is 0, then jump to instruction M. halt: Halt execution.

Expressive Power of RAMs

Theorem 3 : Anything computed on a RAM can be computed on a Turing machine. Proof. We outline a proof sketch in next.

Capturing State of RAM

- In order to simulate the RAM, the TM stores contents of registers, memory etc., in di erent tapes as follows.
- Instruction Counter Tape: Stores the memory location where the next instrcution is stored; initially it is 1.
- Memory Address Tape: Stores the address of memeory location where a load/store operation is to be performed.
- Register Tape: Stores the contents of each of the registers.
- { Has register index followed by contents of each register as follows: #hRegisterNumberi hRegisterValuei# . For example, if register 1 has 11, register 2 has 100, register 3 has 11011, etc, then tape contains #1 11#10 100#11 11011#
- Memory Tape: Like register tape, store #hAddressi hContentsi# { To store an instruction, have opcode; hargumentsi
- Work Tapes: Have 3 additional work tapes to simulate steps of the RAM

Simulating a RAM

- TM starts with the program stored in memory, and the instruction location tape initalized to 1.
- Each step of the RAM is simulated using many steps.
- Read the instruction counter tape
- Search for the relevant instruction in memory
- Store the opcode of instruction and register address (of argument) in the nite control. Store the memory addres (of argument) in memory address tape.
- Retrieve the values from register tape and/or memory tape and store them in work tape { Perform the operation using work tapes
- Update instruction counter tape, register tape, and memory tape.

Example: ADD instruction

- Suppose instruction counter tape holds 101.
- TM searches memory tape for the pattern #101 .
- Suppose the memory tape contains   #101 haddi; 11; 110#
- TM stores \add", 11 and 110 in its nite control. In other words, it moves to a state q_{add} 11;110 whose job it is to add the contents of register 11 and 110 and put the result in 11.
- Search the register tape for the pattern #11 . Suppose the register tape contains #11 10110# ; in other words, the contents of register 11 is 10110. Copy 10110 to one of the work-tapes.
- Search the register tape for pattern #101 , and copy the contents of register onto work tape 2.
- Compute the sum of the contents of the work tapes
- Search the register tape for #11 and replace the string 10110 by the answer computed on the work tape. This may involve shifting contents of the register tape to the right (or left).
- Add 1 to the instruction counter tape.

5.8 COMPOSITE TURING MACHINE

Two or more Turing machines can be combined to solve a collection of simpler problems, so that the output of one Turing machine forms the input to the next Turing machine and so on. This is called as composition.

e.g. We can combine two Turing machines to convert into the decimal form the GCD of two unary numbers. For realizing the composite Turing machine the transition functions of the components of Turing machines are combined by increasing and relabelling I and suitably branching to an appropriate state rather than the halt state at the completion of the performance of each component Turing machine.

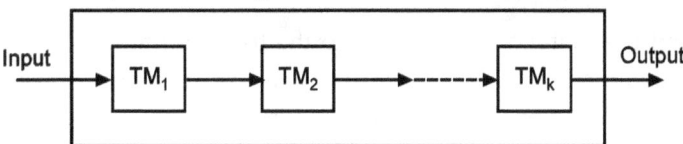

Fig. 5.28 : Composite Turing Machine

5.9 UNIVERSAL TURING MACHINE (UTM)

In the previous sections we have seen Composite and Iterated Turing Machine, and they solve the very complex problems. So the question arises "can we construct a Turing machine which is powerful or universal ?". Universal means, it is capable of doing anything that any other Turing Machine can do. In other words, the Universal Turing Machine (UTM) should have the capability of imitating any Turing Machine T, given the following information in its tape.

(i) The description of T in terms of its transition function (operation or program area of the tape);

(ii) The initial configuration of T, i.e. starting state and the symbol scanned (state area of the tape.)

(iii) The data to be fed to T (data area of the tape).

This means that the UTM should have an imitation algorithm to correctly interpret the rules of operations of T.

The UTM can simulate T, one step at a time as follows :

It is guided by a marker to indicate the point on its tape at which the description of T begins, and it keeps a complete account of how the tape of T looks like at every instant. It also remembers the state of T and the symbol T is reading. It then looks at the description of T to carry out what T is supposed to do. In order to exhibit this behaviour, the UTM should have a table look-up facility and should perform following steps.

Step 1 : Scan the square on the state area of the tape and read the symbol that T reads and the initial state of T.

Step 2 : Move the tape to the program area containing the functional description of T and find the row in the transition matrix headed by the symbol read in step 1.

Step 3 : Find the column headed by the state symbol in which T resides, and read the triple (i.e. the new state, symbol to be replaced and direction of the movement of the tape) in the intersection of this column with the row found in step 2.

Step 4 : Move the tape to the appropriate cell in the data area, replace the symbol, move the head in required direction, read the next symbol and finally reach the state area and replace the state and scanned symbol. Go back to step 1.

In order to convert this imitation algorithm into the transition/functional matrix of the UTM we have to note some points. Since we have only a one-dimensional (linear) tape on the UTM, we cannot directly put on this tape, the two-dimensional description of T unless we use some coding to convert the two-dimensional information into one-dimension. We will now discuss this type of encoding called Turing machine codes.

A universal Turing machine (UTM) is a Turing machine that can simulate an arbitrary Turing machine on arbitrary input. The universal machine essentially achieves this by reading both the description of the machine to be simulated as well as the input thereof from its own tape. It is also known as universal computing machine, universal machine (UM).

5.9.1 Turing Machine Codes

Let $M = (Q, \{a, b\}, \{a, b, B\}, \delta, q_1, B, \{q_2\})$ be a Turing Machine. Assume $Q = \{q_1, q_2, \ldots q_n\}$.

We will now call symbols a, b and B as X_1, X_2 and X_3 respectively. Also the directions of head movements will be called as D_1 and D_2 for L and R respectively.

Now consider the following generic move

$$\delta(q_i, X_j) = (q_k, X_t, D_m)$$

The move can be encoded by the binary string

$$a^i\,ba^j\,ba^k\,ba^l\,ba^m \ldots \ldots \qquad \ldots (I)$$

A binary code for Turing machine M is

$$bbb\ code_1\ bb\ code_2\ bb \ldots bb\ code_n\ bbb,$$

where each $code_i$ is of the form (I) above, and each move of M is encoded by one of the $code_i$'s. Each of the $code_i$'s can be found as there are no two consecutive bb's in (I). These codes begin and end with bbb. Thus the coding will be unique.

Consider the following Turing Machine

$$M = (\{q_1, q_2, q_3\}, \{a, b\}, \{a, b, B\}, \delta, q_1, B, \{q_2\})$$

The moves are

$$\delta(q_1, b) = (q_3, 0, R) \qquad \delta(q_3, 0) = (q_1, b, R)$$
$$\delta(q_3, b) = (q_2, 0, R) \qquad \delta(q_3, B) = (q_3, b, L)$$

Then the machine M can be coded as

bbb<u>abaabaaababaab</u> b<u>aaababababaabaabb</u>

<u>aaabaabaababaab</u> b<u>aaabaaabaaabaababbb</u>

Observe that the code begins and ends with bbb. The underlined portions represent one move of the Turing Machine.

QUESTIONS

1. Design a turing machine which computes 2's complement of given binary number.
2. Write short notes on :
   (i) Multiple turing machine
   (ii) Universal TM
3. Define the TM in terms of tuple. Explain each tuple in brief.
4. Design post canonical system which accepts the string of a and b having odd length and the element at the centre is 'a'.
5. Construct TM that recognizes the languages
   (i) $L = \{0^n, \perp^m, i^n, m >= 0\}$
   (ii) $L = \{x \in \{0, 1\}^* \mid x \text{ ends in } 00\}$
6. Let T be the TM defined by the 5-tuples
   $(S_0, 0, 0, S_1, L)$
   $(S_0, 1, 0, S_1, L)$
   $(S_0, B, B, Halt, L)$
   $(S_1, 0, 1, S_0, L)$
   $(S_1, 1, 1, S_0, R)$

   For each of the following initial tapes, determine the final tape when T halts, assuming that T begins in initial position.
   (i) 110B (ii) 0011B (iii) 0101 B
7. Design a TM to replace string 110 by 101 in binary input string.
8. Design the post machine which accepts the strings with an equal number of 0's and 1's.
9. Construct TM to accept the language.
   (i) $\{w \in \{a, b\}^* \mid w \text{ contains the same number of a's and b's}\}$
   (ii) $\{w \in \{a, b\}^* \mid w = w^R\}$

10. Design a TM for following languages
    (i) {www | w ∈ {a, b}*}
    (ii) {aⁿbⁿcⁿ | n ≥ 0}
    (iii) {aⁱbʲ | i < j}
11. Design a TM that computer

    $$F(m, n) = \begin{cases} m - n & ; \text{ if } m >= n \\ 0 & ; \text{ otherwise} \end{cases}$$

12. Explain the variants of TM in detail.
13. Compare FA, PDM, PM and TM with each other with suitable example.

◈ ◈ ◈

UNIVERSITY QUESTION PAPERS
Formal Language and Automata Theory
May 2015

Time : 3 Hours   Total Marks : 80

Attempt any two out of a, b, c in each questions.

UNIT - I

1. (a) Define the following terms with example.
   - (i) Sets
   - (ii) Relations
   - (iii) Graphs
   - (iv) Trees   [08]

   (b) Design FSM to check whether a given binary number is divisible by five   [08]

   (c) Construct a minimum state automaton equivalent to a given automaton M whose transition table is given below.   [08]

State	Input	
	a	b
q_0	q_0	q_3
q_1	q_2	q_5
q_2	q_3	q_4
q_3	q_0	q_5
q_4	q_0	q_6
q_5	q_1	q_4
ⓠ$_6$	q_1	q_3

Unit - II

2. (a) Find the regular expression corresponding to the automaton given in Fig.1 below. [8]

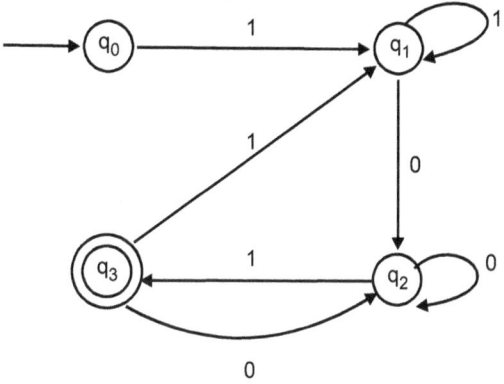

Fig. 1

(b) Construct DFA accepting language represented by,
    (1.(00)*.1 +0.1*.0)* [8]
(c) State and prove pumping Lemma for regular sets. [8]

Unit - III

3. (a) Remove 'ε' production from the following grammar G given as [8]
    S → XYX
    X → OX|ε
    Y → Y|ε
   (b) Find the reduced grammar equivalent to the grammar G whose productions are [8]
    S → AB | CA
    B → BC | AB
    A → a
    C → aB|B
   (c) Explain Decision algorithm for context-free language.

Unit - IV

4. (a) Construct PDA that accepts the language generated by the CFG S → SS |aa [8]
   (b) Writhe the PMT system which can generate the string 'bbbba' [8]
   (c) Design markov algorithm to generate odd parity bit for the string or 0 and 1. [8]

Unit - V

5. (a) Design Turing machine for decimal number is divisible by three. [8]
   (b) Design Turing machine to computer square of a unary number. [8]
   (c) Explain Halting problem of Turing machine. [8]

www.ingramcontent.com/pod-product-compliance
Lightning Source LLC
Chambersburg PA
CBHW080242170426
43192CB00014BA/2534